JULY 2, 1903

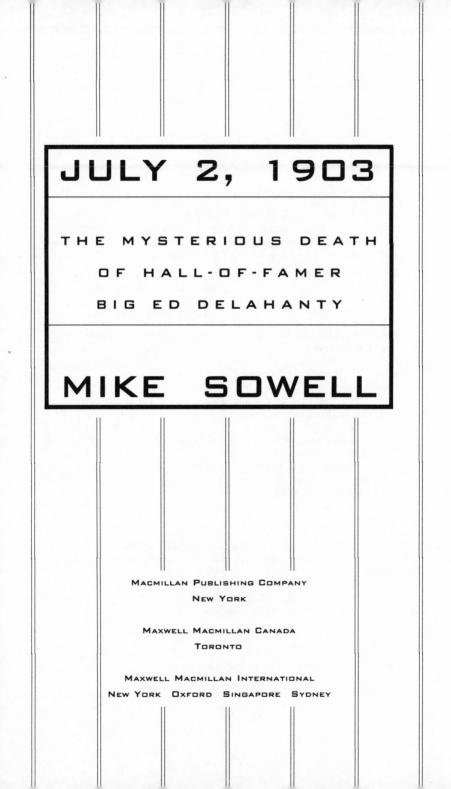

JULY 2, 1903

THE MYSTERIOUS DEATH OF HALL-OF-FAMER BIG ED DELAHANTY

MIKE SOWELL

MACMILLAN PUBLISHING COMPANY
NEW YORK

MAXWELL MACMILLAN CANADA
TORONTO

MAXWELL MACMILLAN INTERNATIONAL
NEW YORK OXFORD SINGAPORE SYDNEY

Macmillan Publishing Company   Maxwell Macmillan Canada, Inc.
866 Third Avenue   1200 Eglinton Avenue East
New York, NY 10022   Suite 200
                                      Don Mills, Ontario M3C 3N1

Macmillan Publishing Company is part of the Maxwell Communication Group of Companies.

Library of Congress Cataloging-in-Publication Data
Sowell, Mike.
     July 2, 1903: the mysterious death of Hall-of-Famer Big Ed
Delahanty/Mike Sowell.
          p.   cm.
     Includes bibliographical references and index.
     ISBN 0-02-612415-7
     I. Delahanty, Ed, d. 1903.   2. Baseball players—United States—
Biography.   I. Title.
     GV865.D45S69   1992   91-37556   CIP
     796.357′092—dc20
     [B]

Macmillan books are available at special discounts for bulk purchases for sales promotions, premiums, fund-raising, or educational use. For details, contact:
                              Special Sales Director
                              Macmillan Publishing Company
                              866 Third Avenue
                              New York, NY 10022

10   9   8   7   6   5   4   3   2   1

Printed in the United States of America

BOOK DESIGN BY DIANE STEVENSON/SNAP•HAUS GRAPHICS

FOR ELLEN,
MY HALL OF FAMER

Contents

ACKNOWLEDGMENTS

There were many people who helped make this book possible. I am especially indebted to Doug Roberts for the many phone calls he made tracking down leads and gathering information on the investigation into Ed Delahanty's death and the resulting lawsuit, as well as his frequent trips to the National Baseball Hall of Fame in Cooperstown in search of material. Also, to Joseph Overfield for lending his expertise on baseball history and the Buffalo–Niagara Falls area, and for taking the time to read the manuscript and offer his suggestions, which helped improve the text. Also, to Fred Schuld for volunteering his time to research material on the city of Cleveland and the Delahanty family.

I also am grateful to Rick Wolff, senior editor at Macmillan, and his assistant, Jeanine Bucek, for all their help and encouragement, and to my agent, Mel Berger.

I also would like to thank the National Baseball Hall of Fame Library and the members of the Society for American Baseball Research, especially Rob Neyer, Bill James, Mike Shannon, Lloyd Johnson, and Allen Pfenninger for their assistance; Mike Sparrow and Mark Alvarez for their work with the SABR microfilm lending library; the other Muggsy McGraw; Pat Carr; the National Baseball Hall of Fame Library; Mike Shannon of *Spitball* magazine; Dr. Jerrold Casway for sharing the materials he gathered while doing his own research on the Delahanty family; Jim Detjen of the *Philadelphia Inquirer*; and Frank McMillan, my "baseball pal," for his support throughout this project.

I

THE GREAT BASEBALL WAR

THE CONSENSUS OF OPINION IS THAT BAN JOHNSON IS THE NEW MOSES, WHO HAS LED THE PLAYERS OUT OF BONDAGE INTO THE LAND OF FAT SALARIES AND SOFT SNAPS.

ANONYMOUS

In the summer of 1903, the game of baseball, like the country itself, still was coming of age. The players wore baggy, drab, wool uniforms and played their games in ninety minutes, although some contests dragged out as long as two hours now that some pitchers wanted to warm up between innings and catchers often held up play to don such new protective devices as shin guards and face masks. Efforts were being made to control the "rowdyism" that had plagued the game the previous decade, but many players still bullied umpires, fought with each other on the field, and sometimes fled for their lives in the face of angry crowds. In Philadelphia, a young catcher named Red Dooin hit upon a more pleasant way to express his disagreements with umpires: While behind the plate, he would sing his objections to balls-and-strikes calls in the fine tenor voice he used on the stage in the off-season.

"Smart baseball" was in vogue that year. Outfielders backed each other up, and infielders played shallow or deep depending upon the situation. There was a tactic known as the "hit-and-run," introduced twenty years earlier by Cap Anson's Chicago White Stockings as "teamwork at bat" and popularized in the 1890s by the Baltimore Orioles. The bunt, or "self-sacrifice," was gaining in popularity, although many of the old-time players scorned it as a "baby play." Signals were flashed from catcher to pitcher through a series of finger signs or, in some cases, by rapidly winking the eyes or staring in a certain direction. Among the weapons in the pitchers' arsenals were the incurve, outcurve, reversing curve, drop, inshoot, jump ball, rising ball, downshoot, and disguised change of pace.

On days they did not work, pitchers stood at the admission gates to take tickets from the patrons arriving at the ballpark. Baseball in 1903 was a game attended by workmen as well as clerks, some decked out in top hats with canes and cigars and others in shirt-sleeves with derbies or caps. The fans were known as "cranks," and some brought with them noisemakers and megaphones. In New York, a man named Frank H. Wood would simply jump to his feet and shout out, "Well, well, well!" after a good play. Occasionally, he would voice his support for his Giants by singing a ditty: "McGraw, McGinnity, and McGann! Upon the word of the Well-Well Man!"

There were two big leagues that summer. The National League was in its twenty-eighth season, and the upstart American League was three years old. There even were two teams in New York for the first time in more than a decade. Minor-league ballplayers advertised their services in the *Sporting News* in classified ads that read, "Catcher—Late with New Orleans. Am at liberty," or "Infielder—Good hitter, good reference. State best terms." In return, ball clubs listed their needs in the "Players Wanted" column: "Battery, infielder and outfielder of ability." "Young players of ability. Long season. Lowest terms in first letter."

The ballplayers came from all walks of life. Some were country boys and some were city slickers. There were college men and there were illiterates. All of them spoke the same language. To kick was to complain. To throw down was to pull the double cross, while to trot on the square was to play it straight. To guy a fellow player was to kid him, which the funsmiths on the team often did. To roast was to criticize. Eyes were called lamps, and hats were known as lids. A rookie was a yannigan, unless he happened to make an ass of himself, in which case he became a donkey. At the other end of the spectrum, when a player no longer was effective he became a back number and resided in Hasbeen Valley.

Many of these ballplayers had become national heroes. In Cleveland, there was the dark and handsome Napoleon Lajoie, a big Frenchman who once hit a ball so hard it broke the pitching rubber. A brilliant but eccentric left-hander named Rube Waddell had landed in Philadelphia, where he often skipped pitching assignments to march in parades, shoot marbles with the neighborhood kids, or simply wander off to go fishing. Pittsburgh boasted the slugging Honus "Hans" Wagner, an all-around star whose hands were so huge that when he picked up the ball to peg it across the diamond he also would scoop up great chunks of dirt and pebbles and throw them, too. The incomparable Cy Young, thirty-six years old, still was delivering his "cyclone" pitches in Boston. In New York, five-foot, four-inch, 140-pound outfielder Wee Willie Keeler not only knew how to "hit 'em where they ain't" but also how to track them down with such skill that it was said that any ball batted into his area was as likely to be caught as if it "were dropped into a barrel."

But no player was greater or more well known than the legendary Big Ed Delahanty, the undisputed "King of Swat." It was Delahanty who hit the ball so far that home runs by other, mere mortal batters were referred to as "Delahanty bunts." It was Delahanty who was said to have a clause in his contract forbidding him to bunt, lest he deprive his team and the fans of one of his mighty drives. It was Delahanty who once hit a low line drive that broke a third baseman's ankle, and it was Delahanty who was reputed to have struck a ball with such force it actually split in two. They said there was nowhere a pitcher could throw the ball that Big Ed could not hit it. He could hit the ball out of the dirt with the end of his bat or he could stand on his tiptoes and still reach out and strike the ball with enough power to send it over the fence.

It was Delahanty who had staged the greatest batting display ever witnessed, hitting four home runs and a single in a memorable game at Chicago's West Side Park in 1896. That was only ten fewer home runs than the league leader would hit for that entire season, and Big Ed did it in just nine innings.

As a member of the Philadelphia Phillies, Delahanty had won a National League batting championship, and playing for Washington he had won the American League crown.

And then, one day in that summer of 1903, while Connie Mack's Philadelphia Athletics were battling Jimmy Collins's Boston Puritans for the American League lead and John McGraw's revived New York Giants were challenging the powerful Pittsburgh Pirates for first place in the National League, while Lajoie was recovering his batting stroke following an off-season illness and a handsome young pitcher named Christy Mathewson was gaining fame in New York, the great Delahanty simply disappeared.

It was as if he had vanished from the face of the earth. He walked out on his Washington teammates during a series in Detroit on July 2, and no friend, relative, or fellow ballplayer ever saw him alive again. For seven days, there was no trace of Delahanty. At first, few people took the matter seriously. A notorious drinker and horseplayer, Del had been known to go on binges before. "He'll probably show up at the track drunk as soon as the horses start running," joked one teammate. A newspaper writer poked fun at the big slugger by noting that upon the team's arrival in Washington following its western trip, "a count of noses was taken [and] that one that is attached to the King of Swatville was 'conspicuous by its absence.' "

But as each day passed without word of Delahanty's whereabouts, there was a growing concern over the ballplayer's disappearance. A headline in the *Washington Post* echoed the question asked not only in that city but throughout baseball: "Where is Del?"

The answer came on July 9, one week after Delahanty first vanished. The horribly mangled body of a man was found just below Niagara Falls on the Canadian side of the Niagara River. One leg had been ripped off, either by the force of the roaring waters as the man was swept over the waterfall or by being caught in the blades of the sight-seeing boat *Maid of the Mist*, which was docked near the site where the body was found. The only clothing that remained on the body was a necktie, socks, and shoes. That man, as investigators soon discovered, was Ed Delahanty, baseball's "King of Swat."

It did not take long to piece together the immediate circumstances leading up to the ballplayer's death. Delahanty, drunk and disorderly, had been put off a train late one night at a way station just across the Niagara River from Buffalo, New York. Shortly afterward, he had plunged off the International Bridge into the waters below, where he was swept downriver and over the powerful waterfall.

But there were more questions about Delahanty's bizarre and gruesome fate than there were answers. People wondered what happened on that bridge that night to send the famous ballplayer to his death. Some thought it was an accident and some thought it was suicide. Others wondered if there was foul play involved. People also wondered what had led Delahanty to that bridge in the first place.

There were many questions about Delahanty's death that would never be answered. And there were others that some people did not want answered.

• • •

One evening in June 1900, four men sat talking in a Chicago hotel room. It was a warm night, but they were careful not to stand next to the open window or step outside in the hallway where they might be seen.

One was a large man who weighed close to three hundred pounds, and he did most of the talking, speaking in a very forceful and direct manner. He was Ban Johnson, thirty-seven years old and a minor-league baseball executive.

The others in the room were John McGraw and Wilbert Robinson, two of the most famous baseball players in the country, and Charlie Comiskey, a former baseball star and a long-time Johnson ally.

It was Comiskey who had arranged the meeting, which was being held in the strictest secrecy. The participants had arrived at the hotel by circuitous routes, one by one, leaving their horse-drawn taxis or dropping off their street cars several blocks from their destination and walking the remainder of the way so as not to be noticed.

The clandestine nature of the gathering was dictated by the nature of their business. Johnson was plotting the formation of a second major league in baseball. Comiskey, forty years old and a statuesque man with a stately head of hair which he combed straight back, was one of his principal backers. McGraw and Robinson, who had been members of the famous Baltimore Orioles before moving to St. Louis of the National League that season, were being recruited to invest in the venture as well as sign on as players in the new league.

Johnson, who was surprisingly agile for a man of his bulk, made an immediate impression on the two ballplayers. He struck McGraw as "young and imaginative and fearless," and while Johnson treated the players with respect he did not "butter them up." Despite all their fame, he never let them forget he was a league president.

Johnson's rise to such a lofty position had been both rapid and unexpected. A former college baseball player, he had dropped out of law school to take a job as a sportswriter for the *Cincinnati Commercial-Gazette*. An unabashed fan of the Cincinnati National League team, Johnson became drinking buddies with Comiskey, the team's star player and manager. Johnson also was an outspoken critic of team owner John Brush, whom he labeled a pinch-penny and a scoundrel. It was Comiskey who, in 1893, convinced Brush that the best way to get Johnson out of town was to get him appointed to the vacant post of secretary, treasurer, and president of the Western League. Brush, who also owned a team in the Western League, finally agreed, and at twenty-eight years of age Johnson became head of the organization.

The Western League thrived under Johnson's leadership, and by 1896 it was regarded by many baseball writers as the "strongest minor ever." The success of the league led Johnson to eye other, more lucrative markets. The circuit had started with teams in the western outposts of Indianapolis, Toledo, Detroit, Grand Rapids, Milwaukee, Minneapolis, Sioux City, and Kansas City. Later, Comiskey entered the league by purchasing a franchise in St. Paul, which replaced Sioux City. When the National League dropped Cleveland in the fall of 1899, Johnson announced his intentions to place a team there. He also gained the National League's permission to move a team run by Comiskey into Chicago, where the old White Stockings, now known as the Orphans or Cubs, still operated. As an indication of his long-range plans, Johnson renamed his circuit the American League in 1900. It still had a regional flavor, but the league's growing strength was reflected in its member cities: Chicago, Cleveland, Detroit, Minneapolis, Milwaukee, Kansas City, and Indianapolis. The league was gaining in popularity because of its high caliber of play and its efficient operation, and now Johnson was ready to expand his horizons again.

He outlined his proposal to McGraw and Robinson in a clear, firm voice.

"The National League is being administered to death," he said. "The American League is the only thing that can keep baseball alive."

The two ballplayers did little talking, but they liked what they heard. Johnson planned to operate an efficient, tightly-knit league free of the internal squabbles and political infighting which had wracked the National League. He also wanted to stamp out "rowdyism," the bullying, intimidating style of ball which had become so common in the older circuit. Johnson wanted a well-played, clean brand of baseball in his league, and those who got out of line would be dealt with swiftly and harshly.

Surprisingly, McGraw, perhaps baseball's most notorious umpire baiter, expressed similar views.

"The umpires should be firm and completely in charge," he told Johnson.

However, McGraw was quick to add one point.

"The player always has a right to challenge the umpire on a point of rule or interpretation," he noted.

But all talk of rowdyism and umpires was secondary to Johnson's master strategy. He planned to establish franchises in several Eastern markets and claim major-league status for his organization. And one of the cities he had chosen for a team was Baltimore, which had been abandoned by the National League after the 1899 season.

McGraw was offered the chance to return to his old city not only as a ballplayer and manager, but also as an investor in the franchise.

The ballplayer jumped at the opportunity, promising to put up seven thousand dollars to invest in the franchise. Robinson, McGraw's best friend and long-time teammate, agreed to buy a smaller block of stock.

The deal was consummated with nothing more than a hand-shake between the men involved. Not wanting to tip off the National League to his intentions, that was how Johnson conducted all of his business in the summer of 1900.

That night, as McGraw and Robinson sat up late in their hotel room and talked enthusiastically about the new venture, they knew they had become staunch American Leaguers.

• • •

Johnson believed that in recruiting McGraw to his cause, he had scored a major victory. The Baltimore third baseman not only was one of the top drawing cards in the National League, he also was one of baseball's brightest young managers.

McGraw was a small man, only five foot seven, who had used his toughness and his cleverness to succeed in a big man's game. When he arrived on the big-league scene in 1891, he was a frail, baby-faced kid who weighed barely 130 pounds. His manager, Billy Barnie of the Baltimore Orioles of the old American Association, stared at his new recruit a full minute before he could speak.

"Why, you're just a kid," said Barnie. "Can you play ball?"

"If you don't think so, get me out on the field," shot back McGraw. "I'm bigger than I look."

Johnny McGraw backed up his tough words with his tough play. He was an expert at finding ways to get on base, whether it required pushing a bunt down the foul line or fouling off dozens of pitches to wear out the pitcher and work him for a walk. One year, McGraw reached first base by hit, walk, error, or being hit by a pitch two out of every three times up, a record that no one ever has approached.

It was McGraw as much as anyone who turned baseball into a science. By the mid-1890s, he and Hughie Jennings, his roommate, met every night with teammates Wee Willie Keeler, Joe Kelley, and Wilbert Robinson to scheme up ways to beat the opposition. The Orioles perfected the hit-and-run play to advance runners and they introduced the Baltimore chop, a ball hit into the ground near home plate so that it bounced high in the air, allowing the batter to reach first base safely.

In the field, McGraw was a master at trickery. He knew how to discreetly hold on to a runner's belt to keep him from tagging up on a fly ball, and he could discreetly bump a passing baserunner to throw him off stride. The Orioles even went so far as to keep the outfield grass so high in their ballpark that they could keep an extra baseball hidden there to slip into play whenever necessary. This practice ended only after the time left-fielder Joe Kelley threw the spare ball to McGraw at third base in time to retire a runner. To the Orioles' chagrin, a moment later center fielder Steve Brodie ran down the ball that actually was in play and pegged it back to the infield, also.

When all else failed, the Orioles attempted to bully anyone who got in their way. They fought with opposing players, brawled with fans, and made enemies wherever they went. Umpires were subjected to special abuse, often forced to soak their feet for hours after McGraw and his cronies kicked and stomped them with their spikes.

The Orioles were a perfect fit for Baltimore as the nineteenth century was drawing to a close. H. L. Mencken had written of the city, "Baltimore, by 1890, was fast degenerating, and so was civilization." The same could be said of baseball itself.

The style of ball played by the Orioles became known as "rowdyism," and other teams began to follow their lead. There were protests that baseball was slipping into ruin, but there was no denying the Orioles' success. They won three consecutive pennants from 1894 through 1896 and finished second to Boston the next two years.

McGraw, the captain and ringleader of the Orioles, became a local hero in Baltimore. In 1896, he and Robinson, the Orioles' catcher, became partners in an establishment known as the Diamond Cafe. It featured a dining room in the front and a small bowling alley in the back, and it became the popular meeting place for the city's sports crowd.

The city also provided a lasting nickname for McGraw. When he arrived on the scene, there was a local politician named "Muggsy" McGraw, and it was rumored the young ballplayer was his son. The newspapers began calling the Orioles infielder "Young Muggsy" McGraw, and the name stuck. McGraw hated it, but he never was able to shake his new identity.

Of all the hecklers he faced around the league, the only one who ever got on McGraw's nerves was a fan in Cleveland who picked up on the nickname. Whenever McGraw would make an error or an out, the man would jump from his seat and run back and forth shouting at the top of his voice: "Oh, Muggsy! Oh, Muggsy! Look at your face! Aren't you a beauty! Oh, Muggsy!"

McGraw asked the writers to quit calling him by the name, but to no avail. "You could stop them saying it if you really wanted to," prizefighter Jim Jeffries once told him. "If I was you, I'd stop them quick enough."

"No you wouldn't," said McGraw. "But if I were you, nobody would have the sand to tie a name of that kind on me."

Otherwise, McGraw reveled in the attention he received in Baltimore. And his stature in the city became even greater in 1899 when he took over as manager after Ned Hanlon jumped to Brooklyn and took most of the team's stars with him. McGraw, with Robinson as his right-hand man, led the badly depleted Orioles to a surprising fourth-place finish that year.

But misfortune lay ahead for McGraw. His problems began that summer while his team was in Louisville. He received word his wife, Minnie, had suffered an inflamed appendix, and he rushed back to Baltimore. By the time McGraw's train arrived, his wife had taken a turn for the worse. The appendix had ruptured, and three days later Minnie was dead.

Not long afterward, McGraw learned the National League was cutting back from twelve teams to eight. One of the franchises being dropped was Baltimore. Within a matter of weeks, McGraw lost his wife, his managerial position, and his ball club.

The next setback came early in 1900. McGraw and Robinson were traded to St. Louis, the westernmost outpost in the league. Not wanting to play ball more than eight hundred miles away from their business interests in Baltimore, the two men fought the move. When they finally signed their contracts with the Cardinals, they did so only after the club agreed to drop the "reserve clause." A standard part of all National League contracts, the reserve clause gave the ball club the option to renew its claim on the player, binding him to the team indefinitely.

The season already was three weeks old when McGraw and Robinson arrived in St. Louis. McGraw's salary of ten thousand dollars was said to be the most paid a player in a decade, but because of reporting late he would receive only ninety-five hundred dollars of it. Robinson, on the downside of his career, would be paid five thousand dollars.

Despite the money, the play of the two ex-Orioles was uninspired, and much of their time was spent at the racetrack across the street from the ballpark. When he was injured McGraw did not even bother to show up at the game, preferring instead to attend the races. Finally, Frank de Haas Robison, the St. Louis owner, became so incensed he ordered manager Patsy Tebeau to inform McGraw that he belonged where he drew his pay. So McGraw returned to the ballpark, where he continued to place his wagers on the horses by dispatching couriers to the track between innings.

The turning point for McGraw came in Chicago when he met Ban Johnson. The American League president made a lasting impression on the young ballplayer. While National League owners are fighting each other, McGraw thought to himself, Johnson is fighting for baseball as a game first and for territorial growth next.

After that meeting, McGraw and Robinson talked frequently about Johnson and the American League. For the first time in their lives, McGraw told his friend, they had been privileged to see a blueprint of sound and sincere baseball administration.

That summer, Johnson's agents quietly went about their business, signing up players in every National League city. All of the deals were worked out under the table, and the National League magnates never caught on to what was happening right under their noses.

McGraw was a particularly effective recruiter in his travels around the circuit. He signed underhand pitcher Iron Man Joe McGinnity of Brooklyn to a contract scribbled on the back of a piece of scratch paper. In Chicago, he landed catcher Roger Bresnahan. In Pittsburgh, he got infielder Jimmy Williams.

McGraw's St. Louis Teammate Turkey Mike Donlin, an outfielder, also agreed to make the jump.

When the season finally ended, McGraw and Robinson were
so happy to get out of St. Louis, they tossed their uniforms
into the Mississippi River while their train slowly made its
way east over the long bridge. As they watched the clothing
disappear into the darkness below, the two ballplayers believed they were leaving the National League behind them for
good.

• • •

It all fell into place with surprising ease for Ban Johnson.
The turning point came in December 1900, when he sat impatiently in his room at the Lafayette Hotel in Philadelphia. With
Johnson was Charles Somers, who had become his right-hand
man in the American League.

Somers, thirty-one years old, was the heir to a lucrative
Cleveland coal and shipping empire. A shy man, he was an
enthusiastic baseball fan. When Johnson had gone to Cleveland
the previous year looking for local backing for the team he
wanted to place in that city, Somers had jumped at the opportunity to become a baseball owner. His father disapproved of
"such a foolish and unprofitable thing as baseball" and urged
his son to devote more of his time and energy to running the
J. H. Somers Coal Company. Charles refused to listen, instead
becoming more and more active in his baseball pursuits. He
became one of Johnson's most trusted allies and provided him
with the financial clout needed to carry out his plans for the
American League. It was Somers who helped finance the
league's move into Chicago, and when Johnson set his sights
on the East, Somers again made his money available.

Buoyed by the success of the 1900 season, Johnson had
begun to reveal his intentions that fall. In September, he made
known his plans to expand into the East by shifting the Kansas
City franchise to Washington and placing a team in Baltimore,

both territories abandoned by the National League. He also would move into National League territory in Philadelphia, but if he could prevent hostilities with the older organization he would scrap his plans to move his Buffalo franchise to Boston. The western wing of the American League would consist of Chicago, Detroit, Cleveland, and Milwaukee.

The announcement was timed to coincide with the end of the National Agreement which his league had signed with the National League ten years earlier. The agreement, the foundation on which organized baseball rested, gave the National League the right to draft American League and other minor-league players without restriction, upon payment of five hundred dollars per player. By letting the document expire, Johnson was revealing his league's claim to major status.

Now, the two men had come to Philadelphia seeking a peaceful solution to the baseball situation.

The National League was holding its annual meeting in nearby New York, and Johnson sent word requesting an opportunity to make an appearance before the owners to explain his plans.

For all of one day, Johnson and Somers waited with growing impatience for a reply. A second day passed and still no word from the National League magnates.

Meanwhile, in New York, the National League owners were busy preparing their response to Johnson. In an effort to sabotage his efforts, they were plotting a two-pronged attack against him. First, they adopted a sympathetic stance toward another group that was attempting to beat the American League to the punch by reviving the old American Association as the second major league. The National League owners indicated they would look kindly on the association's desire to place franchises in the East. Second, the owners attempted to undercut Johnson by awarding his Kansas City and Minneapolis territories to a new Western League.

Finally, after hours of waiting, Johnson received a reply to his messages. The National Leaguers told him he could stay in Philadelphia "until hell froze over."

• • •

There was another showdown looming in New York that month. The Protective Association of Professional Baseball Players had planned its winter meeting to coincide with that of the National League, and the players were demanding an audience with the owners. The timing of events could not have worked out better for Ban Johnson.

The association had been formed only the previous June, the result of years of player discontent following the death of the old brotherhood a decade earlier. The players, who paid five dollars for initiation fees and two dollars in monthly dues to belong to the organization, assured the owners they did not have radical intentions. They sought primarily to correct three grievances—the reserve clause binding a player to a team in perpetuity, the twenty-four-hundred-dollar salary limit, and the practice of "farming out" or "lending" players without their consent. The owners, secure in their monopoly, were not even inclined to take the players seriously.

Arthur Soden of Boston spoke for many of his colleagues when he proclaimed: "I do not believe in labor organizations or unions. When a player ceases to be useful to me, I will release him."

The association, however, continued to gain in strength. At its second meeting, in July, almost a hundred players attended.

The players attempted to keep the identities of their officers secret for fear they would be singled out by the owners as "shining marks," but eventually the names leaked out. Chief Zimmer, a catcher for Pittsburgh and Cy Young's old battery mate, was president. Clark Griffith, a pitcher for Cap Anson's Chicago Orphans, was the vice president. The other officers were first baseman Hughie Jennings, one of the stars of the old Orioles now playing for Brooklyn, and catcher Boileryard Clarke, another former Oriole now with Boston.

From Johnson's standpoint, the key man in the organization was Griffith, who was known among the players as "the Old Fox." He had acquired his nickname because of his trickery in the pitching box, as well as his background as a hunter and trapper while growing up in the prairie country of the Midwest. Griffith's favorite stunt as a pitcher was to shield the ball behind his leg in his windup and drag it across his spikes. The resulting tears and nicks on the ball's surface caused his pitches to take a wide assortment of sudden hops and twists as they neared the plate. On one occasion, Griff's handiwork was so blatant the opposing team sent him a bill for eleven dollars to cover the cost of the eleven balls he cut in two ball games. Griffith also was one of the innovators of a new pitch known as the fadeaway, which later came to be known as the screwball, and he threw a sinker ball which he had learned from 1880s pitching great Old Hoss Radbourn.

Griffith was well qualified for his post in the players' organization. Seven years earlier, as a member of the Oakland Oaks of the Pacific Coast League, he had led a successful players' strike against the team owner for back pay. He also was clever enough to realize the growing weakness of the National League and the need for a second major league to save baseball. In those days, a player who pitched one day would serve as a ticket-taker on the gate the next day. Through such duty, Griffith saw firsthand the declining attendance throughout the league. One day, he had counted only fifty-six people in the stands.

Although still under contract to the Chicago Nationals, the Old Fox already had agreed to become manager of Charles Comiskey's Chicago Americans the following season. And through his position with the Players Association he was able to open the door for even more defections.

Unknown to the National League owners, Griffith had called a meeting of the players late in the season when all the clubs were in the East. At that time, it was agreed they would not sign contracts with their teams for 1901 unless advised to do so by the association officers following the December meeting.

That fall, Griffith met with Johnson and Comisky at the Polk Street Cafe on Chicago's West Side. The decision to seek major-league status had been made, but Johnson was unsure if they could sign enough established players from the National League to achieve credibility. Griffith advised him to delay his next move until December, when he could report on the player situation.

The answer would come quickly enough.

At its December meeting, the association drew up a petition demanding that the league salary limit be raised to three thousand dollars and that clubs provide the players with their uniforms. Griffith, Zimmer, and Jennings then took the document to the National League meetings, where they were granted an audience with the owners.

They had just entered the room when Griffith heard someone trying to attract his attention. He looked over to see "Uncle Nick" Young, the elderly league president, sitting on a trunk just inside the door.

"Son, they ain't going to give you anything in this meeting," whispered Young. "I just thought I would tell you."

Griffith nodded his thanks to the old man. One look at the podium was all it took to understand what was happening in the meeting. Presiding over the hearing was Boston's Arthur Soden, the league's vice president. A clean-shaven New Englander who often was mistaken for a Catholic priest, Soden was a dictatorial boss who treated his ballplayers with cold indifference. It was said that not one out of three men who played for him had ever spoken to Soden, and though he knew each of his players by sight, when he passed them on the street he would do no more than nod as if they were only casual acquaintances. Soden's presence at the head of the meeting was a sure sign the owners were in no mood to accept the players' demands. Whenever they wanted to side-step an issue, it was their practice to go around Young, a weak and ineffective leader.

The owners listened with impatience while Griffith listed the players' grievances, and they promised to give the matter their full consideration. The hearing then ended abruptly, and Griffith, Zimmer, and Jennings were ushered outside.

While waiting for the owners' response, they went downstairs to the hotel bar for a round of drinks. They had been sitting there less than five minutes when Griffith looked up to see Soden coming down the stairway hoping to slip out the back way. The Boston owner was startled to hear Griffith call out to him and ask him to join the ballplayers for a beer.

Soden had no choice but to accept. He blamed his premature departure on another appointment, but as he reached for his drink a document fell out of his pocket. It was the manuscript of the players' demands.

Griffith accused him of lying to the players, but Soden insisted the owners would give the matter their full attention. Flustered, the owner hurried from the room.

Unwittingly, the National League magnates had just played into Johnson's hands. The association announced through the newspapers that their demands had been rejected. They also advised their fellow players to respect their pledges and refuse to sign their 1901 contracts.

That evening, Griffith contacted Johnson by telephone to tell him the news. Not even the static on the line could hide the excitement in Griff's voice.

"There's going to be a new major league if you can get the backing," he shouted, "because I can get the players!"

• • •

These were heady times for twenty-seven-year-old John McGraw. In November 1900, he officially became a baseball executive, meeting with Johnson and Somers to sign the documents giving him the rights to form an American League franchise in Baltimore. The three men celebrated the occasion by dining on pheasant and drinking champagne. A week later, the franchise was incorporated with a capitalization of forty thousand dollars.

The problem of securing playing grounds was overcome when the club gained a lease on the site where the old Orioles of the American Association had played ten years earlier. Work on Oriole Park began February 16, 1901, a cold and windy day. It was a triumphant scene as McGraw and his partners, joined by Johnson, used a silver spade fastened to the handle with nine gold nails to turn the ceremonial first shovelful of dirt, marking the beginning of the project. In just seven weeks, the Orioles would have a single-decked ballpark which would accommodate eighty-five hundred fans in its brick grandstand and wooden bleachers.

The next day, McGraw left for Hot Springs, a favorite training area of ballplayers. A resort town located in the Ouachita Mountains of western Arkansas, Hot Springs was famous for its steam baths and mineral waters. After a winter of inactivity or drinking, many players found it a much-needed curative prior to the rigors of a baseball campaign. The Chicago White Stockings under Cap Anson had been the first team to train in Hot Springs back in the 1880s, and others soon followed. Over the years, other attractions besides steam baths and ball playing had sprung up to keep the visitors occupied. There were a horse track and numerous clubs and bars, making Hot Springs a haven for gamblers and other sportsmen. For a man of McGraw's tastes, it was an ideal spot to stage a training camp.

In the spring of 1901, Hot Springs was swarming with ballplayers and there was even more excitement than usual. The town had become an American League stronghold, and everywhere people were talking about the "new" major league. A few National League agents worked the hotel lobbies and bars, but they received a cold reception.

McGraw set up headquarters in a suite at the plush Eastman Hotel, and spent his afternoons at the Arkansas and Southern clubs or at Oaklawn, the local racetrack. He was in his full glory that spring, strutting about town, cutting deals, dining in splendor, reigning over the pool rooms, and boiling out in the mineral baths. "The doughtiest magnate of them all could [not] cut a wider swath than does the little Pooh Bah of the American League," noted one admiring writer.

Putting together his team had proven to be the easy part for McGraw. On his way to Arkansas, he had stopped in St. Louis to meet his old pitcher, Iron Man Joe McGinnity, and firm up the deal they already had struck.

"The money good, Mac?" asked McGinnity.

"Good as gold, Joe. Every penny."

That was all the assurance the underhand pitcher needed. He signed for twenty-eight hundred dollars. McGinnity had been offered almost twice that to return to Brooklyn, but he turned it down out of loyalty to McGraw.

Second baseman Jimmy Williams arrived from his home in Denver on a train ticket sent him by his old National League club in Pittsburgh. "I not only lose Williams, but I pay his fare east for McGraw to steal him from me," grumbled Pirates owner Barney Dreyfuss.

Also jumping the National League to join McGraw were Cy Seymour, who had both pitched and played the outfield in New York; utility man Roger Bresnahan from Chicago; shortstop Bill "Wagon Tongue" Keister and outfielder Turkey Mike Donlin, teammates from St. Louis; and Brooklyn pitchers Jerry Nops and Handsome Harry Howell, both former Orioles. In addition, there was Wilbert Robinson, who would catch as well as serve as McGraw's right-hand man.

All told, 111 of the 185 players the American League lined up to play that season were former National Leaguers.

McGraw almost landed another ballplayer who would have made the American League an even more revolutionary venture than it already was. His name was Charley Grant, and McGraw had spotted him working out on a diamond adjacent to the hotel. It was immediately apparent that Grant was an outstanding player who could step right into the Orioles' lineup. There was just one catch. Grant was a black man. He played second base on the Columbia Giants, a Negro team out of Chicago, and was spending his off-season in Hot Springs working as a bellhop at the Eastland Hotel, where McGraw was quartered.

There had been black ballplayers previously in the major leagues. In 1884, brothers Moses Fleetwood Walker and Welday Walker had played for Toledo of the American Association, then a major league. But the bigotry of many of the most influential baseball people, most notably former Chicago White Stockings manager Cap Anson, had led to an unwritten rule that blacks were not allowed on the same playing field as white men.

McGraw, however, was less interested in Grant's race than in his abilities as a ballplayer. He wanted Grant on his team, and he cooked up a scheme to try to get him. Grant had straight hair and sharp features, so McGraw tried to pass him off as "Chief" Tokahoma, a full-blooded Cherokee Indian from the Indian Territory adjacent to Arkansas.

McGraw promised Grant he would send for him once the team returned to Baltimore and got the season underway, but the call never came. Charlie Comiskey of Chicago got wind of the scheme and protested that "this Cherokee of McGraw's is really Grant, the crack Negro second baseman, fixed up with war paint and a bunch of feathers." If Grant were allowed into the league, said Comiskey, he would "get a Chinaman of my acquaintance and put him on third." Once the ruse was uncovered, McGraw abandoned the idea and Grant had no choice but to return to his old team. Baseball's color line remained intact.

It proved to be only a minor setback to McGraw. As his first American League season neared, he turned his attention to the matters at hand. There was plenty to do in running a ballclub to keep him busy, and he anticipated an exciting season in the following months. As it turned out, there would be more excitement than he could have imagined.

• • •

In Philadelphia, a solitary figure sat in the clubhouse of the National League ballpark a few days prior to the start of the 1901 season. He picked up a large bat and carefully inspected it, then put it down and picked up another. Some players claimed that all bats looked alike. Ed Delahanty strongly disagreed. He had his bats made by a carpenter in his hometown of Cleveland according to a detailed list of weights and measurements, and he carefully guarded each one. "My bat is like my hat," Delahanty once told a reporter. "It must fit, or it don't go."

He continued his preparations for the upcoming season, arranging equipment in his locker and trying on the new sweater which he had been issued by the Phillies.

Delahanty did not share in the euphoria of his fellow ballplayers over the American League. While others had been quick to jump to Ban Johnson's organization, Del preferred to take a more cautious approach. After thirteen years in the major leagues, he had learned the dangers involved in acting too quickly.

And Delahanty could afford to wait and see how the upstart league fared before he acted. He already had struck a deal to take care of himself. Just one year earlier, in this same room, he had taken part in one of the most publicized and controversial contract signings in baseball history. Delahanty got the money he wanted, but it had not come easily.

• • •

Ed Delahanty was a dark-haired, powerfully built man with broad shoulders, muscular arms, and sturdy legs. He was not an exceptionally large man at six feet and about two hundred pounds, but he had about him a presence that made him seem larger than he was. The other ballplayers called him "Big Ed," which was as much a testament to his exploits as his physical size.

Del was a throwback to another era of baseball, when old-fashioned slugging was in vogue. He was the last in a long line of sluggers that had included the likes of Cap Anson, Pete Browning, Big Sam Thompson, and Roger Connor.

Delahanty struck fear in a pitcher's heart, standing at the plate in a majestic pose with his bat held high. When he swung his big bat, it made a whistling sound as it cut through the air and tore into the ball. No one hit the ball harder than did Big Ed, as evidenced by the numerous pock marks his line shots left as they struck the outfield fences.

Unlike most sluggers, Delahanty rarely struck out. He was a patient hitter, waiting for a pitch he liked and then driving it to any field. One year, he went the first two months of the season without striking out, and yet he finished as the league's top slugger with nineteen home runs, seventy-two extra-base hits and 146 runs batted in. In 1894, when he batted .400 for the first time, he struck out only sixteen times in 497 at-bats.

But Delahanty did things in a big way, and even his occasional strikeouts became the topic of stories. In the early 1890s, there was a brash young pitcher known as Crazy Schmit who entertained the fans with his bizarre antics and boastful ways. Schmit got a lot of attention around the National League for keeping a notebook in which he recorded the strong and weak points of every batter. Opposite Delahanty's name, however, was a blank. When asked why, Schmit replied: "When you pitch to Delahanty, you just want to shut your eyes, say a prayer, and chuck the ball. The Lord only knows what'll happen after that."

While pitching for Baltimore one day, Schmit's prayers were answered when he threw three strikes past Delahanty. As the third strike was called, Schmit sank to his knees and spread his arms as he cried out, "Who says I'm not the greatest pitcher on earth?"

And Del seemed to get better as he got older. At age thirty-one in 1899, he hit his peak by leading the National League with a powerful .410 batting average, achieved on a league-best 238 hits and 55 doubles.

For such a phenomenal season, Delahanty was paid only twenty-four hundred dollars—the most money allowed under the National League salary limits. That wasn't good enough for Big Ed. He had batted over .300 for eight consecutive seasons, and in that time his annual salary had increased by only two hundred dollars.

Nor did the ball club's treatment of its players sit well with him. The Phillies were owned by Alfred Reach, a former baseball great, and Colonel John I. Rogers, a Philadelphia lawyer. As treasurer, Colonel Rogers ran the ball club, and he had a reputation as one of the most tight-fisted owners in the National League.

The Colonel liked to write "abstinence and rebate" clauses into his players' contracts, and he determined whether the required standards had been achieved. If a player was ejected from a game, the Colonel docked his pay by fifty dollars. When pitcher Wiley Piatt, who had won forty-seven games over the previous two seasons, fell ill and had to be hospitalized in 1900, he received no salary for the time he spent away from baseball. It was not because the player was sick, Rogers explained, rather it was because he had not put forth a sufficient effort prior to his illness. When third baseman Billy Lauder did not receive a promised bonus for the Phillies' strong showing in 1899, he was told neither his performance nor that of the team merited such a reward. Lauder, twenty-six years old, responded by quitting baseball.

In Delahanty's case, the money was not so much an issue as the manner in which he received it. Colonel Rogers was willing to boost his pay to three thousand dollars by giving him a six hundred dollar bonus for serving as captain of the ball club. But Del feared he might be summarily relieved of his position as captain and thus have to forfeit the additional money. He insisted on receiving the six hundred dollars as "a gift."

To force the ball club to meet his demands, Delahanty made an unusual pact with one of his teammates. The Phillies had a young infielder named Napoleon "Larry" Lajoie, who had batted over .300 all four years he had been in the league. Claiming he already was being heralded as "a wonder," Lajoie also wanted to be paid three thousand dollars. He and Delahanty agreed neither player would sign until both got what they wanted.

In the spring of 1900, while John McGraw and Wilbert Robinson were employing similar tactics against St. Louis, Delahanty and Lajoie reported to the Philadelphia training camp but refused to play in any exhibition games. Colonel Rogers retaliated by fining both men for each game missed and threatening them with suspensions. Finally, just as the season was about to begin, Delahanty was summoned to the Philadelphia ballpark. Waiting for him was Billy Shettsline, the manager of the Phillies.

Shetts, a big, portly man, greeted Delahanty warmly, then got right down to business. He offered Del the maximum twenty-four hundred dollars plus a guaranteed six hundred dollars disguised as his captain's pay. As manager, Shettsline's primary duties would be to oversee the players and handle travel and hotel arrangements. As captain, Del would be in charge of the team on the field. When Delahanty agreed, Shetts told him to relate the same terms to Lajoie.

Later, the two players met the manager at Delahanty's house. They agreed to the deal, although they had one additional demand. It was standard practice for players to buy their own uniforms, which cost about thirty dollars each. Delahanty and Lajoie wanted the ball club to pay for their baseball clothes.

"I'll see what I can do," Shetts promised them.

The papers were drawn up and waiting to be signed at the ballpark. Del arrived first and scribbled his name on his contract, which called for a total of three thousand dollars. Later, Lajoie sat down while in uniform and looked over the figures on his contract. He would get the twenty-four hundred dollar maximum plus an extra two hundred dollars for a total of twenty-six hundred dollars. Believing this to be the same deal Delahanty got, Lajoie picked up a lead pencil and wrote his name on the document.

The terms of that deal would become a source of great debate, and it never was determined who was responsible for the double cross on Lajoie. But one thing was certain. The damage to the Phillies and the National League would be far greater than the four hundred dollars the ball club saved through its deception.

• • •

Opening Day 1901 in Philadelphia was cold and gloomy, and there was the threat of rain in the clouds overhead. Not even the bright red sweaters which the hometown Phillies wore as they marched onto the field offered much cheerfulness.

As captain of the ball club, Delahanty stood at the head of the procession while a brass band played and a new flag was run up the flagpole. To many it seemed a bad omen when the banner would not unfurl despite three attempts to get it up. Sure enough, Brooklyn scored six runs in the top of the first inning and romped to a 12–7 victory.

But for the Phillies, a more important showdown would come two days later, on April 20. And the setting would be a Philadelphia courtroom, not a baseball field. On that date,

Larry Lajoie would be at the center of the first big legal battle between the National and American leagues.

• • •

There was a ballpark atmosphere surrounding Philadelphia's Common Pleas Court No. 5 that Saturday. The crowd outside cheered and whistled when Larry Lajoie arrived, and the ballplayer, surrounded by his lawyers, had to push his way into the building. A big man with dark good looks and an air of superiority about him, Lajoie said little as he entered the courtroom. He sat at the defense table and listened impassively as Colonel Rogers, a long-time Philadelphia lawyer, rose to give the opening argument for the ballclub.

The Colonel spelled out the case against Lajoie, who two months earlier had signed a contract with the Philadelphia Athletics of the American League. Rogers argued such an action was illegal since the ballplayer already was under contract to the Phillies. The basis of this claim was the reserve clause, which, as Rogers explained, gave the ball club the right to renew the player's services.

The ball club also contended the loss of a star ballplayer such as Lajoie would greatly depreciate the team's revenues. That afternoon, Billy Shettsline, the Philadelphia manager, was called to the stand to testify to Lajoie's abilities.

One of the Colonel's attorneys asked Shetts whether one ballplayer could be "more expert" than another. When the manager answered affirmatively, he was asked if Lajoie was such an expert. His emphatic reply caused even the judge to smile.

"I think he's the best thing that ever happened!" blurted out Shetts.

• • •

Even before his celebrated court case, Larry Lajoie had been a controversial figure in Philadelphia. His brief career was marked by stormy outbursts and disciplinary problems, but through it all Lajoie had proven himself to be one of the best young hitters in the game.

The son of French parents, he had gotten a late start in professional baseball, signing his first contract at age twenty-one in January 1896. At the time, Lajoie was working as the town cabby in his hometown of Woonsocket, Rhode Island, for $1.25 a day and playing baseball for recreation. He had a chance to go to the College of the Holy Cross in Worcester, Massachusetts, to play ball and obtain an education, but he turned down the opportunity in the hopes of playing pro ball. Even as an unproven amateur, he was brash enough to make clear his intentions in the game. One day, he received a telegram from the owner of a nearby club asking what it would take to sign him. Lajoie's terse reply on the back of a postcard was a blunt reminder in the language of ballplayers that he intended to get as much money as possible. "I am out for the stuff," he wrote.

Shortly afterward, owner Charley Marston of the Fall River team in the New England League picked up Lajoie, signing him on the back of an envelope.

Later that year, the Phillies acquired Lajoie as part of a fifteen hundred dollar deal that also included outfielder Phil Geier. It had been Geier who first had attracted the Phillies' attention, but after making the acquisition Philadelphia manager Billy Nash wired the club: "This Lajoie is a find. He will be the grandest player of them all."

But Lajoie, like all rookies, also faced a tough battle to gain the acceptance of his teammates. The Phillies were a rough, veteran ball club, and they didn't treat newcomers kindly. Earlier in the season, rookie pitcher Harry "Beans" Keener became so discouraged when not a single member of the team would speak to him after he reported, he was ready to quit on the spot.

Lajoie tried to gain the friendship of the Philadelphia ballplayers by proving himself a "good fellow." In doing so, he fell under the influence of a bad element on the team. He gained a reputation as a drinker and a scrapper and got involved in numerous ill-advised escapades.

His second year on the team, Lajoie was sitting on the team bus after a game in Washington when he got into an argument with a spectator. Lajoie reached out and punched the man, and promptly was placed under arrest and hauled off to jail.

Later that year, he showed up drunk at the ballpark one day and committed a costly first-inning error. George Stallings, then the manager of the Phillies, pulled him off the field and suspended him from the team. Only after Lajoie promised to stay out of trouble was he allowed back on the squad.

But for all his misadventures, Lajoie proved himself a tremendous hitter. Once he even threw his bat at a pitch on a hit-and-run play and still managed a single to right field.

He was best known as Larry Lajoie, but he also had a number of colorful nicknames. In the early days, the players called him "the Slugging Cabby," because of his background driving a hack, or, more majestically, "King Napoleon." Eventually, they settled on "the Big Frenchman," a title which would stay with him throughout his career.

As Lajoie's reputation as a hitter spread, so did the tales of his quirks and odd behavior. Before he stepped to the plate, he had the superstitious habit of drawing a line outside the batter's box. And one year, Lajoie shocked his teammates by showing up at the ballpark with his forty-five-pound brindle bulldog, which he paraded around the field while posing for pictures.

Most of all, the Big Frenchman had a quick temper and an unforgiving nature.

After he and Delahanty ended their dual holdout in 1900, the Phillies charged to the front of the National League race. But one day early in the season, Delahanty carelessly left out one of his pay receipts while he and Lajoie were rooming together. When Lajoie saw the figures on the paper, he realized he had been double-crossed by the ball club. He confronted Colonel Rogers's office and demanded he be given an extra four hundred dollars to bring him even with Delahanty as promised, but the Colonel refused. Lajoie would never forgive Rogers for the betrayal.

It was not long before the ball club felt the effects of Lajoie's anger. The Phillies had a wiry young outfielder named Elmer Flick, who had arrived in Philadelphia two years earlier with a bat he had turned on a lathe at his home in Ohio. The veteran players scoffed at him, but Flick soon won their admiration with the wicked line drives he hit. Only Lajoie refused to warm up to the young ballplayer.

On Memorial Day 1900, the Phillies swept a doubleheader from defending champion Brooklyn to strengthen their hold on first place. In the clubhouse the next day, Flick got into a dispute with another player over the ownership of a bat. Lajoie began needling Flick, and soon there were harsh words between the two men. Some other players stepped between them to prevent a fight, and it appeared things had cooled off when Lajoie unexpectedly took a swing at Flick. Flick ducked and Lajoie's hand hit a grate, breaking his thumb. Although four inches taller and almost thirty pounds heavier than his adversary, the Frenchman also emerged from the fight with a black eye. When the two men finally were separated, Flick stormed out of the clubhouse, vowing never to play on the same team as Lajoie again.

At first, the absence of the two ballplayers from the lineup was attributed to injuries "suffered in pregame practice." But it was not long before the true story leaked out, and Lajoie came under heavy criticism for his actions.

Flick, who was batting over .400 at the time, stayed away three days before Shettsline finally was able to talk him into rejoining the team. Lajoie would be out of action for more than a month. By the time he returned in July, the Phillies had fallen out of the lead and were slumping badly.

Philadelphia finished in third place that season, eight games behind Brooklyn, and Colonel Rogers blamed Lajoie for the team's failure to win its first pennant.

"We knew the pennant was gone right there," Rogers later said of Lajoie's fight with Flick. "The people in Philadelphia were up in arms that Lajoie should take such foolish chances over matters so trivial. Some demanded a fine of one thousand dollars. Others suggested many intemperate things."

The Big Frenchman was in no mood to listen to such talk. In his mind, Rogers still owed him four hundred dollars as well as the money he still had not received for his baseball shoes and uniform.

That winter, sports editor Frank Hough of the *Inquirer* in Philadelphia relayed word to Lajoie that the new American League team in Philadelphia was willing to pay him sixteen thousand dollars over the next four years. Before accepting the offer, Lajoie gave Colonel Rogers one last chance to make up the difference in the money paid him and Delahanty. Again, the Colonel stubbornly refused.

On Valentine's Day 1901, Lajoie made the jump, signing a four-year deal with Connie Mack of the Philadelphia Athletics. It was one of the best bargains the American League ever got.

• • •

The Lajoie trial lasted for two Saturdays. At times, the bitterness between the two sides became evident. Larry Lajoie took the stand and related the events surrounding the contract he had signed with the Phillies in 1900 and how he had been led to believe he was being paid the same amount as Ed Delahanty. The ball club's lawyers doggedly tried to establish that Delahanty received the most money because he served as the team captain.

"Wasn't Delahanty paid six hundred dollars extra for captaining the team?" demanded one of Colonel's attorneys. "Wasn't he the captain of the nine?"

"I don't know," Lajoie answered dryly. "He was supposed to be the captain. I heard it said that he was the captain."

The man feigned surprise. "Oh, no? Did Delahanty act as captain?"

"No, he did not."

"Well, who did?"

Lajoie glanced across the room at Shettsline, who was listening intently to the exchange. "Why, Shettsline. He seemed to manage and captain from the bench. He wanted to be the whole thing."

On May 17, one month into the season, Judge Ralston issued his ruling. In a stunning decision, he refused the injunction requested by Colonel Rogers on the grounds a baseball contract lacked mutuality.

"If the Court were to enjoin the defendant for the balance of the period for which he agreed to play for the plaintiff," reasoned the Judge, "there would be no way to compel the plaintiff to employ him or to pay him a salary for more than ten days."

There was an outburst of clapping and cheering in the courtroom, and a huge smile crossed Lajoie's normally stoic face. He shook hands with each of his lawyers, and as he made his way toward the door he continued to shake the hands of every one of the well-wishers who wanted to congratulate him. The ballplayer now was free to rejoin his new team and resume his career.

Across the room, Colonel Rogers quickly packed up his papers to leave. A stubborn and unyielding man as well as a shrewd lawyer, he was determined to continue the fight. He did not know when he was beaten.

• • •

In Baltimore, the Orioles began the season in fine fashion. Rain forced the postponement of the scheduled opener, and the honor of staging the American League's first game as a major circuit went to Chicago, where the White Sox defeated the Cleveland Bronchos, later known as the Blues, by the score of 8–2. Baltimore finally opened its season two days later amid much hoopla. People lined the streets to cheer the players during a forty-carriage parade to Oriole Park, where the enthusiastic fans presented them with flowers and other gifts. There were 10,371 spectators on hand, and the above-capacity crowd was rewarded with a 10–2 victory over the Boston Puritans. McGraw made the day an even greater success by making two hits himself. Among those on hand to congratulate him afterward was Ban Johnson, who had been there to throw out the ceremonial first ball.

The team McGraw had put together lacked the talent of the old Orioles clubs, but it played with that same spirit. It was a fast, hustling team, with six .300 hitters in its starting lineup and a strong frontline pitcher in the tireless McGinnity. The Orioles played well early in the season, and for a while showed signs of being a pennant contender, once winning eleven games in a row.

But it did not take long for trouble to develop. Two weeks into the campaign, McGraw had his first run-in with one of Ban Johnson's umpires. At a game in Philadelphia in early May, he forced umpire Jim Haskell to back down and reverse a decision. The next day, McGraw tried the same bullying tactics. This time, Haskell ordered him off the field. McGraw immediately sent a wire to league headquarters complaining about Haskell's incompetence. In reply, Johnson told newsmen that "those who I hear are getting to be rather boisterous and rowdy [might] have their wings clipped right off."

A week later, the league president backed up his talk by

slapping a five-day suspension on McGraw for his conduct in a series against the Athletics in Baltimore.

McGraw did not endure such treatment lightly. Nor did he appreciate how Johnson conducted other league business. Johnson's autocratic power was so great he even handled travel arrangements for all American League teams. The Orioles were about to leave Boston for a trip to Milwaukee that spring when McGraw received a telegram from the league president instructing him to travel by rail to Buffalo. There, he would be met by an envoy who would furnish the tickets for the remainder of the journey west. But when the Orioles arrived, the league representative was not there, having missed his connections. While McGraw fumed, the team had to stay over in Buffalo an entire day waiting for the man. As a result, the Orioles arrived late in Milwaukee and had to play the first game there without any rest.

There was another ugly incident in Detroit. Orioles pitcher Handsome Harry Howell got ejected for arguing a call at home plate, and Turkey Mike Donlin responded by firing the ball at umpire Jack Sheridan's back. When McGraw ordered Howell to return to the mound in defiance of the umpire, Sheridan forfeited the game to the Tigers. McGraw complained that Sheridan and others of Johnson's umpires were incompetent. And without competent umpires, reasoned McGraw, Johnson could not expect discipline on the field.

With each such incident, the animosity grew between the league president and the Baltimore manager. McGraw was angry Johnson was treating him only as one of eight hired managers rather than the club owner he also was. And for his part, Johnson was beginning to have doubts about McGraw's loyalty to the American League.

• • •

Although running a ball club kept him busy that season, John McGraw found time for other activities. An early June morning found him on the platform of the Indianapolis train station. It was not yet dawn, and the station was dark and nearly deserted as McGraw took his bag and began walking down the street. After he had gone two blocks, he came to a waiting carriage. Inside was an attractive young woman, who greeted him by name and motioned him to climb aboard. They drove away from town and soon came to a heavily wooded eight-acre estate.

By now, it was growing light, and McGraw was able to inspect the luxurious surroundings. He had seen the place before, and he was well aware of the story behind it. Seven years earlier, an Indianapolis businessman had won the hand of a twenty-four-year-old actress named Elsie Lombard, whom he had first seen while she was starring in the New York stage play *A Temperance Town*. He built the house for his new bride, and the estate had been christened "Lombardy" in a toast by James Whitcomb Riley, the "Hoosier poet." McGraw now was being escorted to that house by the former Elsie Lombard herself.

He had been summoned to Indianapolis by John T. Brush, one of the most powerful owners in the National League. At the end of each of the past two seasons, Brush had offered McGraw the job as manager of his Cincinnati Reds. Both times, McGraw had turned him down. Now, Brush had an even better offer to make the cocky young ballplayer and magnate.

Brush, a gaunt man with a bent nose and a sad expression on his face, looked older than his fifty-six years. He suffered from a progressive disease of the nervous system known as locomotor ataxia, and he was in constant pain and often walked with two canes. Many nights he could not sleep because of his discomfort, and he would sit up hours playing solitaire card games, one after the other.

Brush had made his fortune through a department store he had opened in Indianapolis when he was only thirty years old. It was one of the earliest stores of its kind outside Chicago and the big Eastern cities, and Brush built it into a lucrative business through his successful promotions and bargain prices. One day, he took a book away from one of his clerks he caught reading while on duty. Upstairs in his office, Brush himself became interested in the book, which outlined the rules of baseball. After reading it all the way through, he decided that baseball was a growing sport and would be a useful vehicle to advertise his business. This led him to purchase the Indianapolis franchise, which then competed in the American Association and later joined the National League. Even when the National League dropped Indianapolis in 1890, Brush managed to buy stock in the Giants. The next year, he became owner of the Cincinnati Reds, at the same time maintaining his holdings in the New York team.

It was such cross-ownership, or "syndicate baseball," which led Brush to become the target of Ban Johnson's barbs in the *Cincinnati Commercial-Gazette*. The remarks, noted one observer, "had the crack of a black snake whip." It was the beginning of a growing enmity between the two men.

Brush had made other enemies in baseball, and even his fellow magnates were suspicious of him. Brush preferred to stay out of the public view, and his secretive methods created a sinister air about him. Said one critic, "Chicanery is the ozone which keeps his old frame from snapping and dark-lantern methods the food which vitalizes his bodily tissues."

One of Brush's staunchest adversaries had been the bombastic Andrew Freedman, principal owner of the New York Giants, and the two men had clashed often over the years. But the arrival of the American League in 1901 forced a truce between them, and that summer they had allied themselves against the common enemy.

It was this unlikely alliance that prompted Brush to meet with McGraw. The old man had an offer to make the ballplayer. Once again, he wanted to hire him as a manager. But this time the position Brush had in mind was not with the Cincinnati ball club. He wanted McGraw to take over the New York Giants. It might not have been the first time such a proposition had been made. On at least two occasions earlier in the year, McGraw had met with Freedman, touching off rumors he had been asked to manage the Giants.

But there was more to this deal. Brush told McGraw he also could sell his Baltimore club to the National League for a handsome profit. The National League then would drive the American League out of business and would return to a twelve-team circuit by reclaiming Washington as well as Baltimore and adding Indianapolis and Detroit.

McGraw listened intently as Brush laid out the scenario. It had been one of McGraw's goals to run a ball club in New York. He had hoped to do so by moving his Baltimore club there when the American League was ready to invade that territory, but his recent troubles were making him uneasy about Ban Johnson's intentions. There was talk Johnson intended to abandon McGraw by dropping Baltimore from the league and establishing another team in New York.

In McGraw's mind, he was only being prudent by responding to Brush's overtures. He agreed to relay the proposal to fellow American League managers Jimmy Manning of Washington and George Stallings of Detroit.

Later, McGraw sneaked out of Indianapolis the same way he had arrived—under the cover of darkness.

• • •

The war between the two leagues took many strange twists and turns that summer. In the American League, they played with baseballs that bore the famous brand of A. J. Reach & Co. The founder and president of the company was the former baseball great Albert Reach, who also happened to be the president of the Philadelphia Phillies of the National League. This apparent duplicity by Reach was a result of Ban Johnson's shrewdness. When he decided to place a team in Philadelphia, Johnson did so by recruiting Ben Shibe, Reach's partner in the sporting-goods firm. As part of the deal to get Shibe to buy into the American League, Johnson also offered to make the Reach & Co. baseball the official ball of the organization. That put Reach in the curious position of owning a National League ball club while his signature appeared on the baseballs used by the rival league. To add to the intrigue, Reach's son, George, was married to Shibe's daughter, Mary.

The relationship between the two teams was further complicated when Hughie Jennings, the famous first baseman, left Brooklyn and arrived in Philadelphia intending to join Connie Mack's Athletics. Instead, he found himself in the plush furnishings of the hometeam clubhouse at National League Park, where he scribbled his name to a contract with the Phillies on Friday morning, June 21.

Surrounding him were spacious lockers and shower baths, and in the basement below was a large swimming pool. The players called the clubhouse "Fort Rogers" in deference to its builder, Colonel Rogers of the Phillies. Jennings still remembered the first time he laid eyes upon the facility following its completion five years earlier. "Why, I wouldn't kick much on paying thirty dollars for the conveniences here," he had marveled.

The red-haired Jennings was an intelligent and cocky man, always smiling and laughing. He came from the coal-mining regions of western Pennsylvania and while playing ball he had earned a law degree from Cornell in the off-seasons. He also was a tough man, having survived three skull fractures during his playing career.

Jennings broke into the major leagues as a first baseman, and later switched to third and then shortstop. It was at shortstop that he attained his greatest fame as the captain of the great Baltimore teams of the 1890s. When Orioles manager

Ned Hanlon moved to Brooklyn in 1899, Jennings went with him and helped the Dodgers win pennants that year and the next. At the same time, he made a remarkable comeback from an arm injury that threatened to end his career. A sore right arm forced him to move to first base, and Jennings feared the arm was going dead. He responded by teaching himself how to throw left-handed. Eventually, his right arm recovered sufficiently to use it so he abandoned his ambidexterity, but not before he had mastered throwing accurately and for some distance with his left arm.

In the spring of 1901, Jennings joined the exodus of players from the National League, signing with Connie Mack's Philadelphia Americans for thirty-five hundred dollars. But before Jennings could report to his new ball club, his old pal John McGraw managed to sabotage the deal.

McGraw and Jennings had been roommates on the old Orioles, and it was during their late-night sessions talking baseball that most of the team's trademark plays had been devised. The two became fast friends, even going so far as to stage an annual celebration for their birthdays, which fell five days apart in April.

Upon learning that Jennings had signed with Mack, McGraw objected on the grounds his friend already had agreed to play for him in Baltimore. When the dispute first broke out, Jennings said he would honor his contract with Mack. But after talking with McGraw, he threatened to return to the National League if he couldn't play in Baltimore. McGraw tried to work out a deal with Mack, but the Athletics manager refused as a matter of principle. Neither side would back down, so Jennings didn't suit up for anyone.

Finally, two months into the season, Jennings issued an ultimatum. He would play in Baltimore or he wouldn't play in the American League. Mack, insisting he had a signed contract with the player, still would not release Jennings.

The next day, Jennings signed with the Phillies for $140

less than he was supposed to get with the Athletics. When word of the deal reached Ban Johnson, the American League president was furious. This time, McGraw's actions had deprived the league of a valuable player. In Johnson's mind, the time was coming to teach the upstart manager a lesson.

• • •

Every city had its special rooters. In Philadelphia, there was a man known only as Smith who always was on hand to greet the visiting National League teams when they arrived at the Hanover Hotel. He boasted that he knew almost every man who ever played in the National League and the old American Association. The ballplayers described him as a true "You can't lose me Charley." A blind comedian named Max Arnold also was a regular at the ballpark, where he sat in the stands and followed the action by listening to the cheers of the crowd and the narrative of nearby spectators.

Gamblers could be spotted with increasing frequency. They congregated on the roof of the clubhouse to place wagers ranging from ten dollars to one hundred dollars and up on the outcome of the games as well as the results of certain plays. As the size of the crowds grew, the practice spread to the grandstand, and the right-hand section of the cantilever became the favorite spot for the bettors. On days doubleheaders were played, the gamblers could be seen almost falling over each other in a hurried effort to get their wagers down between games.

Early in the 1901 season, the Philadelphia fans had thrown their loyalty behind Connie Mack's Athletics, but by mid-August they were coming back to see the Phillies. More than 132,000 fans had flocked to National League Park at Broad Street and Lehigh Avenue, while the Athletics had drawn only 114,500 to their Columbia Park in the Brewerytown section of Philadelphia.

The Phillies played in a ballpark they called "the Hump"

because the grounds had been elevated to compensate for damages caused by a railroad tunnel that had been built beneath the outfield.

It was one of the grandest structures in baseball. The original facility on these grounds had been built in 1887, but seven years later a fire started by a plumber's stove had damaged much of the framework. Rather than replace it with another of the wooden ballparks then in vogue, the Phillies erected a steel-and-brick structure that drew visitors from all over the country.

In an effort to increase profits and capitalize on the growing popularity of bicycling, a quarter-mile bike track fifteen feet wide had been added around the edge of the playing field. As a result, the outfielders had to run up the banked turns on the track to pull down long fly balls.

A modern marvel in many aspects, the Philadelphia ballpark was an example of old-fashioned practicality in others. To keep the grass trimmed, three sheep grazed in the outfield between games.

Hughie Jennings walked onto the field in a Philadelphia uniform for the first time the day he signed, and the 765 spectators on hand gave him a standing ovation. Still out of shape from his long layoff, Jennings sat on the bench and watched his first game with the Phillies. He led the cheers when Ed Delahanty drove a ball into the gallery for a home run in the 4–1 victory over St. Louis.

The scene in the clubhouse afterward reflected the renewed enthusiasm on the team. Players joked and laughed with one another and there was bold talk of a pennant. Although they were in fifth place with a won-lost record of 24–24, the addition of a proven winner such as Jennings had given the Phillies a shot of confidence.

Ed Delahanty shared in the celebration. His moods were determined by his hitting, and this had been a particularly good day for him. In four at-bats, he had hit a single, double, and home run to raise his batting average to .357, fourth best in the league. The home run had been a most impressive shot, sailing over the outfield wall and into the crowd in the left-field stands.

But the camaraderie the Phillies shared that afternoon would not last long. Unknowingly, Jennings had just set into motion the sequence of events that would lead to the team's ruin.

• • •

The next day, Ed Delahanty stood in the outfield lazily shagging fly balls. At the time, Del could not have been happier over the new addition to the ball club.

Big Ed was a versatile fielder, and during his thirteen seasons with Philadelphia and one with Cleveland of the Players League, he had played every position in the infield and outfield. Most of that time had been spent in the outfield, where he covered a surprising amount of ground for such a big man. He had no superior in playing left field, according to many. Philadelphia newspaperman William G. Weart claimed Del had "an eye as keen as a hawk to judge the direction a ball would take" and "an ear that was trained to instinctively estimate by the sound of the crack of the bat how far the ball would travel."

Delahanty moved to first base when he developed a sore arm in 1900, but the recovery of his arm along with the arrival of Jennings to play first base allowed Del to return to the outfield.

Delahanty responded to the switch by going on a batting rampage. He got four hits his first game back in the outfield, with Jennings making his debut for the Phillies at first base. The Phillies won six games in a row before losing to the first-place Pirates, and in that stretch Del made twenty-one hits in thirty-nine at-bats. Twice he hit drives deep into the left-field gallery, which few other players had reached. Once, he hit a ball onto the roof of the center-field clubhouse, scattering some gamblers who had gathered there.

Not even a three-game sweep by the Pirates, dropping the Phillies back to fourth place, discouraged the players. They were at the train station preparing to leave on a three-week western trip, and Jennings was holding court with some of the newspaper writers.

"I may be mistaken," he said, "but I feel sure the Phillies will land in first place within the next two weeks. If we reach there, they will never dislodge us."

Standing nearby, Delahanty said nothing. But already there were signs of strain showing between the two men. Jennings recently had replaced Del as team captain, a move that had become a hot topic of gossip around the league. Some observers, among them Franklin Richter of *Sporting Life*, claimed that Delahanty was glad to hand over the job "as he never was fond of the honor, except the extra money there was in it." Others believed differently. There were reports that Del was upset over being replaced and a feud was brewing between him and Jennings. And Del, the senior member of the team, had a lot of friends on the club who were loyal to him.

• • •

Ban Johnson sensed a double cross that July. Two of his managers, Jimmy Manning of Washington and George Stallings of Detroit, had come to him with curious reports. Both men claimed to have been approached by a Baltimore newspaperman on behalf of John McGraw. Supposedly, this reporter delivered a message of a plot to destroy the American League. If Manning and Stallings would take part, they were told, the Washington and Detroit teams would be added to the National League.

The two men immediately tipped off Johnson to the scheme. It did not take the American League president long to decide how to respond to the threat. He would conduct another player raid on the National League, only this time he would do so in a way that would be especially damaging. He would leave the Pittsburgh team intact, thus destroying the competitive balance in the older league, while recruiting only star players on the other clubs. And, adding a special twist, he would target one National League club for destruction by a wholesale raid on its players.

And finally, Johnson would attempt to discredit McGraw by revealing his treachery. In early August, Johnson leaked a story accusing the Baltimore manager of "flirting" with John T. Brush or other National League magnates about jumping back to that organization.

"We want no Benedict Arnold in our midst," Johnson proclaimed indignantly.

When the story reached McGraw, he denied the charges against him and lashed back at Johnson.

"So the 'Julius Caesar' of the American League calls me a 'Benedict Arnold,' does he? I should like to know upon what evidence he bases that assertion."

• • •

Frank Hough, sports editor of the *Inquirer* in Philadelphia, accompanied the Phillies to New York in early August to report on the team's drive for its first pennant. On August 4, he watched as the Phillies swept a doubleheader against the Giants in the Polo Grounds to post their fiftieth victory and move within one and a half games of the first-place Pirates.

But Hough had more than the pennant race on his mind. Although he dutifully filed his stories on the games, his primary concern in New York was serving as an agent for the American League.

The previous week, Washington manager Jimmy Manning had slipped into Philadelphia to talk to some of the Phillies. In all, he met with as many as ten of the players, among them Ed Delahanty and his roommate, pitcher Jack Townsend, as well as another of Del's close friends, pitcher Al Orth. The others included Elmer Flick, the hard-hitting outfielder who had fought with Larry Lajoie the year before, and third baseman Harry Wolverton. The team's three catchers—Ed McFarland, Klondike Douglass, and Fred Jacklitsch—and another pitcher, Frosty Bill Duggleby, also were approached.

It was Hough's task to follow up by acting as the middleman for some of the American League interests who wanted to make an offer to Delahanty. The two men met secretly in New York, and Hough outlined the offer to Del. The Washington ball club would go as high as four thousand dollars to sign him, but as part of the deal Delahanty had to get Wolverton to make the jump with him. Del listened carefully and told Hough he would get back to him.

After the series in New York, the Phillies had a day off before playing in Boston. It was at this time that Ed Delahanty and Harry Wolverton were spotted at the Bingham House in Washington, accompanied by Jimmy Manning and Connie Mack. Also with them was Frank Hough, a newspaperman who not only reported the baseball news but also helped make it.

• • •

In Boston, Fred Tenney of the Beaneaters collided with Harry Wolverton of the Phillies, sending the Philadelphia third baseman sprawling in the dirt. When he got to his feet, Wolverton was clutching his right shoulder in pain. He could barely lift the arm, but the stocky infielder refused to leave the game.

Wolverton was a loud, aggressive ballplayer, constantly talking and yelling and taunting the opposition. From the time he broke into the National League with Chicago in 1898, he began to make a name for himself. In one of his first games, Dan McGann slid hard into him at third base and in retaliation Wolverton bounced the ball off the player's bald head.

His first year in the league, the brash young Wolverton even was foolish enough to challenge Ed Delahanty. In a game against the Phillies, Wolverton noticed Del make a feint to bunt. On the next pitch, Wolverton crept in on the grass to be ready to field the ball. To his surprise, Delahanty crossed him up by swinging away and sending a vicious line shot right at him. The ball almost tore off Wolverton's leg, and from then on he always made sure to play Del on the back edge of the infield.

When Wolverton joined the Philies in 1900, he and Delahanty used to laugh about the incident. The two men became friends but ultimately Wolverton would find other reasons to try to distance himself from Del.

In mid-August 1901, news of the American League raid on the Phillies leaked into the newspapers. There were reports that seven of the Philadelphia players had signed or promised to sign with the rival league and more were to follow their lead. Delahanty and Wolverton were identified as two of those who already had made deals with Washington.

Over the next few days, the Philadelphia ballplayers were marched into Colonel Rogers's office and interrogated one by one. Delahanty denied all the allegations against him, including the rumor he was acting as an agent for the American League, and the Colonel could come up with no proof of the charges. Nor did any of the other players admit to any wrongdoing.

Eventually, most of the suspicion was centered on Wolverton. Twice the third baseman was interrogated by Colonel Rogers, who tried to bully him into confessing his duplicity. These were stormy sessions, punctuated by loud shouts and threats. Rogers claimed the player had violated paragraph 5 of his contract, which forbade negotiations or contracting with any other club during the playing season. Wolverton refused to be intimidated, neither admitting nor denying he had signed with the American League. Colonel Rogers seethed but he was too prudent to take immediate action. Wolverton was batting .300 and playing an aggressive brand of ball at third base. Not wanting to disrupt his ball club while it still had a chance to win the pennant, the Colonel bided his time.

But in Boston on August 22, Wolverton made a costly mistake. He hurt his shoulder. He got two hits that day as the Phillies lost, 5–4, to fall two games behind the Pirates, but his shoulder was so sore afterward it was obvious he would have to be sidelined. Suddenly, he was expendable.

Wolverton was unusually quiet on the ride back to the team's hotel that afternoon. He went to the front desk to get his room key, and there he was handed a message. With his one good arm, he opened the paper to discover it was a written notice from the ball club of his suspension without pay for the remainder of the season.

That evening, the other players watched silently as Wolverton left to return to Philadelphia. There was a sense of uneasiness on the ball club that had nothing to do with the pressures of the pennant race. Before leaving, Wolverton informed his teammates Colonel Rogers told him that before any man on the squad received his pay he would be required to sign an affidavit swearing he had not signed or agreed to sign with the American League for the following season.

• • •

In Buffalo, President William McKinley was greeting visitors to the Pan-American Exposition on September 6 when a young anarchist named Leon Czolgosz rushed forward and shot him with a pistol concealed in a handkerchief. McKinley, hit twice in the abdomen, lingered for eight days before dying. He was buried September 19 in his hometown of Canton, Ohio. On that day, all games in the National League were postponed out of respect to the slain president.

Ed Delahanty, a longtime admirer of McKinley, awoke that morning at a hotel in Pittsburgh feeling feverish and weak.

Still, he got out of his sickbed long enough to attend a memorial service at a nearby church.

The pennant race was all but over. For weeks, the Phillies had doggedly pursued the Pirates, once winning ten games in a row. The final showdown between the two teams came in Pittsburgh. The Pirates won the first three games to deliver the knockout blow. Two days after McKinley was buried, Delahanty knocked out a double and two singles to help the Phillies salvage the final game of the series, 4–2, but by then the Pirates had an insurmountable eight-game lead. Pittsburgh would become the first western team in fourteen years to win the National League pennant.

Back in Philadelphia, Harry Wolverton continued to report to the ballpark every day, hoping to lay the grounds for a lawsuit against the club. He also appealed to the Players Protective Association for help in his fight against what he believed was an unfair and illegal suspension. Two of the three members on the grievance committee favored calling a strike on Wolverton's behalf, but the association's president, Tom Daly, counseled against such a rash action.

The last day of the season, the Phillies returned home and lost to Boston, 7–3. The players gave Billy Shettsline a gold watch and chain in appreciation for his services, then collected their final paychecks and said their goodbyes to each other. Despite Colonel Rogers's earlier threats, every man on the team except Wolverton was paid in full and no one was asked to sign an affidavit.

Across town, Ben Shibe, owner of the Athletics, presented Larry Lajoie with an imitation glove filled with gold pieces. It was a fitting conclusion to a memorable season for the Big Frenchman, who had batted an astounding .422 to win the American League batting championship.

That same week, Lajoie received another "gift" in recognition of his services for the American League ball club. He and fellow jumpers Chick Fraser and Bill Bernhard were served formal notice of the Philadelphia National League ball club's renewal of its option on their services. For Colonel Rogers, regaining the services of Napoleon Lajoie had become a matter of principle.

• • •

One afternoon in early October, Ed Delahanty emerged from a hotel lobby and headed down a crowded sidewalk in New York. With him were John McGraw and Clark Griffith, both prominent American Leaguers. There were rumors they were in the city to convince McGraw's former Orioles teammate Wee Willie Keeler to jump from Brooklyn to the American League.

The three men were so deep in conversation they didn't notice the approaching newspaper reporter until it was too late. The ballplayers were evasive when asked the nature of their business in New York, and Delahanty continued to insist he had not yet signed with any team for the coming season.

"If Colonel Rogers wants me to play with his team next year," said Del, "he has got to come to the price I quote. I have not signed for next year, and I am not going to be in a hurry to sign. I don't mind saying that I am out for the money and shall go where I can get the most. I have had offers from several American League clubs but have accepted none."

Griffith, the pitcher-manager who had just won twenty-four games to lead the White Sox to the first American League championship, laughed derisively at the mention of the Phillies owner.

"Rogers's Philadelphia (National) League team of next year won't be fit to play in a minor league," Griff sneered.

Evidence of such a claim could be found in the contracts already in possession of Ban Johnson at American League headquarters in New York. The player raids on the Phillies had produced spectacular results, with ten players agreeing to jump to the American League.

Washington had been the main beneficiary, landing Delahanty, Wolverton, and pitchers Al Orth and Jack Townsend. Despite Del's repeated denials, the American League office already had received his signed contract calling for him to receive $4,000 in both 1902 and 1903. That was an increase in salary of $1,000 per year over what he had been paid in Philadelphia. Wolverton received a 50 percent increase to $3,250, while Orth's pay jumped by one-third to $3,259. Townsend doubled his salary to $2,400.

Del's contract had been drawn up by Louis Hutt, a Philadelphia lawyer. It seemed there was no way the ballplayer could lose on the deal. The way the contract was worded, Ed Delahanty would have to die to lose any part of the money.

II
THE KING OF
BATTERS

MEN WHO MET HIM HAD TO ADMIT HE WAS A HANDSOME FELLOW, THOUGH THERE WAS AN AIR ABOUT HIM THAT INDICATED HE WAS A ROUGHNECK AT HEART AND NO MAN TO TAMPER WITH. HE HAD THAT WIDE-EYED, HALF-SMILING, READY-FOR-ANYTHING LOOK THAT IS CHARACTERISTIC OF A CERTAIN TYPE OF IRISHMAN.

ROBERT SMITH

L ong after he had become a famous ballplayer, Ed
Delahanty returned to his hometown of Cleveland one day
and walked to an old fire station on St. Clair Street. Above
the entryway was a sign which read Engine House No. 5. Next
to the station was a vacant lot, where a baseball field had been
laid out.

Ed could look out across the ballfield and let his thoughts
take him back to his childhood. This was where he had
learned to play baseball, and it was here the legend of Ed
Delahanty had begun.

The Delahanty family lived in a house just around the corner, on Phelps Street, later East 34th, between St. Clair and
Superior. Ed was born on October 30, 1867, the son of James
Delahanty. The Delahantys were of Irish origin, although the
family line also contained some French and Norman blood
and the family name originally was spelled "de la Hante."

As a young boy, Ed used to hang around the fire station.
Firemen were among the biggest baseball fans, and the men
at the St. Clair station were no exception. They manicured a
baseball diamond on the adjacent lot, and once winter ended
they never let the field get out of shape. They worked on it
between alarms, and the games played there drew kids from
all the surrounding neighborhoods.

As soon as he was old enough, Ed began taking part in the
games and before long he became a hero to the local firemen.
He always was big for his age, and he could hit the ball amazing distances.

"That boy can hit the ball farther than any player in
Cleveland, that's what he can," boasted the fire captain.

Ed would play late into the evening, and invariably one of
the younger Delahantys would come down the street yelling
that he was wanted at home.

"When I get through batting this ball," Ed would yell back.

"But Ma says come on now."

"Get away from me, I'm busy!"

More often than not, the younger brother would end up staying, either to break into the game himself or, failing in that, to shag the ball for the older players.

Ed also hung out at Kennard Street Park, the home of Cleveland's National League team, and he got to field balls from such well-known ballplayers as Pebbly Jack Glasscock and Fred "Sure Shot" Dunlap. Eventually, Ed got good enough to cross over to the west side of the Cuyahoga River, where the best Cleveland amateur teams played. The peak of his amateur career came when he joined the Shamrocks, a crack team which played everyone in northern Ohio and occasionally even took on the major-league teams. His manager, Charles Salen, liked to claim that Ed was the team's most expensive player, owing to the fact he hit so many home runs from the Riverbed grounds into the adjacent river or the nearby shipyards. Ed played catcher, and one year the Shamrocks had a hard-throwing pitcher named P. H. Callahan. Years later, Callahan, who went on to become a prominent banker, would brag that whenever the team had money to divide, as pitcher he got ten dollars while the great Delahanty was given only five.

The name Shamrocks was a fitting title for a baseball team. Baseball already was the American Game, but no group embraced it with more enthusiasm or played it with more skill than did the Irish-Americans. In the early days, they so dominated the sport it generally was assumed they simply were natural-born ballplayers.

The Irish influence on the game had begun in the cities of the North and Northeast, where the immigrants gathered. In 1870, roughly one-third of the U.S. population of 38.5 million people was Irish born, and half of these Irish-Americans resided in the three states of New York, Pennsylvania, and Massachusetts. Generally poor and uneducated, they faced terrible discrimination. They competed with the better-educated German immigrants of the period for work and usually were forced to take the more menial jobs. Many of the men became laborers and found themselves singled out for derision by other city dwellers, taunted for their ways and ridiculed for their speech. The Irish often said "me" for "I" and "ye" for "you," and commonly used such grammar as "I seen" for "I saw." They mispronounced such words as "join," which became "jine," and "believe," which became "belave." In return, Irish men were disparagingly referred to as "Micks," a version of the common Irish name Michael. There were other terms of derision. A wheelbarrow became an Irish buggy, a shovel an Irish spoon, and bricks Irish confetti.

But one area where the Irish gained respect and even admiration was on the ballfield. Though they were considered undisciplined and easily discouraged, no one questioned the skill and cunning of the Irish ballplayers. Not even the Germans, considered to be reliable pitchers and "heavy and plucky" batsmen although "slow thinkers," could match the Irish on the diamond.

There were so many Irishmen in the game that many young ballplayers adopted Irish surnames or called themselves "Mickey" in the hopes of attracting attention. From the beginning, baseball rosters were full of such Irish names as McVey, Fogarty, McCormick, Kelly, O'Leary, and O'Brien.

But baseball wasn't in the plans Ed's mother had for her son. He attended Cleveland's Central High School, which had been established in 1846 as the first public high school west of the Alleghenies. Along with the other students, Ed studied such subjects as English, mathematics, natural science, bookkeeping, rhetoric, mental philosophy, analytical geometry, and mechanics. Many of the young men from Cleveland's Irish-American community went to work as hard laborers at the steel mills or shipyards. Mrs. Delahanty had bigger plans for her eldest son. After graduation from high school, he began attending St. Joseph's College on Woodland Avenue and taking a course in bookkeeping.

That same year, a state baseball league was being formed in Ohio, and eight cities were starting teams from scratch. Quality ballplayers were needed, and applicants were asked to send letters listing their qualifications and terms.

Ed Delahanty was one of hundreds of young ballplayers to respond to the advertisements. He wrote down his batting and fielding averages and his positions played and mailed in his application. He was nineteen years old at the time.

When the reply came back offering Delahanty a spot on the Mansfield club, Ed's mother threw the letter in the stove and burned it. She was dead set against her son becoming a professional ballplayer.

It was only because Mansfield also wanted Phil Osborne, a pitcher for the Shamrocks, that Ed learned about the letter. Del sent word to the manager that from then on all his mail should be directed to the fire station.

Before setting off to make his mark in baseball in 1887, Ed Delahanty went to his mother and announced, "I'm goin' to quit you and play ball in Mansfield."

"Drat baseball," shot back Mrs. Delahanty. "It's ruinin' the family."

In a final attempt to win her approval, Ed reminded his mother of the money there was to be made in the game.

"I'm comin' home with 'rocks' in me pocket," he said.

Mrs. Delahanty remained unimpressed.

"And many's the time ye've come back with rocks on the side of yer thick head," she answered.

• • •

This same year, a Philadelphia businessman went to his young son one day and asked, "How would you like to take a drive?" The boy agreed, and so they set off in their carriage and drove from their house in Frankford into the city. When they reached the corner of Huntingdon and Broad streets, the man stopped the horse-drawn buggy and pointed to the adjacent field.

"George, what do you think of that for a ball ground?"

Looking out at the dirty stream that ran through the middle of the site and the tin cans and other debris which were scattered about, the boy began to laugh.

"I know, Father, you are joking and having some fun with me."

"Not at all," answered the man in his clipped English accent. "What's more, I intend to erect a ballpark here of which we all may be proud."

The man was Alfred Reach, and he would make good on his word. A few months later, on April 30, 1887, his new ballpark was completed, and more than 20,000 spectators crowded into the wooden stands or pushed up behind the ropes which ringed the outfield. To mark the occasion, the hometown Phillies and their opponents, the New York Giants, arrived at the grounds after parading down Broad Street in decorated carriages accompanied by a marching band. Swept up in the enthusiasm of the event, the Phillies christened the structure in spectacular fashion when their first nine batters hit safely en route to a 19–10 victory.

The ballpark was a testament to the success of Al Reach and to the game of baseball itself. Reach was born in London in 1840 and had come to America as a young boy. His arrival in the country coincided roughly with a key date in the development of the game of baseball. On June 19, 1846, on the Elysian Field in Hoboken, New Jersey, two amateur teams played a form of the game under rules established by Alexander J. Cartwright, a young New York surveyor and the descendant of British sea captains.

Cartwright's game had its roots in the English game of rounders or, going back even further, to similar contests played by the ancient Egyptians, but Americans would claim it as their own. "The game of base ball is pre-eminently an American invention, intended for Americans," insisted Seymour R. Church, a turn-of-the-century baseball historian. To give credit to the Egyptians or English or anyone else, he added, would be a gross distortion of fact. "As well credit the ancient Egyptians with the invention of the steam engine," reasoned Church, "because they may have been the first to smelt iron, of which Fulton made his steam-driven machine centuries later."

As a young man in New York, Cartwright himself previously had played a game called "base ball" on 27th Street, later the site of one of the Madison Square Gardens. In drawing up the rules for his new game, he had dropped the requirement that a runner be struck by the ball to be retired and adopted the use of nine players per side and nine innings per contest.

Reach played baseball as a youngster in Brooklyn in the 1850s, and as the popularity of the game spread, so too did his reputation. A left-handed second baseman, Reach was a quick, sure-handed fielder and a skillful batter. He first came to prominence as a member of the powerful Eckford Club, which was made up of a group of workers for Brooklyn shipbuilder Henry Eckford.

At the time, baseball was an amateur sport, and most of the sixty or so clubs on the membership rolls of the National Association of Base Ball Players were formed according to occupation. The Mutuals of New York were firemen for the Mutual Hook and Ladder Company No. 1, the Manhattans were New York policemen, and the Metropolitans were schoolteachers.

Inevitably, the emphasis on winning led to abuses of the system, and it was not long before some of the top players began to receive offers of political favors, gifts, and even cash in return for their services. Foremost among these players was

Reach, who gained popular recognition as baseball's first "professional" ballplayer.

Reach staked his claim to the title in 1863 when he let it be known he would leave the Eckfords for a price, touching off a bidding war between a Baltimore club and the Philadelphia Athletics. Reach, who ran a small jewelry store in New York, chose the Philadelphia club so that he could be closer to his business. In exchange, he received twenty-five dollars a week "for expenses."

The hiring of a ballplayer was unprecedented, though it later was revealed that star pitcher Jimmy Creighton had been receiving under-the-table payments from the Brooklyn Excelsiors in 1860. But Creighton would leave behind a more tragic legacy. The first pitcher to develop a snap throw enabling him to fire the ball to the plate with great speed, he also was a powerful batter, and this proved to be his downfall. While straining to run out a home run in 1862, Creighton felt a sharp pain in his midsection. He staggered across the marble plate and turned to the catcher with a startled look on his face. "I must have snapped my belt," he said. "I guess not," answered the catcher. Creighton then collapsed into the man's arms, suffering from internal hemorrhaging. According to news accounts, he swung so hard in hitting the ball he ruptured his bladder. The great Jimmy Creighton, only twenty-one years old, died in terrible agony a few days later, the game's first casualty.

Reach was to enjoy a much happier fate. His signing opened the door for others, and by 1869 clubs such as the Athletics, New York Mutuals, and Chicago White Stockings were openly involved in professional baseball. Another, less prominent, team even went one step further. The Red Stocking Club of Cincinnati, under the leadership of Harry Wright, placed every one of its players under contract for an entire season's play and embarked on a historic cross-country tour. The Red

Stockings' final scorecard read sixty victories and one tie, and their success encouraged other clubs to follow suit. Two years later, in 1871, baseball's first league, the National Association of Professional Base Ball Players, was formed.

For Reach, the National Association was the stepping stone to even greater financial rewards. Under his direction, the Athletics won baseball's inaugural championship and with it a pennant paid for through the ten dollar membership fee assessed each of the nine clubs. By the time he stepped down as an active player five years later, Reach's reputation as the greatest second baseman in baseball history was solidified by his selection to the first All-American team.

Though his greatest glory was behind him, even greater success lay ahead for Reach. Capitalizing on the fame he gained on the diamond, he opened a cigar store which became a popular gathering place for Philadelphia sportsmen. Later, he turned it into a sporting-goods store, A. J. Reach & Co., located on Market Street in Philadelphia. As his retail, wholesale, and mail-order business grew, Reach brought in Ben Shibe, a former leatherworker, as a partner. Where once he had made whips and other leather goods, Shibe now concentrated on balls and the increasingly popular fielder's mitts. He developed the two-piece baseball cover and the cork-center baseball, two innovations which enabled A. J. Reach & Co. to corner the market on the manufacturing of balls.

Reach and Shibe first made their baseballs in a one-story frame building near the corner of North and Fifth streets in Philadelphia, where they turned out only a few dozen balls each day. Soon, they moved to a large, five-story factory in nearby Kensington, and through the use of assembly lines and special machinery they began producing balls by the hundreds. As baseball continued to prosper, so too did Reach, his name stamped on thousands of balls in play around the country.

Reach's departure as an active player in 1876 coincided

with another significant event in the development of baseball. In Chicago, a wholesale grocer named William Hulbert had gained control of the White Stockings. Fiercely loyal to his city, Hulbert once had proclaimed, "I would rather be a lamp post in Chicago than a millionaire in any other city." It was this civic pride that prompted Hulbert to break up four-time champion Boston's monopoly of the National Association by signing the "Big Four" of Albert Spalding, Ross Barnes, Deacon White, and Cal McVey away from Beantown. To complete his daring player raids, Hulbert also lured star first baseman Cap Anson away from Philadelphia.

The key to the deal had been Spalding, the game's top pitcher as well as one of if its shrewdest players. Hulbert attempted to assure Spalding that all the players involved would get their money regardless of any action by their old ball clubs, but still the pitcher feared he and the others might be expelled from the association for their actions.

Hulbert pondered this a few minutes and then hit upon a bold idea. "Spalding, I have a new scheme. Let us anticipate the Eastern cusses and organize a new association before the March meeting, and then see who will do the expelling."

The two men proceeded to hammer out the plans for a new league, which they called the National League of Professional Base Ball Clubs. The charter was drawn up at a dramatic organizational meeting in New York's Grand Central Hotel. Hulbert ushered the other baseball men into a room, locked the door, and, with a sweeping gesture, placed the key in his pocket. This was done, he explained to his guests, "to make it impossible for any of you to go out until I have finished what I have to say." When the meeting ended, the National League had been born.

The success of the National League, as well as that of the rival American Association, founded in 1882, convinced Reach there was money to be made in operating a ball club. So, he went into partnership with Colonel John I. Rogers, a noted Philadelphia lawyer, and formed a team which they called the Phillies.

The Phillies joined the National League in 1883, and the following year were boosted by the addition of the famous Harry Wright as manager. Each season the team became more powerful, and when he built his new ballpark, Reach did so in anticipation of flying the league championship banner overhead.

• • •

Ed Delahanty arrived in Mansfield in the spring of 1887 and was greeted by a one-armed pitcher named George England. The two became life-long friends. England was a tough, clever pitcher who never complained about his handicap. Del played every position on the team except pitcher and posted a .355 batting average.

Del also hooked up with Bob Allen, a local player whose boyhood friends included a fellow by the name of Warren Harding. Both Allen and Harding were destined to become leaders in their chosen fields. Allen eventually became president of baseball's Southern Association. Harding became president of the United States.

The Ohio League collapsed at the end of that season, and the next year the remnants of the organization lined up with some other clubs to form the Tri-State League. Del was picked up by the team in Wheeling, West Virginia, and he arrived in town in the spring of 1888 after hopping a freight train. It was a rough town known as "the Nail City," but Delahanty, big and rugged, quickly won over the fans with his powerful batting and clever fielding at second base.

Del played for Al Buckenberger, only twenty-seven years old but already on his way to becoming one of the game's top managers. Buck was an easygoing man but he had a strict set of rules which he rigidly enforced. He required his players to report to the playing grounds for practice every morning at 10 o'clock when they were at home. On the road, they had to show up by 8 o'clock sharp. They had to retire no later than 11:30 at night.

Players assigned ticket duty at the gate were not allowed to leave their posts. Drinking "intoxicating liquors" was prohibited, as was playing practical jokes, which the manager believed could lead to "discord."

Buckenberger demanded one other thing of his players. They had to conduct themselves as gentlemen at all times. "Do not let everybody in the hotel dining room know that you are ball players," he warned. "It is hardly a place for talking base ball."

Although he was mild-mannered, Buck knew how to enforce discipline. Once a team he was managing was playing on an unbearably hot afternoon, and late in the game the center fielder stationed himself up against the fence where it was shady. The catcher kept signaling him to move in, but the center fielder kept sneaking back into the shade. This went on for a while before Buckenberger impatiently ordered the catcher to move the fielder in where he could get to the ball.

"I've tried to, but he won't leave the shade," said the young catcher, by now almost in tears.

Angered, Buckenberger walked halfway onto the field and motioned for the center fielder to move in. The player just shook his head and stood in the shade, fanning himself with his cap. Finally, Buckenberger yelled out, "You are fined twenty-five dollars for standing in the shade!"

That got the center fielder's attention, and he worked the rest of the game in the sunlight. Still, the fine stood.

The Tri-State League was one of the fastest in baseball, and it also was one of the most progressive. There was an unwritten rule against black, or "colored," players in organized baseball. The Zanesville team defied the ban by recruiting catcher

Dick Johnson, a black, and the league allowed him to play on the grounds he "had been signed in due form and his contract officially promulgated."

But no one in the league attracted as much attention as Ed Delahanty. He knocked out hit after hit, and through twenty-one games he had been "Chicagoed," or shut out, only twice. At a game in Kalamazoo, Michigan, he slammed three hits and stole three bases to lead Wheeling to a 4–2 victory. That same day, a member of the Philadelphia National League club arrived in town. Already, Del's fame was spreading.

• • •

In Philadelphia, there was a pitcher who carried with him a large chest of assorted medicines. He was Charlie Ferguson, a marvelous athlete and a tremendous pitcher but a man strangely obsessed with his health. Ferguson was a chronic complainer, always fretting over real and imaginary ailments, and he took enough of his various medicines to kill an ordinary man.

Invariably, he would complain of being too sick to play, but his teammates would goad him into trying and before long he would be firing strikes past batters and running about the diamond as spry as ever. It got to be a joke on the team that whenever Fergy said he was sick it was a sure sign of victory for he always played his best ball at such times.

Ferguson had joined the Phillies in 1884, and over the next four seasons he won ninety-nine games, sixteen of them in a row, and once threw a no-hitter. He had an overpowering fastball, and he took particular pleasure in "knocking out" new catchers who were put in to receive his pitches. Then the Phillies got a tough young left-handed catcher named Jack Clements, who handled everything Fergy threw up to the plate, and the two became closely linked as Philadelphia's "Ferocious Battery."

For all his skills as a pitcher, Ferguson was perhaps the

most versatile performer in the game. There was nothing on a baseball diamond he could not do well. He was a crack hitter, a speedy base runner, a sure-handed infielder, and a brilliant outfielder. On occasion, he was called upon to play center field, and he displayed a strong throwing arm and excellent range. Later, he filled in at second base, where he ranked behind only Chicago's "Unzer Fritz" Pfeffer in fielding prowess. A left-handed batter, Ferguson ran with long strides which made his speed deceptive. In 1887, he won twenty-two games as a pitcher and hit .412 as a batter. Walks were counted as hits that season, inflating his batting average, but even subtracting the bases on balls he posted an impressive .337 mark.

Ferguson performed so well at so many positions that manager Harry Wright's greatest dilemma was deciding where the star player could best serve the team. Finally, in the spring of 1888, the Phillies chose to make Ferguson their full-time second baseman. And then one day prior to the opening of the season, Fergy began to complain of feeling poorly. No one seemed concerned as the ballplayer once again began taking his medicines, but this time it was no imaginary illness. Ferguson had contracted typhoid fever and was confined to his bed, where he grew steadily weaker.

He never made it back to the baseball field. On April 29, nine days into the season and just twelve days past his twenty-fifth birthday, Charlie Ferguson died.

The flags at the Philadelphia ballpark were lowered to half staff, black crepe was placed above the team benches, and each Phillies player wore a black band on his arm.

Demoralized by the death of their teammate and robbed of their best player, the Phillies struggled to recover. Philadelphia, a second-place ball club the previous season, fell into last place by the end of April. The losses continued to mount in May, and Charlie Bastian, Ferguson's replacement at second base, was particularly ineffective.

In desperation, Al Reach and Harry Wright began searching for a new second baseman. The name they came up with was Ed Delahanty.

An agent was sent to see Delahanty play, and the reports that came back were so positive Reach himself traveled to West Virginia to secure the player's release. It cost Philadelphia a reported two thousand dollars to make the transaction, a record purchase price for a minor-league ball-player. It was the first of many records Del would set in his career.

• • •

Ed Delahanty stood in the outfield at Chicago's West Side Park and surveyed the scene around him. It was May 22, 1888, his first day in the National League. He looked up and saw the White Stockings' championship pennants flapping in the breeze—one each for the seasons 1876, 1880, 1881, 1882, 1885, and 1886. Legend had it that yet another banner lay beneath the playing field, buried there by the New York Giants as a symbolic gesture after their pennant hopes died in a dramatic last-day showdown against the White Stockings to end the 1885 season.

Looking around the grandstands in the bathtub-shaped ballpark, Del could see the private boxes for team officials, newspapermen, and special guests of the ball club. Western Union had its own box to receive scores from other National League parks, and club president Albert Spalding had a telephone in his private box to allow him "to conduct details of the game" without leaving his seat.

Shortly before game time, there was a loud roar from the crowd and Del turned to see the White Stockings marching ceremoniously onto the field. At the head of the procession was Chicago's legendary player-manager, Adrian "Cap" Anson, a powerfully built six-foot, 220-pounder with striking blue eyes, blond hair, a bushy moustache, and a dominating presence.

Anson was the game's first great slugger, carrying to the plate a long, thick bat reputed to be the heaviest ever used by a player. "About as heavy as a telegraph pole," claimed veteran ballplayer Sam Crane. Behind Anson strode the other Chicago players, handsomely outfitted in wide trousers, silk stockings, and tight sleeveless jerseys with "CHICAGO" emblazoned across the front. There was the powerfully built but acrobatic shortstop, Big Ned Williamson. Next came second baseman Fred "Unzer Fritz" Pfeffer, who had a face like the German leader Bismarck, and tough little third baseman Tommy Burns, the other members of the famous "Stone Wall" infield.

While the appearance of the White Stockings got the crowd excited, the Phillies proceeded to entertain the fans with a lively pregame warmup which manager Harry Wright had introduced to replace the standard practice of simply tossing around a ball to loosen up. Each Phillie raced from his position in the field to the plate, swung at twelve pitches, and then ran back to his defensive station. All the while, a fungo hitter stood down the baseline and batted fly balls to the outfielders. And when the Phillies first took the field, the starters marched nine abreast to first base and from there sprinted around the diamond, each man dropping off at his position.

Delahanty played second base that day. Although he went hitless in three at-bats and committed two errors in the field, the Phillies prevailed, 4–2. The next day, Del lined a single off Chicago pitcher George Borchers for his first hit, and he was on his way.

• • •

Ed Delahanty had entered a world of excitement and glamour but one that also could be rough and hazardous.

The ballplayers hustled from city to city by railway, dozing fitfully while being bumped and jolted aboard sleeper cars. The train engines burned four-foot logs for fuel, and there were piles of the logs stacked at intervals along the tracks.

The trains would stop to refuel, and when they did the ballplayers would get out to help load the wood. The players even managed to turn this into a game. Coming to a crooked piece, they would yell, "Look out, here's a curve!" or, for a straight piece, "Here's a hot one!" Other passengers considered it a sign of good fortune to have a baseball team aboard the train, for ballplayers had uncanny luck in avoiding railroad wrecks. No ballplayer ever had been killed or injured in a railroad accident, though some narrowly averted disaster. A delay once prevented the White Stockings from making a connection in New York, and the train which they were to have ridden was involved in one of the worst railway accidents ever in New England.

Teams generally stayed in the "swellest" hotels, two men to a room. Each player anted up fifty cents a day for room and board.

From the hotel, the players rode to the ballparks in uniform aboard horse-drawn carriages, a ceremony known as the "tally-ho." Fans and curious spectators lined the route to cheer or taunt them, while boys ran alongside calling out their names. At times, the ride could get rough. After an important victory in Detroit one year, the White Stockings were returning to their hotel when an angry mob on Woodward Avenue began pelting them with stones. Anson ordered his men to stay put and keep their heads down, but the words no sooner were out of his mouth than a quid of tobacco hit him square in the face. That was more than King Kelly and Tommy Burns could take. They sprang from the carriage and waded into the crowd, swinging their fists. The police arrived to break up the melee, but not before Burns suffered a broken wrist and several toughs in the mob had their heads cracked and their noses bloodied.

It could be a rough game on the field, too, as players bullied and intimidated each other, howled at umpires, and schemed up new ways to circumvent the ever-changing rules. But baseball also was a colorful, wildly exciting game.

The pitchers stood in a four-foot by five-and-a-half-foot "pitching box" only fifty feet from home plate and fired a 5- to 5 ¼-ounce ball—the standard weight throughout the game's history—toward the batsman. Some could throw a swift underhanded curveball, a phenomena which had been stumbled upon by Arthur "Candy" Cummings two decades earlier. While tossing clam shells into the water at a beach near his home in Brooklyn, Cummings was intrigued by the irregular path followed by the shells. He applied the same principles to throwing a baseball, and soon was baffling opponents with a mysterious pitch that one batter described thusly: "It came at us and then it went away from us." Where once they had been required to throw the ball in an underhand motion, pitchers now were allowed to use a full overhand delivery which enabled them to gain speed and put a variety of spins on the ball. In 1888, the batters were making the further adjustment to the new three-strike rule, which many believed tipped the scales too far in favor of the pitchers.

"Coachers" stood in their boxes along the two foul lines, screaming and cursing the fielders, taunting the pitcher, and shouting at runners, "Give them the spikes!" Arlie Latham, known as "the Freshest Man on Earth," was the king of the coachers, chattering constantly, making monkey faces, and joking with the crowd. Doggie Miller of Pittsburgh bellowed in such a loud voice he became known as "Foghorn." At Louisville, a player by the name of Skyrocket Smith took the practice one step further. When the batter hit the ball or a runner started to steal, Skyrocket emitted a loud, screeching howl as if he were in mortal agony.

In New York, Giants manager Jim Mutrie would leave the team under the direction of catcher Buck Ewing and join the fans in the stands. Outfitted in a stovepipe hat, frock coat, gloves, and spats, Mutrie would roam up and down the aisles shouting, "Who are the people?" In response, the cranks would yell back, "We are the people!" And so, the Giants became known as "the people's team." It also was Mutrie who had given the team its name when he became so enthused during a rally that he jumped off the bench and cried out proudly, "My big fellows! My giants!"

In Boston, Mike "King" Kelly, the son of an Irish paper-hanger, strutted down the street wearing London-tailored clothes, pointed high-button shoes, and a tall silk hat. He had a handsome face, thick dark hair, and a mighty handlebar moustache. He was "the King of Baseball," a dangerous hitter and daring base runner who had been the most flamboyant member of Cap Anson's great Chicago White Stockings. After Kelly's drinking and escapades got to be too much for Anson, he was sold to Boston for the record price of ten thousand dollars. He became known as the "Ten-Thousand Dollar Beauty," the title by which actress Louise Montague was being billed in Boston at the time. When he showed up at games drunk, Kelly would stagger under fly balls only to see them bounce off his mitt. "By Gad," the King would call out cheerfully, "I made it hit me gloves, anyhow!"

In Detroit, there was a slugging catcher named Charlie Bennett, who celebrated the team's championship in 1887 by happily racing around the bases pushing a wheelbarrow full of five hundred silver dollars which the fans had presented to him.

On Delahanty's first trip to Washington, he fell victim to a stunt by Senators catcher Connie Mack, who discreetly tipped Del's bat to throw off his swing. Mack also liked to place baseballs in an ice box overnight to deaden them and then slip them into play when the other team was batting.

There was an eccentric outfielder named Cliff Carroll, who traveled around the league with his pet monkey in tow. When the monkey died, it was buried under home plate in the

Pittsburgh ballpark. In Indianapolis, infielder Tommy "Dude" Esterbrook walked the city streets with a green parrot on his shoulder. The other players claimed Esterbrook was "nutty, screwy and full of tacks."

In Pittsburgh, Del marveled at the blazing speed of a slender, boyish-looking outfielder named Billy Sunday. In the outfield Sunday could cover enough ground for two men, and on the bases his wild and reckless running caused more wild throws than anyone. "Hurry it up!" fielders would shout anxiously whenever Sunday hit the ball. But it wasn't just his speed and mild appearance that made Sunday stand out among such a rough crew. While playing for the White Stockings a year earlier, he had been sitting on a street corner, drunk, when he heard the singing of a Salvation Army gospel group. Touched by the sound of the hymns, Billy turned to his companions with tears streaming down his face. "Boys, it's all off," he said in a voice choked with emotion. "We have come to where the roads part."

With that, he walked off to answer the calling of the Lord. Behind him, he could hear the taunts of his teammates: "Look out, Billy, you better not take a chance! They might get hold of you and spoil a good ballplayer!" From that moment, Billy Sunday lived a life of piety, carrying his Bible wherever he went and using his fame as a ballplayer to draw crowds to the religious talks he gave at cities around the league. And when his traveling companions got too boisterous with their cursing, gambling, and card playing on the train, Billy would rise from his seat and go back to talk to them about the Lord, only to be greeted with their gruff cries of "Go back and read your book!"

• • •

Success in this fast-paced game did not come easily for Ed Delahanty. That first season, the pitchers threw him high curveballs around the neck and he flailed wildly at them. He would walk back to the bench cursing and swearing at himself. "If I could only hold myself like that old crab Anson, I would bat better than he ever did!" he complained to anyone who would listen. Then Del broke a finger, which further handicapped his batting. In the field, runners discreetly bumped him off balance as they raced past, and he made forty-seven errors in just seventy-four games. At the plate, his batting average was a weak .228.

But Del was tough, standing up to base runners and refusing to be intimidated by pitchers who threw the ball in on him. And for such a big man, he was surprisingly fast, covering the ground in big, lumbering strides. Del stole thirty-eight bases that first season, and he liked to boast he could beat any man on the team in a footrace. Once he went so far as to spot teammate Arthur Irwin five yards in a hundred-yard race, losing twenty dollars when he came up just short of overtaking the speedy shortstop.

For a twenty-year-old boy, it had been a fast and spectacular ride to the top. In October 1888, just eighteen months after he had left home to chase a dream, he returned to Cleveland a bona fide major-league ballplayer. He would never forget the greeting that awaited him. When Ed stepped off the train, a crowd of friends and supporters waiting on the platform began to serenade him.

• • •

Elsewhere in Cleveland, two men shook hands on a deal that would make them business partners. One was a big, jovial fellow who wore ill-fitting suits. His name was Albert Lofton "Al" Johnson, and at twenty-six years of age he already was a wealthy streetcar magnate and entrepreneur. With him was Dr. Edwin Beeman, a Cleveland physician who was struggling to capitalize on a discovery he had made a few years earlier. A specialist in digestive disorders, Dr. Beeman learned through his research that pepsin, an extract from the stomach of hogs, provided humans with relief from indigestion. He began to manufacture pepsin as a powder, selling it in his trademark blue bottle with the picture of a pig on the label.

But Beeman needed money to expand his operation. Johnson and a couple of other investors agreed to put up the cash to form the Beeman Chemical Co. Not long afterward, a bookkeeper at the company spilled some of the powder on a stick of chewing gum. This gave Beeman an idea. By adding the pepsin to gum, he could sell more of his product. This led to the introduction of Beeman's Pepsin Gum, and that turned out to be even more popular than the indigestion powder. Eventually, Beeman would become a millionaire, known across the nation as "the Chewing Gum King."

Al Johnson made many such investments in his life. He was a shrewd businessman but also an idealist, as was his brother and close companion, Tom, who was destined to leave a lasting mark on Cleveland as its reform mayor after the turn of the century.

Al and Tom Johnson came from a prominent Kentucky family. Their uncle was Richard M. Johnson, who in the War of 1812 gained fame by killing the great Shawnee Indian Chief Tecumseh and in 1836 became the only U.S. vice president chosen for the office by the Senate. Their father was a Confederate colonel whose Kentucky cotton plantation was wiped out during the Civil War.

The brothers had no formal education, but they proved to be very hard-working and resourceful. Tom got a job at a street-railway company in Louisville, and by the time he was seventeen he had worked his way up from office boy to secretary of the firm. He also invented a see-through fare box which earned him a small fortune of thirty thousand dollars. Al Johnson pooled what money he had with Tom's substantial bankroll, and the two brothers bought a floundering railway company in Indianapolis. They turned it into a profitable business, sold out, and then moved to Cleveland to enter the streetcar business in that city. There, Tom Johnson took on railway magnate Mark Hanna and the two brothers used their political maneuvering and astute management to build up a streetcar empire of their own, making millions of dollars along the way.

In addition to his business interests, Al Johnson also was a noted sportsman and enthusiastic baseball fan. He regularly attended games at Cleveland's Kennard Park, often traveled out of town to important contests, and frequently placed sizable wagers on the outcome of these games. But most of all, Johnson enjoyed keeping company with the ballplayers. He liked to play cards with them, drink with them, and swap stories with them.

Johnson's favorite ballplayer was King Kelly, who was the subject of a tale Al enjoyed relating to his friends. A few years earlier, the White Stockings had been in Cleveland and Johnson gave Kelly the keys to his apartment on Superior Street. After the game, Kelly and some of his pals showed up at the place with a large supply of what the ballplayers liked to call "wet groceries." The players proceeded to get drunk and boisterous, and toward midnight Kelly and Big Ned Williamson began a "hat-smashing expedition." They stomped just about every hat in the room, but Fred Pfeffer managed to save his baseball cap by tossing it out the window. Kelly was so "lushed" he jumped out after the cap, not realizing there was a hundred-foot drop to the stone-paved court below. Johnson and Piano Legs Gore barely grabbed the King in time to pull him to safety. When he sobered up later and realized what had happened, Kelly fainted.

Johnson also played a role in Billy Sunday's famous "prayer catch." Shortly after his religious conversion, Sunday had saved an important game in Detroit by making a miraculous catch of a Charlie Bennett drive by racing into the crowd lining the outfield to track down the ball. "God, I'm in an awful hole," Sunday prayed as he made his mad dash through the crowd. "Help me out, if you ever helped mortal man. Help me get that ball. And you haven't much time to make up your mind, either!" With that, Sunday made a desperate stab for the ball and felt it hit in his mitt as he tumbled forward and landed beneath a team of horses. Sunday never would forget what happened next. As he jumped up and held the ball aloft, Johnson raced up to him and happily shoved a wad of bills into his hand. "Here's ten dollars, Bill," Johnson said enthusiastically. "Buy yourself the best hat in Chicago. That catch won me fifteen hundred dollars!"

Before long, Johnson's friendship with the players and his sporting nature led him to make an even more daring gamble. There was a revolution brewing in baseball, and both Al Johnson and Ed Delahanty were about to be swept up in it.

• • •

In Washington, President Grover Cleveland, a 250-pounder with a bull neck and double chin, greeted the Chicago White Stockings at a reception at the conclusion of the 1888 baseball season. One by one, the famous ballplayers stepped up to shake the president's hand.

It came Silver Flint's turn, and the rugged catcher stuck out a hand that was bent and gnarled, its fingers twisted grotesquely. Flint had come up in the days when catchers received the ball barehanded, and it was said that every bone in the ball of his hand had been broken. The president clasped the catcher's hand in his meaty paw and shook it vigorously. He then thrust his hand into his coat pocket and felt around as if he were searching for something. When the President pulled out his hand he was surprised to see it was empty.

"Oh, I beg pardon," he said to Flint. "I thought you had given me a handful of walnuts."

The presidential sendoff marked the beginning of one of the most fantastic journeys ever taken by a group of ballplayers. Under the direction of Albert Spalding, the White Stockings president and a wealthy sporting-goods magnate, the Chicago team and a squad of All-Americans were embarking on what was to become a world baseball tour.

Over the following months, the players sailed the South Pacific to Australia, then northward through the Indian Ocean to Egypt and from there on to Europe. They played games in the shadow of the Egyptian pyramids, incurred the wrath of Italian authorities with their boisterousness in Naples, and swatted fly balls against the backdrop of the Eiffel Tower in Paris. In England, Spalding shocked the crowd by pulling up a chair next to Prince Edward and poking him in the arm following an outstanding play. "What do you think of that?" Spalding asked excitedly.

Unknown to Spalding, there also were many times when several players gathered by themselves for late-night meetings held in hushed tones. These were baseball's brotherhood men, and their leader was one of the most prominent members of the tour.

He was John Montgomery Ward, the charismatic and brilliant shortstop for the New York Giants. A handsome man with blond hair and blue eyes, Ward was one of the most versatile performers the game ever would know. He had begun his career as a pitcher, won as many as forty-seven games in one season, and in 1880 had thrown the second perfect game in National League history. When an arm injury threatened to curtail his career, Ward made such a successful switch to the infield that in 1885 he soon became known as "Mr. Shortstop." But Ward was no ordinary ballplayer.

He attended Pennsylvania State College at age 13 and studied law at Columbia University in New York while playing for the Giants. After he was graduated from law school with honors in 1885, Ward received a degree in political science and was honored by Columbia for his work in that field. He was admitted to the New York bar in 1888, the same year he became the first ballplayer to write a book with the publication of *Baseball: How to Become a Player*. And he still found time that season to lead the Giants to their first pennant. On top of all that, Ward was married to Helen Dauvray, the beautiful and famous actress who had donated the Dauvray Cup to be awarded to the winner of an annual postseason series between the champions of the National League and American Association.

At times, Ward angered others with his aloofness and his habit of reporting late to practice, a tactic which became so well known that ballplayers around the league began to refer to any latecomer as a Johnny Ward. But Ward was a natural leader and he had a tremendous following among his fellow players.

He also was the driving force behind the Brotherhood of Professional Base Ball Players, which had been founded in 1885 as the first protective association for ballplayers. Ward was president of the organization, while his brother-in-law, Giants pitcher Tim Keefe, served as treasurer.

And it was not by coincidence that while Ward and several of the other top brotherhood men were out of the country on Spalding's tour in the winter of 1888–89 the owners elected to adopt a revolutionary new plan to restrict player salaries. Under this "classification plan" worked out by Indianapolis owner John T. Brush, players would be rated by their abilities and paid accordingly. The pay scale would range from twenty-five hundred dollars for Class A players down to fifteen hundred dollars for Class E players.

Spalding's tour group steamed into New York harbor on April 6, 1889, five months after its departure. The ballplayers were greeted by boat whistles and the cheers of the two hundred well-wishers gathered on the dock. Among those in the crowd were several brotherhood men. Grim faced, they pulled Ward aside and gave him the news as soon as he stepped off the boat. Ward said nothing as he shoved his way through the crowd of reporters and hopped in a waiting carriage. His response to the classification plan would come soon enough.

• • •

Early in the summer of 1889, Ned Hanlon, the Pittsburgh center fielder and a staunch brotherhood man, called upon Al Johnson at Cleveland's elegant Hollenden Hotel. The establishment featured paneled walls, mahogany fittings, specially designed furniture, incandescent lights, and a hundred private baths. It was an unlikely setting for such a meeting.

The two men exchanged pleasantries, and then Hanlon got down to business. He began by spelling out a bold plan which John Montgomery Ward had devised on behalf of the brotherhood. It was Ward's idea to form a new major league. But this was not to be a conventional baseball league, explained Hanlon. This time, the players themselves would have a say in running the organization.

The basis of the league was a unique alliance between capitalists and laborers. Both sides would agree to participate in the management of the league, and both sides would share in the profits. There would be no owners. Instead, the money would come from "contributors." Gate receipts would pay for salaries first and then operating expenses, with the remaining money counted as profits to be split among the shareholders, whose ranks would include the players.

The brotherhood, more than one hundred men strong and with chapters in every league city, could deliver the players for such an organization. But first, Ward needed to find the necessary financial backing.

Johnson, who was known and trusted by many of the players, was being offered the first chance to invest in the proposed organization. Johnson admitted his interest, but asked first to meet with some of the other players. He wanted to see just how devoted to the cause these men were.

Over the next few weeks, whenever a National League team came to Cleveland, players would secretly meet with Al Johnson at the Hollenden. Sentries were posted in the corridors, and the policemen on the street outside were bribed not to report the comings and goings of so many ballplayers. One by one, these players told Johnson of the abuses they had suffered, of money withheld from their paychecks without warning, of fines and blacklists, and of the indignity of being bought and sold at the whim of others. Most of all, they complained about the hated reserve clause, under which an owner could lay a claim on their services indefinitely.

"I support my wife and family on the money I earn on the field," said outfielder Larry Twitchell. "In 1888, I played with Detroit. This year, I was sold to Cleveland, and told that I must play in that city or leave a business in which I have spent my life to attain proficiency. All of my interests were elsewhere, yet I was forced to play in Cleveland.

"Now, suppose I were a theatrical manager like George Floyd. I signed a contract with the Aronsons. After I had fulfilled my contract with them, they could say to me, 'You must manage our opera house in Hoboken next year or we will drive you out of the business.'

"Well, I guess not. No corporation in the world can say 'you must' or 'you must not' to a man except the ones conducted by the present baseball magnates."

Johnson, an idealist, was appalled by such abuses.

"If the league can hold a man on a contract for any or all time that it may desire," he exclaimed, "why then the laws of our land are worse than those of any other nation on earth, and instead of progressing, as we suppose that every civilized country is struggling to do, the sooner we turn back the better."

As a businessman, Johnson also realized the tremendous financial possibilities in operating a baseball club. He had seen streetcars on rival railways packed with people going to baseball parks on their routes. With his own ball club, he would have the opportunity to put a ballpark on one of his own railway lines. The thought of his two businesses helping each other gave him "visions of millions of dollars of profit."

July 14, 1889, marked the one hundredth anniversary of Bastille Day, when mobs in Paris stormed the infamous prison fortress and touched off the French Revolution. Members of the brotherhood marked the occasion by setting into motion a revolution of their own. It was on that day that Al Johnson appeared before them and announced he had agreed to become the first investor in the new league. The ballplayers greeted the news with cheers and whistles as they rushed to the front of the room to shake Johnson's hand and slap him on the back.

News of the fledgling league finally broke in September. Spalding's response was to brand the brotherhood "an oath-bound, secret organization of strikers."

In Cleveland that month, Al Johnson celebrated with his friend, King Kelly, who was in town with the Boston ball club. They drank several bottles of Pomer Sec, and Kelly was so hung over the next day he was unable to play. Instead, he sat on the bench in a light overcoat, got ejected from the premises for accusing the umpire of robbery, was roughed up by the police, and was put out on the sidewalk. Without the King, the Beaneaters lost to fall one game behind the Giants, which is where they remained when the season ended three days later. The newspapers termed Kelly's costly indiscretion a "jollification."

The pennant race soon was forgotten anyway. On November 6, 1889, more than thirty players and their backers met at the Fifth Avenue Hotel in New York City and formed the Players' National League of Base Ball Clubs.

The announcement of the new league came in the form of a 643-word document known as the Brotherhood Manifesto, which outlined the players' case and asked for the support of the public.

"There was a time when the League stood for integrity and fair dealing," it began. "Today it stands for dollars and cents. Once it looked to the elevation of the game and an honest exhibition of the sport. Today its eyes are upon the turnstile. Men have come into the business for no other motive than to exploit it for every dollar in sight."

In conclusion, the players noted, "We began organizing for ourselves, and are in shape to go ahead next year under new management and new auspices."

• • •

The strength of the brotherhood was such that players on the National League clubs defected en masse, enabling the Players' League to start out with teams that closely resembled the old National League clubs in most cities. The standard practice was for the brotherhood representatives in the various cities to head up these clubs.

In Philadelphia, the famous drop-ball pitcher Charlie Buffinton directed the new brotherhood team, and he took with him the heart of the Phillies ball club. Jimmy Fogarty, the hard-hitting outfielder with the black handlebar moustache, made the jump, as did popular first baseman Sid Farrar. So did John Clements, the left-handed catcher, and Big Sam Thompson, the powerful outfielder.

At this point in his career, Ed Delahanty had done little to distinguish himself. A reckless head-first slide into Cleveland second baseman Cub Stricker in 1889, Del's second year in the National League, had resulted in a broken collarbone and sidelined him much of the season. He batted a respectable .293 but showed few signs of power, and he fielded erratically.

But like so many others, Delahanty became a prized commodity that winter. He signed a standard Players' League contract in November 1889 and later was transferred to the Cleveland brotherhood team. Al Johnson, the backer of the Cleveland club, arranged the deal, believing the young ballplayer would be a big draw in his hometown.

Soon, Colonel Rogers of the Phillies began to launch a counterattack to regain his ballplayers. He offered bribes to lure the defectors back into the fold, and in quick order Thompson, Clements, Joe Mulvey, Pop Schriver, and Al Myers jumped back to the Phillies. Delahanty also pulled the "dinky-dink," or runout, when Rogers offered him $500 plus an increase in his salary of $1,750.

There was turmoil everywhere in the weeks leading up to the 1890 season. The Players' League, National League, and American Association all were scrambling wildly for players to fill out their rosters, and fantastic sums of money were being dangled in front of the players.

Albert Spalding held a secret rendezvous with King Kelly, who was heading up the Boston Players' League team, and placed a ten thousand dollar check in front of him.

"Mike, how would you like that check for ten thousand dollars filled out to your order?" asked Spalding.

Kelly laughed at the notion. "Would Mike Kelly like ten thousand dollars? I should smile."

Spalding leaned forward and told Kelly the check was his if only he would agree to return to the National League. Stunned, Kelly asked for some time to think it over.

For the next hour and a half, the King paced the city streets, wrestling with his dilemma. Finally, he returned to the room with his answer.

"I can't go back on the boys," he said quietly. "Me mother would never look at me again if I would prove a traitor to the boys."

Spalding was so impressed with the display of loyalty he shook Kelly's hand and loaned him five hundred dollars. "I think it was little enough," Spalding later wrote, "to pay for the anguish of that hour and a half, when he was deciding to give up thousands of dollars on the altar of sentiment in behalf of the Brotherhood."

Buck Ewing, the greatest catcher in the game, came under similar pressure when Giants owner John Day offered him a reported twenty thousand dollars in cash and an extended contract calling for eighty-five hundred dollars if he would rejoin his old team. When word leaked out Ewing was wavering on his commitment to the brotherhood, he was besieged by dozens of telegrams urging him to stand by his comrades.

"What is $1,000,000 to the high esteem and honor in which you are held by our associates in this glorious cause?" wired Pittsburgh outfielder Ned Hanlon. "Spurn all offers and stand firm."

Finally, Ewing gave his reply in a dispatch sent to the *New York World*: "I am as strong now as ever, and will not leave until every man goes."

Charlie Comiskey, the St. Louis Browns star who revolutionized the way first base was played by stationing himself away from the bag, turned his back on a six thousand dollar salary in the American Association to become the player-manager of the Chicago Players' League team.

One prominent ballplayer who did abandon the brotherhood was shortstop Jack Glasscock, who was branded a spy and informer when he jumped back to the National League. Once known as "Pebbly Jack" for his habit of picking up and tossing away real and imagined pebbles at his position in the infield, the shortstop acquired a new nickname that year. To the brotherhood men, he became known as "Judas" Glasscock, a name that in baseball circles became synonymous with treachery and betrayal.

It was a testament to the unity of the players that so few of them gave in to the magnates' offers of signing money, increased pay, and a promise to eliminate the reserve clause. Just three months after it was formed, the Players' League had

188 players under contract. By some accounts, the National League had managed to hang on to only 38 of its players. Among the game's top stars, only Cap Anson, who was himself a shareholder in the Chicago club, remained loyal to the older league. Even Clarence Duval, a pint-sized black man who served as the mascot of the White Stockings, jumped to the Players' League to serve a similar role for the Chicago brotherhood team.

The Players' League struck one of its final blows about a month before the start of the season. After training in Florida, the Phillies were on their way north and had just stopped in Charleston, South Carolina. There, Ed Delahanty received a packet from Al Johnson. Inside was a contract for thirty-five hundred dollars, a check for a thousand dollars in advance pay, train fare north, and some "sandwich money" for the journey.

Delahanty, unhappy and anxious to return to his hometown to play ball, packed his trunk and headed for the train station. Harry Wright intercepted him on the way and tried to convince him of the "unmanliness" of his action, but Del could not be swayed. That afternoon, he boarded a train for Birmingham, Alabama, where he would join the Cleveland Players' League team.

Another Phillie, Joe Mulvey, also had returned to the Players' League a few days earlier. Even in the midst of all the contract jumping and double crosses, Delahanty and Mulvey gained special notoriety for their actions. They were the only players to make three jumps between the two leagues, earning them the title of "triple jumpers."

When word of Del's second defection reached Philadelphia, Colonel Rogers reacted with indignation. "That scalawag! I thought he was a man of honor!"

The reaction among the Phillies was of a different nature. The evening Delahanty departed, they drank a toast to the brotherhood.

• • •

Baseball would never experience another season quite like 1890. Somehow, all three major leagues—the Players' League, the National League, and the American Association—fielded teams and played out their schedules amid the resulting confusion, fan disenchantment, continuing player defections, financial woes, mistrust, and angry charges and countercharges of sabotage.

Players wore white uniforms at home and bright, colorful outfits on the road. Teams lied about attendance figures, gave out free tickets at barber shops and saloons, and hit upon such gimmicks as admitting ladies free on Saturdays or staging "Professional's Day" during which actors were given complimentary passes. Chicago's Albert Spalding assigned agents to count the customers as they passed through the turnstiles at brotherhood games, then published these attendance figures next to those given out by the Players' League to discredit his rivals. When a reporter asked for an attendance count at a Chicago National League game one day, the team's secretary replied. "Twenty-four, eighteen." After the man dutifully logged the figure and left, the secretary turned to Spalding and remarked, "There were twenty-four on one side of the grounds and eighteen on the other. If he reports twenty-four hundred and eighteen, that's a matter for his conscience, not mine."

As manager of the Players' League team in Boston, King Kelly gave himself the day off whenever he felt like it and set his own standards on drinking. When one of his players made several errors in a game, the King handed the man some money and ordered him to go get drunk. "When sober, you're the rottenest ballplayer I ever saw," Kelly said with disgust.

At an American Association game, a heckler taunted umpire Larry O'Dea with the cry, "You're rotten, rotten, rotten!" O'Dea halted play and shouted back, "Maybe I am, but you ought to see my brother." But the fans got the last laugh. After they roughed him up three times in one week, O'Dea resigned as an umpire and left baseball.

Over in the National League, the shortage of quality ballplayers was so acute Chicago's Cap Anson called upon a new outfielder who went by the name Pop Lytle. Whenever the ball was hit to Pop, no matter what the situation, he always threw it to second baseman Bob Glenalvin, his old teammate down at Wheeling. In exasperation, Anson finally called time and went out to confront Lytle.

"See here, you!" shouted Anson. "Why do you always throw to Glenalvin? Why don't you throw the ball where it will do the most good?"

"Well," answered Pop, "I throw it to Glenalvin because he's the only man on the team I know."

In Cleveland, the brotherhood team signed a sixteen-year-old pitcher, Kid McGill, and became known as the Infants.

Another of Ed Delahanty's teammates in Cleveland was the popular slugger Pete Browning, a big, friendly man who entertained the other players with his colorful dialogue, odd habits, and numerous superstitions. Old Pete refused to cross puddles and always touched third base on his way off the field, explaining that it made him a better hitter. In conversation, he liked to refer to himself in the third person, if not as Old Pete then as the Gladiator, a title he picked up for the way he fought with fly balls in the outfield. He also was obsessed with his eyes, which he referred to as his "lamps" or "peepers."

"Old Pete never washes 'em with soap and water," he would explain. "It will ruin the best lamps in the world. Pete closes 'em up when he is washing, then he waits until about ten o'clock, when he goes out in the streets and looks right up in the sun two or three times. That opens 'em up good, and then he can line 'em out."

Although he was an illiterate man and knew practically nothing of events outside of baseball, Browning was one of the most knowledgeable hitters in the game. A two-time batting champion when playing for his hometown Louisville team in the American Association, he always insisted his bats be made to his particular specifications. One year, a Louisville man named John Hillerich made him a bat that Browning called his "Louisville Slugger." Soon, other ballplayers began ordering bats from Hillerich, enabling him to open the bat-making firm of Hillerich & Bradsby.

Browning also liked to label his bats with the deeds they had accomplished. His favorite was one that carried the tag: "In '87, at St. Louis, Old Pete put a dent in the centerfield fence for a home run. Three were on the sacks, and it was the last inning, and that four-sack bingle of Pete's won the game."

But Old Pete also suffered from mastoiditis, a painful infection of the middle ear which left him partially deaf and in frequent pain. He turned to alcohol for relief, and eventually his drinking became so excessive he gained such dubious nicknames as Pistol Pete, Distillery Pete, Old Red-Eye, and the Inspector of Red Lights. "I can't hit the ball," Browning once lamented, "until I hit the bottle."

He appeared washed up after the 1889 season, when his batting average dropped below .300 for the first time in eight seasons, but Old Pete jumped to the Players' League vowing to give up liquor and make a comeback. He made good on both counts, staying off the bottle and hitting a robust .373 to win the batting title.

Delahanty also enjoyed his moments. En route to posting a solid .298 batting average, he banged out six hits in a single game off thirty-two-game winner Mark "Fido" Baldwin of Chicago.

The wild season came to an end with the Players' League championship banner being raised over Brotherhood Grounds in Boston while a band played, "Slide, Kelly, Slide!" But that was to be the last hurrah for the ill-fated league.

Weary parties from all three leagues sat down to peace talks that fall, and though the National League was on the verge of collapse, Albert Spalding was able to bluff his way through the negotiations. The Players' League backers, inexperienced in the ways of baseball, began selling out one by one, either to be merged with existing franchises or to be added to a revamped National League.

In January 1891, the brotherhood men gathered one last time at Nick Engel's Home Plate restaurant on West Twenty-seventh Street in New York. A popular hangout for ballplayers, actors, and other sportsmen, the Home Plate had served as the unofficial headquarters of the brotherhood. "Uncle Nick" was a baseball rooter of "the thirty-third degree," and his friendship with the ballplayers dated back to the early days of the game. Photographs of all the greats covered the walls, and in one corner there was a full-length picture of King Kelly which included a telegram from the player informing Engel of an important victory. It was here that many an important conference had been held and many a triumph celebrated by the players. Now, they had come to stage a wake—for the Players' League and for the brotherhood.

The room grew silent as John Montgomery Ward stood and raised his glass for a toast.

"Pass the wine around," he said sadly, "the league is dead. Long live the league."

· · ·

The ballplayers received their contracts in spring 1891 and stared glumly at the figures on them. Cutbacks were the order of the day. Ed Delahanty's new pact called for a salary of twenty-one hundred dollars, a reduction of almost 33 percent from the lofty sum he had been paid the year before. And ominously, the club had extended the period of its option on each player from two to three years. But it was not necessary for the club to re-sign its players if it did not so choose. Colonel Rogers of the Phillies had worked out this new form of contract, option clause and all, and he stated confidently it could be enforced through the courts.

At that, Del was one of the lucky ones. He at least was being taken back by the Phillies. The elimination of the Players' League had flooded the market with players, and the owners were free to pick and choose from those available. In Philadelphia, Delahanty was the only defector allowed back by a vindictive Colonel Rogers.

Everywhere, players were returning to their old clubs, hat in hand, begging for jobs. A sign of the times was an item which appeared in *Sporting Life,* cruelly mocking the once-brash players: "Lost—A big opinion of myself. Please return to Mister Baldwin, pitcher and contract juggler and a fellow who used to be a cocky gent."

And things soon would get worse. At the end of the 1891 season, the American Association, weakened by the effects of the Brotherhood War, also went under. The National League moved to take up the slack by absorbing some of the franchises and expanding to twelve teams. The players called this revamped organization "the big league," leading to the expression "big-league baseball." A writer for the *Cleveland Press* had a better idea. He proposed the league change its name to "the Monopoly."

His suggestion was not without merit. The magnates now ruled the field, and they were free to operate as they liked. The first order of business in 1892 was to slash costs through roster reductions and pay cuts. Roster limits of fifteen men per team were imposed, meaning there were openings for only 180 players. And shortly after the 1892 season began, the National League clubs enacted payroll reductions ranging from 30 to 40 percent.

The magnates did not even try to conceal their disregard for the contracts the players held. Tony Mullane of Cincinnati received a pay cut from forty-two hundred dollars to thirty-five hundred in midseason. When he objected, owner John T.

Brush informed him his contract was not "worth the paper it was written on." Mullane walked out, refusing to play the second half of the season, but few others followed his lead.

Jack Glasscock, who had incurred the wrath of his fellow players by abandoning the brotherhood in 1890, was summoned to the office of St. Louis owner Chris Von der Ahe to discuss his revised pay. Getting up to leave, Glasscock turned to his companions and said, "Excuse me, I'm going into Von der Ahe's barbershop to get my salary shaved."

The final indignity came at the conclusion of the season in mid-October 1892. The standard player contract ran through November 1, so the ballplayers still had two weeks' pay coming. To eliminate this expense, the magnates simply released all of their players and agreed not to negotiate with each other's possessions. At the appropriate time, they reclaimed all their old players. The *New York World* called these "releases that did not release."

In the spring of 1893, every player on the Phillies refused to sign his contract at the terms offered. But the protest did no good. Colonel Rogers refused to budge on his figures, and eventually the players knuckled under. Not a man on the team was paid more than eighteen hundred dollars that season.

The golden age of the late 1880s was a rapidly fading memory. The inning was over for the ballplayers—the magnates were now at bat.

• • •

For all its drawbacks—the abuse by management, the long train rides, the rowdy fans—Ed Delahanty enjoyed the life of a ballplayer.

He liked the excitement, the travel, the contacts, and the companionship of his fellow players. Big Ed was a good-natured and likable sort, a socially inclined young man described by his teammates as a "good fellow."

He made friends easily, was popular with the kids who

hung around the ballparks, and was generous to a fault. Del gave little thought to the future, preferring to live for the moment and enjoy the many rewards that came his way. He liked to bet the horse races, he attended the theater regularly, and during the off-season he was a loyal patron of the opera. It was said he was as regular a first-nighter at Hanna's opera house in Cleveland as Mr. Hanna himself. Social clubs were big in those days, and Ed belonged to several. One was the Ancient Order of Jabawauks, an organization of ballplayers, theatrical and professional men, and newspaper boys which he helped form in 1891. The Jabawauks held feasts every other Tuesday night, at which time they would sing songs and recite such essays as Del's "The Ultimatum of the Usufruct."

But Big Ed also could be hot-tempered and impatient, frequently clashing with manager Harry Wright over some perceived slight. On a trip to Pittsburgh, Del threw a sulk when Wright refused to let him take a young boy with him on the bus to the ballpark. Ed refused to play that day, so the manager fined him one hundred dollars and suspended him indefinitely. By the next day, Del had cooled off enough to apologize for his actions, so Wright reinstated him and reduced the fine to twenty-five dollars.

Another time, Delahanty went to the plate with orders from Wright to lay down a bunt. But Ed got a pitch he liked, so he swung away and sent the ball flying over the fence for a home run. He still had a grin on his face when he returned to the bench only to be greeted by a stern-looking Wright.

"That will cost you twenty-five dollars," said the manager.

Del was flabbergasted. "What for?"

"For not bunting," Wright answered coolly.

Delahanty, who prided himself on his batting eye, also had his run-ins with the umpires, as illustrated by a popular story passed on through the years. In a game against Cincinnati, Ed let an inside pitch from Icebox Chamberlain sail past only to hear umpire Tim Hurst call it a strike.

"Tim, you were off on that one," said Del. "It missed the plate."

Hurst, a pugnacious umpire who was quick to use his fists to settle an argument, said nothing. The next pitch shot across the middle of the plate, and he called it strike two. Then came an offering that appeared just inside, and Hurst pronounced it ball one.

Ed turned slightly and looked back at the umpire. "You sure are off today, Tim, because that one came across just like the one before it, and you called that one a strike."

Hurst jerked off his mask and stepped around the catcher to look Delahanty square in the face.

"It's a real Irishman you are," said Hurst in his thick Irish brogue. "And sons of the old sod always tell the truth. So if you say that last pitch was a strike like the other one was, I'll be taking your word for it. Strike three and you're out! And good day to you, Mister Delahanty!"

But through all the tantrums and outbursts of rage and frustration, one man stuck with Delahanty. Harry Wright, the kind and gentle Philadelphia manager, always was there to calm the hotheaded young ballplayer. And eventually, it was Wright, the grand old man of baseball, who tamed Delahanty and set him on the path to stardom.

• • •

Harry Wright was baseball's most revered figure, known affectionately as the "Father of Professional Baseball." A distinguished-looking man in his mid-fifties, he had a full beard and wavy brown hair. During games he sat on the bench in a dusty brown suit, wearing a straw hat for good luck.

He was not in good health and had not been since a severe eye ailment almost robbed him of his sight during the Brotherhood War of 1890. The illness had been described in the newspapers as a "catarrh of the eyeballs," or an inflammation of the mucous membranes, and it had left Wright bedridden and in intense pain for several weeks. When he finally was able to return to the ball club, Wright could not walk unassisted, his eyes remained swollen, and he could not even see well enough to recognize the many friends who came up to shake his hand.

A year later, his vision still was so clouded and poor that he sat on the bench and watched the game through a pair of field glasses. Occasionally, Wright would whisper instructions to a player sitting next to him, and that man would relay the signals to the fielders.

But some things about Wright had not changed. He was quiet and dignified, a brilliant tactician, and a firm believer in sportsmanship and fair play. And he still got a headache whenever his team lost a ball game.

That was not often, for over the past quarter century Harry Wright had been baseball's most successful and acclaimed manager.

Wright was an English immigrant who had come to this country shortly after his birth in 1835. Harry grew up in New York, and at age fourteen went to work as a jeweler's manufacturer. He also played cricket on a team managed by his father, a former professional, and he was introduced to baseball quite by accident. During a cricket match on the Elysian Fields in Hoboken, New Jersey, Harry and his younger brother George happened to see a game of "base ball" being played on some adjacent grounds. The brothers tried the new game, and liked it well enough to become members of the famed New York Knickerbockers in 1858.

Nine years later, at age thirty-two, Harry Wright accepted a twelve hundred dollar fee to organize and captain the Cincinnati Base Ball Club, which became known as the Red Stockings when he added scarlet stockings to the uniform. This was the club that revolutionized baseball when, in 1869, Harry recruited his brother George to play shortstop, turned the Red Stockings into the first all-salaried team, and embarked on his historic cross-country tour.

He also was an innovator, designing the basic baseball uniform of knee-length knickerbockers instead of pantaloons and patenting the game's first scorecard. And his knowledge of the rules and tactical brilliance were unmatched. The *Cincinnati Enquirer* hailed him as "a base-ball Edison."

"He eats base-ball, breathes base-ball, thinks base-ball, dreams base-ball, and incorporates base-ball in his prayers," said the newspaper.

Two years after his historic tour with the Red Stockings, Wright moved his famous team name to Boston, where he won four consecutive titles in the National Association and two of the first three championships of the National League. Moving to Providence in 1882, he posted finishes of second and third before leaving for Philadelphia.

Taking over a last-place ball club in Philadelphia, Wright turned the Phillies into winners his second year on the job. And though he never realized his ambition of delivering a pennant to the City of Brotherly Love, neither did his teams ever finish lower than fourth after that first season.

Harry Wright's teams always were the best drilled and the best disciplined in baseball. The Phillies practiced every morning, with Wright stationing the players in their regular positions in the field and having each man take six turns at bat, facing each of the six pitchers. They ran on and off the field between times at bat to improve their condition. The outfielders especially found the work tiring as they sprinted to and from their positions six times each workout.

At times, Colonel Rogers complained that Wright was not strict enough with his players, and he urged the manager to levy more fines and on occasion ordered him to give the team "encouraging talks."

But Wright's gentle manner and his kind ways earned him the unquestioned devotion of his ballplayers. And the dignified manager had a calming effect on young players such as Delahanty, who would fly into a rage whenever he made an out and at times became so discouraged he threatened to quit the game and return home.

"Be less impetuous, Edward," Wright would say on those occasions Delahanty returned to the bench cursing and berating himself. "Be less hasty. Calm yourself. Modify your speech. It doesn't do you a bit of good to be too strong in big words. It won't help make you a better ballplayer."

"Damn it, I know it," Del would snap, "but what are you going to do if you don't hit the ball to suit you?"

Finally, in 1892, Delahanty's fifth year in the major leagues, it all began to fall into place. At Wright's urging, Del had given up drinking the year before. He trained feverishly at a gym during the winter and showed up for baseball season twenty pounds lighter. In the words of Cleveland writer Elmer Bates, Delahanty looked "as strong as an ox and as spry as an antelope." Del began to hold his temper in check. He became a patient hitter, waiting for the pitch he wanted rather than swinging wildly at anything near the plate. Suddenly, he was hitting vicious line drives and spraying hits to all fields.

Del slugged a league-leading twenty-one triples that year, and joined the "Society of .300" for the first time with a .306 batting average. He also left his mark in other ways. Against St. Louis, he hit a line shot with such force it broke third baseman George Pinckney's ankle.

• • •

The pitchers reigned supreme in baseball, still shooting the ball toward the plate from a distance of only fifty feet. Ed Delahanty was one of only twelve batters to reach the .300 figure in the 1892 season, and even the great Cap Anson saw his average slip to .272, the lowest mark of his seventeen-year career. While veteran hurlers such as Tim Keefe and John Clarkson continued to baffle the batters, newer and even more dominating young pitching stars were arriving on the scene.

In Cleveland, a big farmboy named Denton Young was acquired by the Spiders for the cost of a new suit of clothes during the Brotherhood War. He arrived with a reputation for being "as fast as a cyclone," and once he began throwing the ball past National League batters he became known as "Cyclone" Young. His famous nickname was shortened to "Cy," and the name Cy Young would become synonymous with pitching greatness after he won a record 511 games over the next twenty-two seasons.

The batters faced an even more terrifying sight in Amos Rusie, a burly, red-haired six-footer who would rock far back on his right leg before hurling himself toward the plate and slinging the ball forward with frightening speed. They called Rusie, an Indiana native, "the Hoosier Thunderbolt," and it was said his fastball was second only to the speed of sound.

When one of Rusie's fastballs shot over the plate one day in St. Louis, the batter stepped back and complained, "That guy ain't no pitcher, he's a cannon."

The batters dreaded facing the big New York pitcher, who won thirty-two games in 1892 despite walking almost as many men (267) as he struck out (288). "If any other pitcher hit a man, the man swore, limped a moment, and went to first base," said Chicago's Jimmy Ryan. "If Rusie hit a man, the man retired from the game, went to the hospital, and sometimes was never again fit to play ball. To be hit by Rusie was worse than to have an ordinary man hit you with a rock."

More than anything else, it was Rusie's incredible speed which prompted the magnates to correct the growing imbalance between pitcher and hitter. The reformists wanted to adopt a plan proposed by sports editor W. R. Lester of the *Philadelphia Record*. Under the so-called Lester Plan, the base lines would be lengthened from ninety to ninety-three feet and the pitcher would be stationed in the geometrical center of the diamond, or sixty-five feet, seven inches from the plate. The magnates were evenly divided on the issue, so they struck a compromise. They left the bases as they were and split the difference on the pitching distance. Rather than move it back ten feet, as they would have on the larger field, they added five feet to the existing fifty-five feet, six inches. Thus, in 1893, the sixty-foot, six-inch pitching distance was established.

Big Ed Delahanty burst into his full glory that season. He hit nineteen home runs, the most in the league, and even achieved the rare feat of belting a drive over the distant left-field fence in Cleveland. He batted .368 and scored more than one run and drove in more than one run per game.

The Phillies were a sight to behold. "Sliding Billy" Hamilton batted a league-best .380 and drove opponents wild with his daring base running. In one game, a Cleveland fielder became so frustrated he picked up the five-foot-six Hamilton, carried him to the edge of the field, and dropped him into the stands. Sam Thompson, a menacing sight at six-foot-two and two hundred pounds with a big black moustache, knocked out 222 hits and gunned down runners from right field with the game's most powerful throwing arm.

More and more teams were resorting to the loud, unruly tactics known as "rowdy ball," but the Phillies relied on quiet efficiency, old-time slugging, and teamwork.

"I like to see your team play ball," treasurer Edward Talcott of New York praised Wright one day, "because the players refrain from howling and yelling and play good, hard ball. The Bostons' method of playing is not liked here."

"I agree with you," said Wright. "I don't approve of noisy coaching and never did. If the Philadelphias can't win without howling themselves hoarse then I don't want them to win at all. This bellowing from the coaching lines isn't baseball."

But for all their precision and powerful batting, the Phillies could do no better than a fourth-place finish. Colonel Rogers feared the game was passing the Phillies by, that Wright's tactics had become outdated.

That December, the baseball world was stunned by the news that Harry Wright, fifty-eight years old, had been turned loose by Philadelphia. The Father of Professional Baseball was gone, and with him, one of the game's last links to its beginnings.

Among those who mourned Wright's firing was Ed Delahanty. His love of the old man was such he told one reporter, "God breathed pure Hibernian oxygen into the heart of Harry Wright."

For an Irishman, it was the highest form of praise when Del added, "Even if he was of English descent."

• • •

It was a new era in baseball. It was becoming a faster, more aggressive game, with speedy little men replacing the big rugged stars of earlier days. Batters relied on "place hitting" and pitchers learned the value of "pitching for catches." It also was becoming a tougher, meaner game.

In Baltimore, cocky little infielder Johnny McGraw was introducing a style of play known as "rowdyism" because of its bullying, belligerent manner. There were fights, threats, and angry words everywhere. A first baseman named Tommy Tucker stopped play once to challenge McGraw to a duel. "You take three balls and I'll take three, and we'll try to wing each other at ten yards," snarled Tucker. "And you—I'll catch your three and kill you with the six."

A similar type of ball was practiced in Cleveland, where they called it "Tebeauism" in honor of Spiders manager Oliver Wendell "Patsy" Tebeau. A notorious umpire baiter and brawler, Tebeau put into practice his oft-repeated boast, "Show me a team of fighters, and I'll show you a team that has a chance."

Nor were these brawling tactics restricted to the playing field. Once, Tebeau and catcher Jack O'Connor brutally beat a Cleveland reporter in a saloon. When questioned about the incident, Tebeau sneered, "What right has a reporter to be in a barroom?"

One by one, the old stars were passing from the scene. King

Kelly was washed up in 1892, his brilliant talents ruined by alcohol. He opened a saloon in New York with former umpire "Honest John" Kelly and made a pathetic attempt to capitalize on his fame by going on stage and reciting the famous poem "Casey at the Bat." His stage debut came at the old Imperial Theater on Broadway, where one critic noted, "There was a lot less applause when he finished than when he started." Still, Kelly hung on. In November 1894, he booked an appearance in Boston and traveled up the coast by boat. On the way, he took ill and a cold worsened into pneumonia. Upon his arrival, he was rushed to a hospital, but as the stretcher bearers entered the doorway one of them stumbled and Kelly fell to the floor. Legend has it the once great ballplayer looked up with a smile and whispered in a hoarse voice, "This is me last slide." Three days later, the King of Baseball died penniless. More than five thousand mourners came to pay their respects as his body lay in state at the Boston Elks Hall.

Big Ned Williamson, the robust infielder on those powerful White Stockings teams, fell victim to dropsy and gained weight at an alarming rate. Prior to his death at age thirty-six in 1894, he had become so fat he had to turn sideways to pass through a door.

They found Silver Flint, the once great Chicago catcher who had turned to the bottle, lying sick on a street corner, stricken with consumption and coughing up blood. He died eight weeks later, wasted away so badly he was recognizable only by his familiar blond moustache.

Charlie Bennett, the slugging catcher, was running to catch up to a train in Kansas while on a hunting trip in 1894. He slipped on some ice, and his companion, pitcher John Clarkson, watched in horror as Bennett fell beneath the wheels of the train. Both Bennett's legs were severed, and he spent the rest of his life in a wheelchair. Clarkson never recovered from the trauma of seeing his buddy maimed. The famous pitcher drifted out of baseball after the next season, and eight years later he would end up at a "hospital for the insane" in Pontiac, Michigan.

Helen Dauvray left John Montgomery Ward and returned to the stage to resume her acting career. Ward managed the Brooklyn and New York teams, then retired from baseball in 1895 to open a law practice in New York. As one of his first acts, he waged a successful fight against the reserve clause in his baseball contract, removing the stigma of having a ball club retain the option on his services.

• • •

One day, Ed Delahanty came to bat against the great Cy Young with two outs and the winning run on base in the bottom of the ninth inning. The catcher signaled for an intentional walk, and Young's first pitch sailed two feet wide of the plate. Del stepped all the way across the plate to hit the ball, knocking it clean out of the ballpark.

Walking back to the hotel afterward, the catcher turned to Young and said, "I told you to let him walk."

"Oh, I know you did," answered Young. "But I had to pitch the ball somewhere, and I thought I had a wild pitch until I saw it going over the fence."

Delahanty had become the "King of Batters." He compiled a batting average of .400 or more two years in a row, in 1894 and 1895, and for the second time in his career knocked out six hits in a single game. The other ballplayers nicknamed him "Mush," for that was what the ball felt like after a Delahanty hit.

But Del was more than just a great hitter. In the outfield, he made brilliant over-the-head grabs with a homemade glove about half the size of other mitts, its thumb held on with some tacks and a few stitches. He called his powerful throwing arm his "whip" and guarded it carefully, lobbing the ball back to the infield except when necessary to cut down a runner or hold a man on base. At such times, he would fire the ball with amazing accuracy and with a speed unmatched by any other outfielder except his teammate, Big Sam Thompson.

Del played wherever his team needed him, whether it was center field, left field, first base, or filling in at second, third, or shortstop.

It was a time of transition for the Phillies. The former short-stop Arthur Irwin returned to Philadelphia in 1894 to take over for Harry Wright as manager, and he brought with him his baseball theories, his many patents, and his smooth, charming ways. Eleven years earlier, prior to the introduction of fielders' mitts, Irwin had been the best-fielding shortstop in baseball. One day, he broke the third and fourth fingers on his left hand during a game, but he refused to leave the game. Instead, he found a large buckskin driving glove, padded it, sewed together the fingers and used the makeshift device on his injured hand to field the ball. That was the first infielder's glove, and Irwin took out a patent on his invention and made a handsome profit by marketing it. Irwin's other interests in-cluded the new sport of football, so he invented a football scoreboard and patented it, also.

The new Philadelphia manager liked to surround himself with people and he always had lots of friends. But few people really knew Irwin and the strange double life he led. He had a wife, Edna, whom he had married in 1883 while playing ball. Edna and the couple's two daughters and one son lived in Boston. Around 1890, Irwin married again, this time to a woman who lived in New York with their son while he was employed in Philadelphia. Neither woman was aware of the other, although at one time Irwin's first wife and children lived with him at the Grand Hotel in New York while his second wife and son resided across town. Both wives consid-ered Irwin a kind man and devoted husband.

The Phillies finished fourth their first year under Irwin and third the next, but that was not good enough for owners Alfred Reach and Colonel Rogers. In 1896, Arthur Irwin resigned and headed back to New York, blaming his failures in Philadelphia on interference from "the directory," as he called the two owners.

Billy Hamilton scored the incredible total of 196 runs one season and stole ninety-nine bases and proved it was no fluke by scoring 166 runs and stealing ninety-seven bases the next year. He asked to be rewarded with a pay raise, so the Phillies traded him to Boston in 1896.

In return, Philadelphia got Billy Nash, a smart, aggressive third baseman who had played on the Beaneaters' championship teams of 1891–93. He took over as manager but instead of instilling some spark and fight in the Phillies he antagonized and alienated them. The other players talked back to him, disregarded his instructions, and laughed at him behind his back.

It was hard for the players to take the new manager seriously. Against Cincinnati, Delahanty stood at the plate and fouled off pitch after pitch while waiting for one to his liking, swinging just hard enough to keep from striking out. It was smart playing on Del's part, but Nash called him down and asked that he stop delaying the game.

The players knocked one another and griped constantly. If they trailed in the ninth inning, they packed their bats and prepared to go to the clubhouse. They accused Colonel Rogers of housing them in cheap hotels and making them travel on cheap railroads, and one year the owner drew their anger by telling them they must dress at the ballpark rather than take the traditional bus ride from the hotel in their uniforms. The Colonel got so disgusted hearing their complaints he snapped that anyone "looking for a soft job should seek it in a sponge factory."

In July 1896, the Phillies went to Cincinnati and dropped three games in a row. The players were getting on the horse-drawn bus at the ballpark when a bystander remarked to one of them, "This is a bad beginning for your western trip, losing three straight."

The player looked back and laughed harshly. "I'll bet you five dollars that we lose every game on the trip."

Arriving in Chicago, the Phillies faced a strikingly handsome pitcher known as "Adonis" Bill Terry. He was nearing the end of a fourteen-year career which would include 197 victories and two no-hitters, but his most famous game would be that one on July 13, 1896.

Cap Anson's team, then known as the Colts, played at West Side Grounds, an oddly shaped ballpark with foul lines that measured 340 feet in left and right fields and a vast center field that stretched 560 feet to the distant fence. In right field there was an "inner fence" inside the regular wall.

His first time up, Del hit a drive over the first barrier in right field, and by the time Chicago outfielder Jimmy Ryan could chase it down between the two fences Delahanty had circled the bases for a home run.

In the third, Del lined the ball up the middle. Shortstop Bill "Bullhead" Dahlen leaped to make the catch, but the ball arrived with such force it ripped off his mitt as it shot past him.

Two men were on base in the fifth when Big Ed hit a towering drive that cleared the right-center-field scoreboard and the canvas screen behind it before it landed across the street. It was "the longest hit of the year at the local grounds," marveled a *Chicago Tribune* writer.

The Phillies trailed, 9–6, in the seventh when Delahanty came to bat with no one on base. In center field was Bill Lange, who fielded his position in such a graceful manner he was known as 'Little Eva." This time, Del drove the ball over Lange's head, and not even the fleet center fielder could track it down in time to prevent Ed from getting his third home run of the day.

The fans were in an uproar when Delahanty came to the plate again in the ninth inning. The Phillies were now trailing by two runs, and everywhere there were loud shouts of "Another one, Del!" and "Another home run!"

In the pitcher's box, Adonis Terry prepared to make his first delivery when he heard Lange calling from center field, "Hold it up a minute!" Terry turned to see his center fielder retreat deep into the uncut grass in the area where the clubhouses were located, a sort of no-man's land where no ball ever had been hit. As he watched from home plate, even Big Ed had to laugh at the sight of the player so far removed from the action.

Finally, Terry fired the ball toward the plate, and this time Delahanty sent a drive rocketing deep into right-center field. The ball kept carrying and carrying, finally landing on the roof of one clubhouse, bouncing over to the other and ricocheting out of Lange's reach. Big Ed already had rounded third and was well on his way toward home when Lange finally caught up with the ball. The Chicago center fielder did not even attempt a throw home. Instead, he took the ball and hid it under the floor of the home-team clubhouse to save for a souvenir.

When Del crossed the plate, Terry was there to shake his hand and compliment him on his feat. The thousand spectators present stood and cheered Delahanty, and afterward the bleachers crowd followed him to the bus calling out his name and slapping him on the back.

Big Ed's final figures for the day were four home runs and one single, accounting for seventeen total bases and driving home seven runs. In that one game, Delahanty accounted for almost one third of his final home-run total of thirteen, which was one fewer than league leader Scrappy Bill Joyce hit.

As a reward for his heroics, Big Ed was presented with four boxes of chewing gum—one for each of his home runs.

• • •

It was a time of labor unrest, of tight money and debates over the gold standard. Jobs were scarce. The country was gripped by a depression.

Umpires came under constant attack from both players and

fans, and in exchange received $250 a month with, as *Sporting Life* noted, "extras in the form of pop bottles, cushions and rip-snorting roasts." When the end of a game was near, it was common practice for the umpire to stand as far back of the catcher as possible so as to get a head start out of the ballpark.

Still, there was no shortage of applicants for the position. "Death on the diamond is preferable to dying of starvation," said one man.

At times, players had to fight for their money. The Phillies went to Louisville, where a last-place club was having trouble drawing enough fans to meet the payroll. Outfielder Fred Clarke and first baseman Luke Lutenberg walked off the field and refused to continue play until they received the cash owed them. They finally got their money, and Clarke responded by getting five hits in five at-bats.

Their fame also made them handy targets for others. Chief Zimmer, the big Cleveland catcher, woke up one night to see two masked men standing above his bed with their pistols pointed at him.

"Do you know us, Chief?" asked one of the robbers.

"No, I don't," said Zimmer.

"Well, we know you all right. You know what we're here for, though, don't you?"

"I guess so. There are my clothes. Help yourselves."

Zimmer lay there and watched while one of the intruders took his sixty-dollar gold watch and about twenty dollars in cash and the other stood guard with his revolver.

As the two men slowly backed out of the house, one of them called out, "So long, Charley."

"So long," answered Zimmer.

There were other hazards. In Chicago's Hotel Worth, where most of Cap Anson's team stayed, a mad dog got loose and sent the players into a panic. Catcher Tim Donahue ran screaming into the dining room and jumped on a table, while Malachi Kittridge scrambled onto a gas fixture and Clark

Griffith hid in a closet. Finally, they were rescued by a husky porter, who killed the rabid animal with an ax.

In Brooklyn, pint-sized outfielder Mike Griffin caught hold of one of Amos Rusie's fastballs and sent the ball rocketing back through the box even faster than it was delivered. The drive caught Rusie flush on his left ear, spinning the big pitcher all the way around and leaving him with a permanent loss of hearing on that side.

Still, Rusie kept firing his thunderbolts toward the plate. In 1894, he and teammate Jouett Meekin, "the Iron Twins," won thirty-six and thirty-three games respectively, alternating the pitching chores down the stretch to lead New York to a second-place finish and a victory over Baltimore in the post-season Temple Cup series.

Rusie arrived in New York prior to the start of the 1895 season and was greeted at the train station by hundreds of cheering fans as well as a marching band and large banners of welcome. He missed curfew one night and was fined a hundred dollars by owner Andrew Freedman. Pitching against Philadelphia a few days later, Rusie spotted the owner in the stands and thumbed his nose at him. That resulted in another hundred-dollar fine.

Rusie refused to pay the fines, so Freedman took the money out of his paycheck. The pitcher vowed not to return the next year until he was reimbursed, and the owner reacted with scorn. "I have offered Rusie twenty-four hundred dollars, and unless he signs and gets down to business, he will not play ball at all. Nor will I revoke the fines."

Rusie sat out all of the 1896 season, then hired John Montgomery Ward as his attorney and filed suit, asking for his release from the Giants and five thousand dollars in damages from the club for depriving him of a livelihood. Not wanting to see the matter go to court, the other National League owners agreed to pool their money to meet the pitcher's demands. Only Freedman and Boston's Arthur Soden refused to contribute to the fund.

Angry over the defeat, Freedman refused to issue Rusie a uniform when he reported in 1897. The pitcher sat in the stands to watch the first game, but the fans raised such a ruckus that after several days he was allowed to pitch. In his first start, he broke a long losing streak by the Giants.

But Andrew Freedman did not forget nor did he forgive. The Giants owner never did speak to his star pitcher again.

• • •

Alfred Reach went to Detroit on a player hunt late in 1896, and there he met an aristocratic young minor-league manager named George Tweedy Stallings. The son of a Confederate general and a graduate of Virginia Military Institute, Stallings seemed to be everything the Philadelphia owner was looking for in a manager. He had studied two years at the College of Physicians and Surgeons in Baltimore, then left school in 1887 to try out for the Philadelphia Phillies. Stallings failed to make the team, but Harry Wright convinced him to give up his medical studies to concentrate on baseball.

It was Stallings's goal to play for Wright, but he never made it, kicking around in the minor leagues for nine years except for a brief stint with the Brooklyn National League club during the Brotherhood War. Given a chance to manage the Detroit team in the Western League, Stallings soon earned a reputation as a stern disciplinarian and a sharp baseball man. Reach was so impressed by his bearing and his no-nonsense manner, he offered the twenty-nine-year-old Stallings the job as Philadelphia manager for the 1897 season.

It was a bad mix. Stallings cursed and derided his players in an effort to whip them into line. He belittled them with his sarcasm and his harsh insults, and he threatened them with fines and suspensions to break up their cliques. He was obsessed by his superstitions, meticulously picking up peanut shells and scraps of paper which littered the bench area.

The players bristled under his command, resenting him not

only because of his tactics but because he came from a minor-league background. They treated him with politeness and respect to his face, then turned on him when he wasn't looking.

"They have patted me on the back until my coat is threadbare," Stallings complained to a friend, "and the ones who have been most active in this taffy giving are the ones who are doing the damage."

Stallings drove the Phillies relentlessly, working them out every morning at 9:30 during the season. One Thursday, the manager was riding his bicycle to the grounds for the morning practice when he collided with a street car and was thrown into the fender of the vehicle. Dazed and bruised, Stallings lay in the street beside his wrecked bike and wondered what hit him. And that proved to be just the beginning of his troubles.

• • •

In the spring of 1897, a fortune teller in Hot Springs, Arkansas, told Cap Anson his team would win the National League pennant. The Chicago manager laughed and replied that was "no great shakes of a prediction," for he had known as much all along.

That same spring, Ed Delahanty dreamed it was Philadelphia that won the championship that season. In the dream, Ed saw himself fingering the money he would receive from the postseason Temple Cup series. It was all so real that when he woke up he even could remember what that money felt like.

Del spent a lot of time thinking about money that year. There were changes taking place in his life, and he was showing signs of settling down. He bought some property in Cleveland that winter, then arrived at training camp with his new bride, Norine. The other ballplayers kidded him about becoming a "benedict," and Colonel Rogers frowned at the news, for he preferred to have only single men on his ball club.

One day, Ed and Norine were on a train when they happened to run into Giants owner Andrew Freedman. The two
men began talking about baseball and boasting of their respective teams. Finally, Del offered to wager all his money that
the Phillies would beat out the Giants in the pennant race.
Freedman respectfully declined the bet.

• • •

There would be no pennant or postseason money for the
Phillies in 1897. Under George Stallings, they began losing
steadily and sinking lower and lower in the standings. The
more the new manager tried to crack down on his players,
the worse the problems became. The Phillies sat on their
bench showing no interest in the game, seemingly not caring
whether they won or lost.

"Stallings has wrecked the team by letting some of the best
men go in foolish trades," one player confided to a newspaperman, "and he has publicly rebuked the rest of us because we
cannot win. No man knows what position he will be asked to
play tomorrow, and we are all disgusted with the way things
have been run this year."

Drinking and misbehaving became the trademarks of the
Phillies, who came to be known around the league as the
"Staggering Stallingites." Only a few of the men escaped
blame for the team's problems. One of those who did was Ed
Delahanty. He was foremost among those players listed publicly as not taking part in the dissipation and demoralizing
tactics ruining the team.

The friction between Stallings and his players came to a
head the following spring. The Phillies had finished tenth in
1897 and started the 1898 season by losing twenty-seven of
their first forty-six games. At that point, a committee of players
headed by outfielder Dick Cooley took their grievances to
owners Al Reach and Colonel Rogers.

"We are fed up with the way Stallings has been riding us

and decided we had enough of him and would regard him as our manager no longer," read their statement. "For weeks he's been handling us like a lot of cattle. We may not be the best team in the league, but we don't intend to put up with Stallings' tactics."

The owners caved in to the demands, buying up the remaining year and a half on Stallings's contract and letting him go. In his place, they installed Billy Shettsline as manager, and under his easygoing leadership the Phillies rallied to post a winning record for the season.

Big and portly, Shetts was a good-humored and friendly man. A native Philadelphian, he got his start with the Phillies more than a decade earlier as a handyman and ticket-taker and from there he worked his way up to bookkeeper and secretary and now manager. All the while, Shetts continued to live in the suburb of Glenolden, where he raised chickens with the same care he raised ballplayers.

• • •

In the newspapers, they spelled the Delahanty name with an e in the middle, making it "Delehanty." It was a source of considerable irritation to Ed.

"My name is spelled D-e-l-a-h-a-n-t-y," he would tell the writers. "I do not think it fair that a man who has won fame as a swatter of shoots and benders should have his name misspelled just because some fellows think it easier to make an e than an a."

A strange pattern was developing in Del's career. His greatest batting feats frequently occurred on the thirteenth day of the month. He hit his first major-league home run on June 13, 1888. He hit four home runs in a game on July 13, 1896. Exactly one year later—on July 13, 1897—he got nine hits in nine at-bats in a doubleheader against Louisville.

The 1899 season began, and once again the number thirteen

came up. On May 13 of that year, Del lined out four doubles in a game against the New York Giants.

To ballplayers, the number was a bad omen. It was bad luck to have thirteen men on a team. No player would stay in room 13 of a hotel. Often, hotels would turn the numbers around and label room 13 as room 31, but even this was to be avoided. Nor would a player travel in section 13 of a train car. Since players drew for their berths the ones who drew No. 13 had to put up with the misfortune unless they could persuade someone else to swap with them.

For Delahanty, the number seemed more of a charm than a curse. In 1899, he knocked out the incredible total of 238 hits to post a .410 batting average and realize his dream of becoming the batting champion of the National League.

At the time, his age was 31. As the ballplayers liked to point out, that was 13 backward.

• • •

Colonel Rogers was a clever man. He had on his payroll a catcher named Morgan Murphy, who rarely appeared in ball games but was a valuable member of the team nonetheless. It was Murphy's job to sit in the Philadelphia clubhouse with a pair of field glasses and steal the signals from the opposing teams. He would pick up the sign from the catcher and, through the use of a piece of blotting paper in the scoreboard, relay it to the Philadelphia batter to let him know what pitch was coming. Murphy liked to brag the glasses we used were powerful enough to see a catcher wink his eye at 250 yards.

The Philadelphia batters put the information to good use. With the aid of their "spy," the Phillies moved all the way up to third place in 1899.

The arrival of the new century brought with it technological advances. A physicist, Reginald A. Fessenden, transmitted spoken words by radio waves. In the U.S., the amount of telephone wires laid increased to more than one million miles.

In Philadelphia, an electrical switchboard was buried beneath the third-base coach's box at the ballpark and connected by wire to a telegraphic device in the clubhouse beyond the outfield. Another wire went to a small metal plate hidden beneath the coach's box. Now, Murphy could relay his signals to the coach by use of the crude telegraph. He would tap out a series of electronic impulses, which the coach could detect by standing with his metal spikes atop a metal plate hidden just below the surface of the coaching box.

The scheme worked perfectly, and the Phillies were well on their way to another third-place finish when the Cincinnati Reds arrived in town in late September 1900. On September 17, Reds captain Tommy Corcoran stationed himself in the third-base coach's box and kept the Phillies nervous by casually digging at the ground with his shoes throughout the first inning. The next inning, Corcoran dropped all pretense and began digging furiously.

There was a shout, and groundskeeper Schroeder, accompanied by a police sergeant, raced frantically onto the field to stop the Cincinnati player. It was too late. As players from both teams gathered around, Corcoran fell to his knees and pulled up the board with the electrical apparatus and wires attached to it.

Arlie Latham, the one-time clown-ballplayer who had turned to umpiring, feigned grave concern as he inspected the device. "Ah ha! What's this? An infernal machine to disrupt the noble National League? Or is it a dastardly attempt on the life of my distinguished friend, Colonel John I. Rogers?"

The rest of the game, the Reds taunted the Phillies with the cry, "We tapped the wire! We tapped the wire!"

That was the end of the buzzer scheme, which the Colonel claimed was no more than a harmless prank. As it turned out, the big loser in the affair was Morgan Murphy. Not only did the team release him a year later, the Colonel never did reimburse him the fifty-two dollars he spent on the field glasses.

• • •

That winter, former Phillies outfielder Dick Cooley, who had been traded to Pittsburgh, returned to his home in Topeka, Kansas. He got a job there as a bartender in a saloon. The name of the establishment was the Senate.

One day in February 1901, Cooley looked up to see a gang of ax-wielding women marching through the front door shouting about the evils of liquor. At the head of the delegation was Carry Nation, the famous prohibitionist. She took a swing with her ax, and Cooley ducked under the bar while the startled customers also scrambled for cover. Later, Cooley joked that he was so busy dodging hatchets and falling mirrors and bottles that he forgot the usual social formalities.

Billy Sunday spent that winter touring the small towns and dusty back roads of the Midwest and preaching the word of God. Seven years earlier, Sunday's knack for memorizing train schedules while a member of Cap Anson's old Chicago White Stockings earned him the job of advance agent for the evangelist J. Wilbur Chapman. The former ballplayer received forty dollars a week, and his duties included putting up tents and straightening chairs after meetings. When Chapman accepted a position as a preacher in a church, Sunday replaced him at a revival in Iowa. He was such a success, he still was preaching the word and railing against the evils of alcohol in early 1901.

That same year, Ban Johnson welcomed John McGraw to the American League and prepared to launch his war on the National League. In Philadelphia, Connie Mack stole Napoleon Lajoie away from Colonel Rogers.

At the house back on East Thirty-fourth Street in Cleveland, there were more Delahantys following in Ed's footsteps. In all, there were six Delahanty brothers, and all were crack ballplayers. Ed was the oldest, followed by Tom, who was five years younger. Then came Joe, who was born three years after Tom. Four years later came Jim, then Frank, and finally Will.

It was said that as babies the Delahanty boys had baseball bats instead of rattles. Like Ed, his younger brothers learned the game at the field next to the St. Clair Street Engine House. "We were practically raised there," Frank would recall years later. They played on the same sandlots as Ed. And when Ed would come to town with the Phillies to play against Cleveland, they all turned out to see him play.

"Why, on the gate in Cleveland," said pitcher Clark Griffith, "when the Philadelphians would come to town, you'd see a long line of young fellows, all with the same statement: 'Let me in. I'm Ed Delahanty's brother.' And they were, too. You could see it in their faces. All looked just alike. I think there were seventy-three of them."

Tom Delahanty was the first to follow Ed into the big league, joining his brother for one game with Philadelphia in 1894 and two years later playing briefly for Cleveland and Pittsburgh.

That was the beginning of what would become baseball's greatest brother act. Eventually, five of the Delahanty brothers would play in the major leagues.

But Ed beat them all, just as the fire captain had predicted. Ed never forgot that old man. He would stop by to visit the captain, and the two of them would stand there next to the ballfield and reminisce about the old days.

One time, Ed took a reporter to the station and showed him the ballfield. The captain wasn't in, so Ed left a box of cigars for him.

As they were leaving, Del told the reporter, "I never go by the engine house that I don't stop in and leave a cigar for the captain, that old bird who told me that I was the best batter for a kid he ever seen."

At the time, Del had just signed a big contract. He wore fancy clothes and sported flashy jewelry. As he had boasted years earlier, Ed Delahanty had come home with rocks in his pocket.

III
THE
DOUBLE
CROSS

As it stands, everything is fair in love, war and baseball.

JIMMY COLLINS

Larry Lajoie arrived in Philadelphia in the spring of 1902 and diligently began training for the upcoming baseball season. He was an orderly man who planned each move carefully and followed a familiar pattern in whatever activity he was engaged.

He liked to swing at the first ball pitched. He played poker once a week with a group of newspapermen. He refused to read newspapers or books on the train for fear of hurting his eyes. He even arranged an elaborate scheme to safeguard his money. When he jumped to the American League the year before, Lajoie demanded that his pay be deposited in the Northwestern National Bank of Philadelphia in an account under the names of his roommate, a man named Johnson, and Frank Hough, the sports editor of the *Inquirer*. Each payday, Johnson and Hough would draw checks for the proper amount and pay Lajoie themselves.

The big Frenchman followed other routines which escaped the public eye. He met a Philadelphia family whose working members had been incapacitated, and for three years Lajoie supported it by sending money at regular intervals.

But not even all his plans and careful arrangements could prepare Lajoie for the storm which he was swept up in on the eve of the 1902 season. On April 21, two days before the Athletics were to play the Orioles in Baltimore, the Pennsylvania Supreme Court handed down a stunning decision in Colonel Rogers's appeal of the Lajoie case. Overturning the lower court rulings, the judges upheld the validity of Lajoie's contract with the Philadelphia National League club and stated that he should be prohibited from playing for any other team than the Phillies. It was a "splendid victory," proclaimed Colonel Rogers. James A. Hart, president of the Chicago Nationals, went so far as to state that if Lajoie continued to play in the American League he would be jailed.

Early the next morning, Larry Lajoie sat quietly in a hotel

room in downtown Philadelphia. With him were Ben Shibe and Connie Mack, owners of the Athletics, and Ban Johnson, who had hurried to Philadelphia upon hearing the news.

Johnson did most of the talking, pacing about the room and speaking out forcefully in his booming voice. The ruling appeared to be a crushing defeat for his league, and already it was creating confusion throughout baseball. Frantic team owners wondered how many of their own players they might lose, and jumpers everywhere read the news and feared they were about to be sent back to their old clubs. But Johnson saw things differently.

The court's decision was not quite the decisive triumph the National Leaguers made it out to be, he explained. It applied only to Lajoie, although in their suit the Phillies also had attempted to regain the services of pitchers Bill Bernhard and Chick Fraser, who also had jumped to the Athletics. Rather than validate the reserve clause as the Phillies had hoped, the supreme court had determined that Lajoie's contract differed from most such documents in baseball. Its reserve clause was limited to three years, and there were other paragraphs in the pact giving the Phillies the right to enforce specific performance and to prevent Lajoie from playing for another team.

Johnson believed his other jumpers still were on solid ground legally. And even Lajoie might be able to prevail in court since the Pennsylvania Supreme Court ruling did not apply outside the state.

But for now, the American League president did not want to take any chances. He looked across the room at Lajoie and suggested he, Bernhard, and Fraser leave town immediately before any legal papers could be served on them. The Big Frenchman nodded his approval.

That afternoon, the three ballplayers were on a train headed to Baltimore, where they would await the rest of the team's arrival for the season opener.

In Baltimore, a crowd of 12,726 turned out at Oriole Park,

which had seats for only two-thirds that number, to witness the game on April 23. Even the partisan Baltimore rooters roared their approval when the Athletics took the field and, in defiance of the Pennsylvania court order, Lajoie ran out to second base and Bernhard trotted to the pitcher's box.

Lajoie batted five times that day and he made one hit, a single off Iron Man McGinnity. Bernhard, who was known as "Strawberry Bill," showed no signs of nervousness over the legal battles, as he methodically disposed of the Orioles batters inning after inning. And then, in the eighth inning, a messenger arrived on the field and delivered a telegram to Athletics manager Connie Mack, notifying him of a preliminary injunction secured against Napoleon Lajoie by the Philadelphia Nationals. Mack had no choice but to pull the ballplayer from the field. Lajoie dejectedly sat on the bench and watched the final two innings of Philadelphia's 8–1 victory. It would be thirteen years before he ever again played in an Athletics uniform.

• • •

That same afternoon, Colonel Rogers appeared at Common Pleas Court No. 5 in Philadelphia. Having succeeded in preventing Lajoie from playing for the Athletics, the Colonel now sought an injunction barring him from competing for any team other than the Phillies. In the wake of the state supreme court's decision, the lower court promptly granted the request. The Colonel emerged from the courtroom with a smile on his face and vowed he would be back to obtain similar papers for the other players he had lost to the rival league.

There was turmoil everywhere in baseball in the following days. Players spent much of their time hiding out, taking late-night trains, appearing in court, or secretly meeting with agents from the rival league. In Washington, twenty-five policemen were on hand for the opening game at American League Park, ready to arrest anyone who interfered with play by attempting to serve legal papers on the players. In Chicago, the fans taunted Brooklyn's Jimmy "the Human Flea" Sheckard, a two-time jumper who had run out on a thousand-dollar loan he had received from the Orioles, with the chant, "Jump! Jump!"

The joke around the American League that spring was, "If you're not figuring in an injunction suit, you're not worth much."

In Cleveland, there was a deaf pitcher by the name of Luther "Dummy" Taylor. He was a demonstrative and outgoing man who had little trouble communicating with others despite his handicap. A few of his teammates learned sign language in order to communicate with him, and at times he resorted to other tactics to make himself understood. When he disagreed with an umpire's call, Taylor would wave his arms over his head in excitement and perhaps throw down his glove and kick it for emphasis. A hard thrower, he jumped from the Giants in 1901 to become the first player to sign a major-league contract with the new Cleveland team in the American League. But in April 1902, following the Lajoie ruling, the Giants determined they would get the pitcher back.

On May 6, Taylor was roughed up for fourteen hits as the Blues lost their home opener to the Chicago White Sox before a record Cleveland crowd of 12,000. That night, the pitcher's roommate, Charlie Hemphill, returned from the theater to discover he was locked out of his room.

"Here is a rummy go," Hemphill thought to himself. "Me with no key and a deaf-and-dumb man to wake up before I can get in the room to go to bed."

It did no good to bang on the door, so the ballplayer went to the front desk and found that a key had been left in the box for him. Returning to the room, he struck a light and looked inside only to find his roommate gone and two Cleveland uniforms laid out neatly on Taylor's bed. Hemphill picked one up and out fell a note in the Dummy's handwriting.

It read simply, "Good-bye, Charlie—I am back with New York."

Dummy had been "kidnapped" by Giants catcher Frank Bowerman, his old batterymate in New York. Bowerman knew how to speak sign language, and he had been dispatched to Cleveland with orders not to return without Taylor. When he returned a few days later with the pitcher in tow, Bowerman acquired a new nickname that was indicative of the times. The writers began referring to him as "Kidnapper" Bowerman.

• • •

Day after day, Larry Lajoie remained trapped in his baseball limbo. He showed signs of wavering in his opposition to returning to the National League, going so far as to put on a Phillies uniform and work out at the Huntingdon Street Grounds. He met with Colonel Rogers and indicated he would rejoin the Phillies if his contract demands were met. The Frenchman wanted a thirty-five hundred dollar salary, but the Colonel was offering only three thousand dollars. When neither man would budge in his position, the impasse continued.

All around him, Lajoie saw his fellow Philadelphia jumpers returning to the ballfield. Chick Fraser gave in and rejoined the Phillies. Elmer Flick, who had left the Phillies to join the Athletics after the past season, fled to Cleveland to hide out after the court decision in the Lajoie case. While he was there, the Blues worked out a deal to purchase his contract from the Athletics and Flick suited up for the Ohio team.

The uncertainty surrounding the jumpers led to rumors. There was a story that Flick had caught a train and was on his way back to Philadelphia to rejoin the Phillies, but the outfielder never arrived. A report leaked out that the Phillies would trade Lajoie to the Giants. Still, nothing happened.

In the midst of the standoff, the Blues arrived in Philadelphia on May 21 to play the Athletics. The Cleveland ball club was a sorry outfit. It had finished seventh the previous season and had lost seventeen of twenty-three games in 1902 to fall into last place. Already, player defections, injuries, and illness had left the Blues so shorthanded that when Flick could not make the trip to Philadelphia, pitcher Addie Joss was pressed into duty at first base in one game.

But the one thing the Cleveland ball club did have was a wealthy and ambitious owner. Charles Somers, the "good angel of the American League," spent his money freely when it came to baseball and he was growing impatient to be rewarded with a winning ball club in Cleveland.

While the Blues and Athletics were in the process of splitting a four-game series, the soft-spoken and shy Somers was busy at work behind the scenes. He sought permission from Connie Mack to negotiate with Lajoie in an effort to keep the star ballplayer in the American League camp. Mack, indebted to Somers for his help in establishing the American League team in Philadelphia, eagerly agreed. Next, Somers made his pitch to Lajoie. Not only was he willing to pay the Frenchman twenty-eight thousand dollars over a four-year period to play ball in Cleveland, Somers also was willing to guarantee the money. Even if legal problems prevented Lajoie from playing ball, he would continue to draw his pay from Somers.

For four days, the two men continued to talk. Ban Johnson arrived in Philadelphia from Atlantic City, and he entered the negotiations. Finally, Somers's persistence paid off. On May 26, Lajoie, as well as pitcher Strawberry Bill Bernhard, agreed to sign with the Cleveland ball club. Fearing legal repercussions, they did not want to do business in Pennsylvania, so late that night the two players slipped out of town by train and headed to Cleveland to complete the deal.

They arrived in the Forest City the next day and immediately headed to the Kennard House, where they would be staying. On the way, a reporter asked Lajoie why he hadn't returned to Colonel Rogers and the Phillies.

The Frenchman scowled as he gave his answer. "He had a chance to do what was right but failed to take advantage of the opportunity."

It took another week to work out all the details, but on June 3 the Blues finally were able to announce Lajoie had signed his contract. When the news broke, the ticket office sold an extra three thousand tickets before that day's game was rained out.

"King Napoleon" finally made his debut for Cleveland on June 4, and a weekday crowd of 9,827 turned out to see the Blues' prize acquisition. Every move Lajoie made was cheered loudly, and he rewarded the fans by hitting a double and scoring a run in a 4–3 victory over Boston. But not everyone in the crowd was happy. Among those in attendance was Frank de Haas Robison, the owner of the St. Louis Nationals and the man who had left Cleveland without baseball in 1900 when he had disbanded the old Spiders of the National League. Robison, accompanied by two lawyers, was on hand not to enjoy the game but to witness Lajoie's "overt act" so that he could testify in court for Colonel Rogers.

No one in Cleveland paid the Colonel or his allies much mind. Before the Philadelphia magnate could get Lajoie in court, he first would have to catch him. And that would prove very difficult. The courts in Ohio and other states refused to honor the ruling by the Pennsylvania court on the Lajoie case. So, on orders from Ban Johnson, the Cleveland jumpers Lajoie, Bernhard, and Flick did not set foot in Pennsylvania the rest of the season. Whenever the Blues traveled to Philadelphia to play the Athletics, Lajoie and his companions would make a side trip to Atlantic City, New Jersey, where they would hide out.

It got to be a familiar routine on the ball club. The Blues would arrive in Philadelphia, and sheriffs would be waiting to meet the train and deliver Lajoie a summons to appear in court. Each time, Cleveland manager Bill Armour would feign ignorance as to the whereabouts of the Big Frenchman.

With a shrug, Armour would smile and say, "I guess he took 'French leave.'"

• • •

It was raining in Baltimore when a cab pulled up outside John McGraw's residence one evening in late June 1902. Inside the horse-drawn carriage was Fred Knowles, secretary of the New York Giants and a personal emissary of team owner Andrew Freedman. Knowles had been dispatched to Baltimore to deliver a proposal to McGraw. For the next few hours, the two men drove around the city in the rain while Knowles made his pitch. McGraw listened with interest but remained noncommittal. When they arrived back at his house, McGraw had only a brief reply for Knowles to relay to his boss.

"Tell Freedman I can't give him a definite answer. I need time to think it over."

The deal being discussed would confirm what many people already had come to suspect. Freedman was offering McGraw the chance to return to the National League as manager of the Giants.

It would not take McGraw long to reach his decision. The events of recent months already had determined his course of action.

• • •

The signs of change in John McGraw's life had been evident since the beginning of the new year. On January 8, 1902, he married Mary Blanche Sindall, the daughter of Baltimore contractor James W. Sindall. At their wedding, the Reverend Cornelius F. Thomas of St. Ann's Church in Baltimore reminded the couple "it is the 'sacrifice hit' that adds to the number of runs and wins the game," and he urged the groom to make his bride " 'steal' her way . . . until she reaches the 'home plate' of happiness."

The next month, John K. Mahon bought a large block of Orioles stock and was elected president of the ball club. Mahon's son-in-law was Joe Kelley, one of the old Orioles who had followed Ned Hanlon to Brooklyn. With his father-in-law in charge of the club, Kelley also bought into the Orioles and jumped Brooklyn to return to Baltimore. That spring, McGraw made it clear that he was the sole authority on the Orioles and he would accept no suggestions from either Kelley or even Wilbert Robinson on running the team. To those who had known him for a long time, this was not the same McGraw who used to enjoy staying up late swapping ideas and plotting new tricks with Robinson, Jennings, and his other teammates on the old Orioles.

The atmosphere in Hot Springs also was different when McGraw arrived in February with his new bride and her younger sister. His primary concern was to nurse his injured knee back to health in the town's many mineral baths and steam rooms. To some of the newspapermen present, it appeared as if McGraw also spent a greater deal of time than usual betting the thoroughbreds and pursuing his leisure activities. "The team that was to represent his beloved Baltimore did not take up much of his time or attention," claimed one writer.

When the season began and McGraw was not in the lineup, there were grumblings in some quarters that his bad knee was not all that was keeping him off the field. The rumor, perhaps spread by his enemies, was that McGraw's wife objected to his playing because it belittled them socially.

But one thing had not changed. McGraw again was in hot water with Johnson over his run-ins with the umpires. The

Baltimore manager did not even make it through the first game of the season before receiving his first ejection from umpire Tommy Connolly.

One week later, umpire Jack Sheridan would not let McGraw take his base after being hit by a pitch because he had not tried to get out of the way of the ball. The next game, McGraw stood at the plate and let pitches hit him five times and not once would Sheridan award him first base. In disgust, McGraw sat down in the batter's box and would not move. That stunt earned him a five-day suspension from Johnson.

The strife resulting from McGraw's constant antics began to come to a head in an incident at Oriole Park in late May. In the first inning, Dirty Dick Harley of the Tigers slid into third base and tore open McGraw's left knee with his spikes. Although badly hurt, McGraw lunged at Harley and landed several blows to his face before being pulled away. McGraw had to be carried to the clubhouse, his pants leg and stocking soaked with blood. The wounds required seven stitches, and this time McGraw's knee would not fully recover.

It was a month before he was able to return to the lineup. His first game back, he again got thrown out by Connolly. So did Kelley, who went so far as to shove the umpire. When McGraw refused to leave the field, Connolly forfeited the game to Boston. That earned both McGraw and Kelley indefinite suspensions.

By now, even some of McGraw's closest friends were showing their resentment of his methods. He and Robinson had not spoken for weeks, and Robbie asked for a dissolution of their partnership in the Diamond Cafe. The falling out had centered on what Robinson saw as McGraw's neglect of his duties as manager. The Baltimore fans and writers also had their doubts about McGraw. Since the start of training camp, McGraw had released first Jack Dunn and then Steve Brodie, and both men immediately signed with the Giants. "McGraw and Freedman seem to be working on the 'community of interest' plan," observed the *Baltimore Press*.

To some people, it appeared McGraw was going out of his way to make his departure from the American League inevitable.

• • •

There was much for John McGraw to think about when he returned from his cab ride with Fred Knowles. He was convinced his days in the American League were numbered. Already, Ban Johnson had relocated one of his franchises, abandoning Milwaukee for St. Louis. The American League president also was planning to establish a team in New York, and at one time had considered moving the Baltimore franchise there with McGraw as its head. But doubts over McGraw's loyalty and business ability had caused Johnson to delay the move to see how the Baltimore manager conducted himself during the 1902 season.

In turn, McGraw had begun to question whether Johnson could successfully pull off such a move. On a scouting trip to New York, McGraw had met with Frank Farrell, one of the proposed backers of an American League ball club in the city. The two men even went so far as to discuss building a ballpark on a vacant lot at 111th Street between First Avenue and the East River. Later, McGraw learned that the land Farrell had picked out had been condemned and was targeted to become a public lot. McGraw suspected the Giants' Freedman had used his Tammany Hall political connections to sabotage the proposed site.

Not wanting to "be left holding the bag" in Baltimore, McGraw began scheming to move to New York on his own terms. But he wasn't content simply to return to the National League as a player-manager. Instead, he had become part of an elaborate plot designed to not only land him in New York but also deal a crippling blow to Johnson's American League in the process.

The principals in the plan were McGraw, Andrew Freedman, and John Brush. The deal would be put into action by McGraw joining the Giants as a player and manager, with the power to recruit and sign his own players. But he would not be working for the notorious Freedman, dubbed by the newspapers as "the most despised man in baseball." As part of a compromise to resolve the deadlock resulting from the power struggle between the two factions of the National League, Freedman had agreed to sell his ball club and leave baseball. In return, Albert Spalding had given up his claim on the office of league president and been replaced by a three-man governing committee.

Freedman's decision to pull out of baseball was prompted by the deteriorating political situation in New York. Mayor Seth Low swept into office the year before by defeating incumbent Robert A. Van Wyck, a Tammany Hall man, and William Travers Jerome, an avowed enemy of the corrupt organization, had become the new district attorney. Tammany Hall was losing its political grip, and Boss Croker, one of Freedman's closest friends and allies, resigned as head of the organization and moved to Europe to live in splendor. Freedman also wisely fled the city to his Red Bank, New Jersey, estate to avoid any process servers.

The new owner of the Giants would be John Brush, the Cincinnati magnate who had opened negotiations with McGraw more than a year earlier. Brush already controlled a block of stock in the New York ball club, and he would buy out Freedman's controlling share for two hundred thousand dollars.

To finance the move, Brush would sell the Cincinnati Reds to that city's "yeast kings," brothers Max and Julius Fleischmann. The older of the two brothers, Julius, was a well-known sportsman and, at age twenty-nine, the youngest mayor in Cincinnati's history. The Fleischmanns had entered the picture through their horse-racing ties with New York's Frank Farrell, the so-called Pool Room King, who ran a string of gambling operations out of his billiard rooms.

It took a series of secret meetings to work out the details of the complex scheme, and throughout May and June, McGraw managed to avoid public detection while slipping in and out of New York, Philadelphia, Wilmington, and even Freedman's Red Bank home in New Jersey.

At one point, the deal almost fell apart because of Freedman's insistence that McGraw's duties with the Giants include running the concessions. McGraw refused, telling Freedman the Giants already had the best concession man in the business in Harry M. Stevens. Reluctantly, Freedman gave in. As it turned out, McGraw's assessment was proven correct. Eventually, Stevens would build his concession business into a large company that catered to ballparks around the country.

• • •

In late June, the suspensions handed McGraw and Kelley for their run-in with umpire Tommy Connolly touched off another round of public sparring between Ban Johnson and the Baltimore manager. Johnson said he was glad Connolly "humiliated McGraw" and "the men who disregard the organization rules must suffer the consequences." McGraw shot back, "No man likes to be ordered off the earth like a dog in the presence of his friends. Ballplayers are not a lot of cattle to have the whip cracked over them."

Unable to suit up with the Orioles because of the suspension, McGraw slipped into New York on July 1 to meet with Freedman. The time had come for Muggsy to make his break. Sitting across a desk from Freedman in his office in the St. James Building at Broadway and Twenty-sixth Street, McGraw signed a contract to become manager and player for the New York Giants ball club at a salary of eleven thousand dollars for four years. That made him the highest-paid player or manager in the game's history. As a precaution, McGraw asked attorney John Montgomery Ward, the former brotherhood leader, to check the wording of the document.

All that remained now was for McGraw to free himself of his contractual obligations to the Baltimore club. He did this with surprising ease. He returned to Baltimore, called a meeting of the Orioles' directors, and demanded payment of seven thousand dollars which he claimed he had advanced out of his own pocket for players' salaries and other expenses. If the money wasn't available, said McGraw, he wanted his outright release from the club. After a day of wrangling, the directors agreed on July 8 to give McGraw his release in exchange for his stock in the team.

That night, McGraw left for New York, where he would formally sign his contract with the Giants. Before leaving, he boasted to Baltimore reporters he would be paid "as much as any ballplayer ever drew" and have "practically unlimited funds" for buying players. As a final pledge to the fans of the Orioles, McGraw added, "I certainly will not draw on the Baltimore team for players."

Despite his words of assurance, McGraw was back in Baltimore a week later to execute the final part of the plan. Acting as a go-between for the two sides, he helped put together a deal in which Freedman would purchase from Orioles director John Mahon 201 of the 400 shares of stock in the ball club. The block of stock sold by Mahon included not only his original shares but also those he had purchased from McGraw and Kelley, who had been brought in on the conspiracy. The transaction left control of the American League club in the hands of Freedman. He then released several key players, who already had been divided up among three National League teams. McGraw and the Giants got Joe McGinnity, Jack Cronin, Dan McGann, and Roger Bresnahan. Kelley, Mahon's son-in-law, went to Cincinnati, where he had been offered the manager's job in exchange for his help in sabotaging the Orioles. Cy Seymour also left to join the Reds.

The outrage in Baltimore was predictable. McGraw was branded a traitor and was referred to in print as "John Muggsy Benedict Arnold McGraw." Wilbert Robinson, at one time McGraw's closest friend and now one of the handful of players left behind in Baltimore, was so discouraged by the turn of events he declared he was leaving baseball.

It took Johnson's quick action to avert disaster for the American League. He arrived in Baltimore on the morning of July 17 and announced that unless the club fielded a team that afternoon for its scheduled game with St. Louis, the stockholders would forfeit their franchise to the league.

Only four Orioles, among them McGraw's one-time friend and partner Wilbert Robinson, were in uniform at game time. The game was forfeited to St. Louis and, in accordance with the American League constitution, the Baltimore franchise was turned over to the league. This effectively terminated Freedman's control over the Orioles and allowed Johnson to salvage the situation. He appointed Robinson manager of the team and filled out its roster with players donated by other American League clubs. This makeshift team would finish last in the league, but Baltimore at least was able to complete its schedule.

Although he had managed to minimize the damage, Johnson would never forgive McGraw for what he considered an act of treason.

• • •

His first day on the job as Giants manager, John McGraw strutted out of the team's headquarters in the St. James Building and was greeted by a crowd of reporters.

"Hey, Muggsy!" shouted one of the newspapermen.

McGraw stiffened as he shot back his reply.

"It is to be no more 'Muggsy.' Just cut that out, and I will show you that I can be a gentleman."

His plea was in vain, but New Yorkers had no complaints about his behavior. McGraw's style fit in well in New York, a city that respected such battlers. Among the celebrities in the city of four and a half million people at the turn of the century were prizefighters, famous journalists such as William Randolph Hearst, and even old gunfighters. Bat Masterson, the legendary frontier sheriff of Dodge City, Kansas, moved to town in 1902 to fill the post of deputy U.S. marshal for the southern district of New York. Later, Masterson would turn to newspaper work, and as sports editor of the *Morning Telegraph* he would chronicle the exploits of McGraw and his ballplayers.

From the moment he arrived in town, McGraw began exerting his power. The team he inherited had a record of 23–50, putting it a distant 33½ games out of first place. At a meeting with Andrew Freedman, the new manager went down a list of the twenty-three men on the roster and began scratching off those he did not want. When he was finished, nine names had been crossed off the list.

"You can begin by releasing these," he said.

Freedman immediately objected, pointing out that those nine players had cost him a total of fourteen thousand dollars.

"They'll cost you more if you keep them," snapped McGraw. "You're in last place, aren't you? I've brought some real ballplayers with me, and I'll get you some more."

One of the players released was rookie outfielder Jack Hendricks. Later, he would brag: "There is a story that McGraw fired me the first day. That is a big lie. It was the second day. I hid in the clubhouse the first day."

Another of the casualties was one of McGraw's old enemies, Dirty Jack Doyle. When he got the news, Doyle, who was batting over .300, told Freedman he was glad to be leaving. When asked why, he said, "I'm going to join my old pal, Tom Loftus, at Washington, where I shall be able to hear someone crack a joke occasionally. I haven't heard one all season here."

McGraw had a different assessment of the situation. He found ballplayers who sang and whistled cheerfully in the clubhouse even after losing ball games. A popular greeting on the team was, "One less day 'til payday." Other times, a player might remark, "Wish it would rain and choke off the game, but stay pleasant over Sunday." There also were deep divisions on the club, one of them reportedly splitting the team between Catholic and Protestant factions and another involving a young pitcher named Christy Mathewson. It was Mathewson's plight that best illustrated the problems plaguing the ball club.

Two years earlier, the Giants had purchased the pitcher from the minor-league Norfolk club for fifteen hundred dollars. In his debut, Mathewson lost to league champion Brooklyn, thanks in part to five errors committed by his teammates. When he also lost his next two starts, Freedman canceled the deal and sent the pitcher back to Norfolk. There, Mathewson completed the season with a phenomenal record of 21–2.

By coincidence, Mathewson's three National League appearances made him eligible to be drafted that winter by Cincinnati's John Brush, a part owner of the Giants, for only one hundred dollars. Norfolk lost fourteen hundred dollars on the deal, but its protests were to no avail. Brush then turned around and traded Mathewson back to the Giants in exchange for sore-armed pitcher Amos Rusie, who had not even pitched since injuring his arm three years earlier. Rusie retired after pitching just three games for Cincinnati.

Meanwhile, Mathewson proceeded to win his first eight games with the Giants in 1901, and finished the season with twenty victories, including a no-hitter, for a seventh-place team.

But Mathewson, a strikingly handsome college man from

Bucknell University, was not popular with his New York teammates, most of whom refused to speak to him. Jack Hendricks initially was surprised by the treatment given the pitcher, but it did not take him long to understand the cause of Mathewson's plight. "He is a pinhead, and a conceited fellow," said Hendricks. As an example, Hendricks cited the time a throw by Mathewson hit Billy Lauder in the head during practice. Lauder collapsed to the ground, obviously hurt, but Matty never even bothered to check on him.

As a result of such haughtiness, the other players "threw down," or betrayed, Mathewson every chance they got. "I can't win! I can't win!" he would moan after every defeat. The other players would just laugh and call out, "To the woods, you big stiff!" and other more profane insults. The problem came to a head early in the 1902 season when Mathewson got so angry at his teammates' poor play he told manager Horace Fogel, "I cannot win with them behind me."

So Fogel, a former sportswriter, moved Mathewson to first base. The other infielders responded by intentionally throwing the ball in the dirt and wide of the bag to make him look bad. Mathewson lasted only three games at the position, so Fogel tried him in the outfield.

Even after he was fired in May, Fogel continued to serve the club in an unofficial capacity as an advisor to his successor, second baseman Heinie Smith. Consequently, Mathewson even was tried at shortstop in addition to his stints in the outfield and his duties on the mound.

One of McGraw's first moves was to make Mathewson a full-time pitcher again and instruct Freedman to get rid of Fogel.

"Anybody that doesn't know any more about ballplayers than he does has no place with a big-league ball club," said McGraw. "Mathewson has as fine a pitching motion as any kid who's come up in a long time."

Another of McGraw's moves was to hire Thomas J. Murphy,

his old groundskeeper from Baltimore. Murphy, an elderly man with a huge moustache, knew how to groom the playing field to McGraw's specifications, tampering with the foul lines and varying the height of the grass as needed. To further endear himself to the manager, Murphy even had made various depictions of McGraw in the Baltimore infield. In New York, the groundskeeper went one step further by picturing McGraw and Freedman in the turf as "the Heavenly Twins."

• • •

The Giants went through their first pregame practice under John McGraw on July 19, 1902. The players ran onto the field, and McGraw kept them hustling the entire time. After just a few minutes of the lively display, one fan was so delighted, he stood up and shouted in a voice that could be heard throughout the Polo Grounds.

"They're awake!"

The game time of four o'clock was designed to cater to the Wall Street crowd, and the El train's baseball special, which ran from Wall Street to the Polo Grounds with only a stop at Forty-second Street, was packed that day. Other fans arrived in hansom cabs or larger horse-drawn carriages, which parked on the running track between the bleachers and the rope fence that ran across center field of the horseshoe-shaped ballpark.

An estimated ten thousand people, the largest crowd of the season, packed into the Polo Grounds for the game with the Philadelphia Phillies. In the stands, waiters in black coats and white aprons carried trays filled with large glasses of beer, which sold for ten cents each. Harry Stevens's concessionaires also sold pieces of pie for ten cents and a frankfurter sausage in a split roll, later known as a hot dog, for the same price. Printed scorecards carrying the lineups, as well as advertisements, cost five cents.

With the influx of old Orioles in the lineup, McGraw's team was dubbed "the Baltimore Giants" or "the Baltimorized New

Yorks." McGraw played shortstop and batted second. The battery consisted of former Orioles Iron Man McGinnity and Roger Bresnahan. Dan McGann played first base and Steve Brodie center field.

Even though they lost, 4–3, the Giants didn't disappoint their fans. McGraw went 1-for-3 and McGinnity pitched a strong game. The Iron Man had only one bad inning, the third, when the Phillies scored all four of their runs. The key hit in the rally was delivered by another former Oriole, first baseman Hughie Jennings.

Afterward, Jennings stood on the sidelines and taunted his old roommate.

"G'wan back to Baltimore where you belong, Mac!"

The New York fans had a far different reaction. They applauded the Giants, and many of them waited outside the clubhouse to cheer the players again. For the first time in years, the Giants had played with spark, and there was a mood of optimism surrounding the Polo Grounds.

McGraw did nothing to dampen the enthusiasm. Despite losing his first game in New York, he remained as cocky as ever as he emerged from the clubhouse.

"The pennant is out of reach, of course," he said. "But look out for us next year."

• • •

One week later, White Sox pitcher Clark Griffith, needing just one more out to complete a one-run victory over the Senators, sent one of his trick pitches spinning toward the plate in Washington. Griff's reputation for trickery and cunning had earned him the nickname, "the Old Fox," but this delivery did not fool the batter. Ed Delahanty lashed out with one of his powerful swings, and the crack of the bat meeting the ball was so loud there were reports it could be heard three blocks away. Griff turned and watched in amazement as the ball shot over the fence, still rising as it sailed out of the ballpark. By the time it landed, the ball had traveled more than a block away.

The dramatic home run tied the game and touched off the most joyful celebration seen at a Washington ballpark in years as the four thousand fans in attendance tossed their hats in the air, clapped their hands, and called out Delahanty's name. Although the Senators went on to lose the game in extra innings, nothing could diminish the impact of Del's feats in his new home. Washington was eager for heroes, and "the Only Del" fit the bill.

When he made the jump to the American League, there had been a derisive joke about Delahanty and the Washington weather. It was said the heat in the capital city would make him so lazy he would have to be given a cold shower bath before and after every game.

Delahanty, thirty-four years old, soon proved his critics wrong. Not even the sultry conditions could affect his batting. He reported late to the Senators after receiving permission to work out with the ball club in New Orleans, where he had enjoyed a lucrative season at the horse track. Once he did arrive in Washington, Del was as spry as the colts he had been betting all winter. He was named captain of the team and he immediately won over the Washington fans, knocking out eight hits his first seventeen at-bats.

The atmosphere Del found in Washington was far different from Philadelphia. When he stationed himself in left field at American League Park, he stood in front of a rickety outfield fence on which whisky signs were painted. In the stands were district clerks as well as powerful congressmen, admirals, and generals. Sometimes, one might spot a famous figure such as Admiral Dewey, the hero of Manila Bay in the Spanish-American War of 1898. Game time was four o'clock but the size of the crowd always increased in the second inning because of the many government workers who arrived late on the single railway line running to the park.

On the sidelines roamed a one-armed man named E. Lawrence Phillips, who would point a megaphone toward the crowd and call out the names of the opposing pitchers and catchers, or batteries. In other ballparks, the umpires handled this chore, often in a voice nobody could hear or understand. Phillips, who owned the scorecard concession in Washington, figured it would be good for business if he kept the spectators informed of who was who. So he began taking his megaphone out to the bleachers and calling out the information to the two-bit customers. He had such a distinctive style, adding extra syllables to players' names and drawing out the word *batteries* to make it "bat-ter-eeze," that one day late in the 1901 season umpire Tim Hurst asked him to handle the announcing. By 1902, Phillips had become a fixture at the games, paving the way for what soon would become a baseball tradition.

It was only one of many baseball traditions which the city had to offer.

• • •

Half a century earlier, the nation's capital had been described by the French minister De Bacourt as "neither a city nor a village nor the country, but a building yard, placed in a desolate spot, where living is unbearable."

The Washington that Ed Delahanty discovered in 1902 had made considerable progress since that dreary assessment. In the ten years following the Civil War, the city had doubled in size and had begun an aggressive renovation. The streets were illuminated and more than 180 miles of the roadways were paved.

By the turn of the century, Washington even had a modern street-railway system that was the envy of other cities. Street cars driven by electrical propulsion ran from one side of the District of Columbia to the other on grooved rails in the street pavement. There were no poles or wires overhead to mar the landscape.

But the city remained an enigma to baseball people. The roots of the game ran deep in Washington, and the city long had been considered a hotbed of baseball. Yet, when it came to professional baseball, the trademarks of Washington were mismanagement, greed, corruption, and ineptitude. Underscoring the city's futility in the professional ranks, no Washington team had managed to finish in the first division of any league in the fourteen seasons prior to Delahanty's arrival.

Such futility was in marked contrast to the game's beginnings in Washington.

Following the outbreak of the Civil War, several regiments of the Union Army either camped in Washington or were based in the city. While there, many of them, particularly the units from New York, entertained themselves by playing baseball. The Seventy-first New York Guards, later beaten at the Battle of Bull Run, played the Washington Nationals on the White House grounds in 1861. A game played on a Washington circus lot the following year was watched by President Lincoln and his son, Tad. Arriving in a black carriage drawn by two black horses, the president took his son by the hand and sat along the first-base line in some sawdust left over from a circus. From there, he watched the action and cheered enthusiastically.

Lincoln was reputed to have been a great baseball fan, the first of many who would occupy the White House. There was a popular tale concerning Lincoln and baseball that said as much about the national game as it did about the nation's leader. According to the story, when Lincoln still was a country lawyer back in Illinois, he was engaged in a game of baseball near his home when a delegation from the Republican National Committee called upon him one day.

"Tell the gentlemen they will have to wait a few minutes until I get my next turn at bat," he said when told of the visitors' arrival. Only after he had batted did Abraham Lincoln learn he had won the Republican presidential nomination.

The Civil War ended, and the 133rd New York Volunteers stopped on their way back from Appomattox to challenge the Washingtons to a game. That same year, the famed Brooklyn Atlantics and Philadelphia Athletics played a game in the capital city. Among the six thousand spectators on hand was Andrew Johnson, who had succeeded the slain Lincoln as president. Johnson was an avid baseball fan, and he ordered the marine band to play at every Saturday game held on the Ellipse, a lot behind the White House.

Ulysses S. Grant entered office in 1869 and he, too, faithfully watched the ball games from a vantage point on the south lawn of the White House.

Another prominent baseball fan in Washington was a former Union soldier named Michael Scanlon, who first learned the game after joining the army as a commissary clerk at the age of fifteen. In 1870, Scanlon moved to capitalize on the game's popularity in Washington by building a five-hundred seat wooden ballpark and charging twenty-five cents for admission. A year later, the Washington Olympics became a charter member of the National Association, and Scanlon's ballpark became the team's home.

The arrival of professional baseball in the city was followed by the poor play and frustration that was to become a symbol of Washington teams. Two separate Washington clubs dropped out of the National Association. The city had brief and unsuccessful flings with the short-lived Union Association and later the American Association. A Washington club was admitted to the National League in 1886, but four years later was booted out after never finishing higher than seventh place.

The city got another chance in 1892 when the National League took in the old Philadelphia Athletics following the collapse of the American Association and transferred the team to Washington. Team owners George and Jacob Earl Wagner, wealthy associates of the Armour meat-packing firm, came to town and proceeded to methodically run the ball club into the ground. They established a board of local directors and then disbanded it, they sold their most promising players to other teams, and in their first three seasons alone they went through five managers.

One of the best-known of the many Washington managers was the famous James "Orator Jim" O'Rourke, who was known for his spectacular handlebar moustache and his verbal duels with the umpires. One game, O'Rourke, playing first base, loudly protested a call and was fined fifty dollars by umpire Silk O'Laughlin.

Shortly thereafter, O'Rourke caught a pop fly, turned to the umpire, and asked sarcastically, "Safe or out?"

"He's out," replied O'Laughlin. "But it just cost you five dollars for the information."

It was a lesson the Washington fans could take to heart. The Wagners did not provide the city with a winner, but they knew how to take its money. They had a handsome young pitcher named Win Mercer whose wavy black hair, striking features, and handsome smile made him popular with the ladies. So the Wagners designated every Tuesday and Friday as "ladies day" and billed Mercer as the pitcher. "The announcement that he would do the honors was a guarantee of a grandstand filled with the fairer sex," proclaimed the *Washington Post*.

In eight seasons, the Senators never finished better than a tie for sixth place. One season, they employed four different managers and at one point J. Earl Wagner went so far as to install himself as a co-manager to help run the team.

When the Wagners finally decided to sell out following an eleventh-place finish in 1899, the National League was only too happy to oblige by buying out the franchise and the lease on the ballpark. Despite all the failures on the field, George and J. Earl Wagner departed with a profit of $230,000 and Washington was left without a ball club.

The city was without baseball for one year, but it got another chance to prove itself thanks to the arrival of the American League. When Ban Johnson declared major-league status for his organization and invaded the East in 1901, he persuaded Jimmy Manning to transfer his Kansas City franchise to Washington.

Manning's club finished only sixth in its first season, but he worked hard to bring the city a winner. In Johnson's estimation, he went too far in his efforts. The American League had a reserve fund for teams to draw on as needed to sign National League players, and Manning made liberal use of the money. His plan was to concentrate his funds on a few first-class players and carry no more than thirteen or fourteen men on his roster in 1902. He signed Ed Delahanty to a four-thousand-dollar deal and also paid heavily to get Smiling Al Orth, Harry Wolverton, and Jack Townsend from the Phillies.

Washington fans were overjoyed by the news of the signings, but it was not long before their euphoria was tempered by reality.

When Manning attempted to withdraw money from the league fund to go after Willie Keeler, he was turned down. Johnson believed he had enough capital invested in Washington, and he wanted to see a return on his money before spending any more. Angered, Manning sold out his shares of the club and left town.

That allowed Johnson to bring in his own man, Tom Loftus, as manager. Of more importance to Washington fans, it also gave the American League president an excuse to raise the cost of grandstand tickets in the city from fifty to seventy-five cents to pay for the expensive new ballplayers. If Washington fans wanted a winning team, Johnson reasoned, they must foot the bill.

• • •

Everything seemed to go Delahanty's way upon his arrival in Washington. In the wake of the Lajoie ruling the first week of the season, Delahanty and the other Philadelphia jumpers in Washington received a telegram from Colonel Rogers of the Phillies. It read: "Supreme Court upholds us in Lajoie case. Decides our contract absolutely binding on you. You are hereby ordered to report forthwith to me at the Philadelphia ball park for performance of your duties under your contract. Refusal to obey this will be at your peril."

Even that worked out well. Wilton J. Lambert, attorney for the Washington ball club, assured the players the ruling applied only to Pennsylvania and to Lajoie but advised them to stay out of that state.

As a result, whenever the Senators traveled to Philadelphia, Delahanty and his fellow Phillies jumpers Al Orth, Harry Wolverton, and Jack Townsend got to enjoy themselves in New York. Taking advantage of the time off, Del went to the horse track one day and placed a twenty-dollar wager on a longshot in the Metropolitan Handicap. His horse, Arsenal, came home a winner, and Big Ed won five hundred dollars.

Another time, Del strolled down a street in New York with Townsend and Wolverton at his side and spotted his old Philadelphia manager, Billy Shettsline. Shetts, good-natured as always, gave the players the glad hand and asked them how things were going in Washington. He told them how much he missed them in Philadelphia and how Colonel Rogers still hadn't given up on getting them back. One thing led to another, and soon Shetts began jollying Townsend.

Townsend was a big, carefree farmboy with an overpowering fastball that he still hadn't learned to control. He had walked as many as seventeen batters in a game, and in his first big-league start for the Phillies in 1901 he was so wild he had to be pulled immediately. He feared he would be released, but he was given another chance and he responded with a three-hit shutout against the defending champion Brooklyn Dodgers. Besides his wildness, Townsend's biggest problem was his inability to take the game seriously. Always laughing and smiling, he was nicknamed "Happy" and there was no more aptly named player on the team. He was a particular favorite of Delahanty's, and on the road the two roomed together.

The more Shetts needled him, the more nervous Townsend became.

"Now that I've found you, you don't have a chance to get away," Shetts said in mock seriousness. "Just as soon as you go to sleep, I'll kidnap you sure."

Townsend eyed the manager suspiciously. "You wouldn't dare. Del has a pistol."

"Never mind Del's gun. It won't be in working order when we go after you when you've gone to sleep."

Shetts paused to let his words sink in before continuing. "I'll have you sure as fate. This is just the chance I've been looking for to get you back, and once I have you in Philadelphia you'll never get another chance as long as you live to get away from me."

The gag had its intended effect. Townsend was so convinced kidnappers would be coming after him, he sat up in a chair in his hotel room all night. He dozed off occasionally, but awoke with a start at the slightest noise.

When Del related the story to the other Washington players, they all had great fun at Townsend's expense. No one laughed louder at the tale of kidnappers than did Ed Delahanty.

• • •

It was open warfare between the two leagues that summer. Shortly after sabotaging the Baltimore franchise, National League raiders slipped into Detroit to attempt a similar stunt.

They were foiled by the alertness of Sam Angus, a minority owner who warned Ban Johnson what was happening and then bought out the other investors before they could sell to John Brush.

At this same time, John McGraw was taking advantage of the rumored sale of the ball club to sign several of the Detroit players while they were on a trip to the East. No one knew for sure how many of the players accepted McGraw's offers, but when it was revealed that Detroit pitcher Roscoe "Rubberlegs" Miller had signed with the Giants he was blackballed from the American League. There were reports that Detroit shortstop Kid Elberfeld also put his name on a New York contract, but these stories were not proven.

In retaliation for McGraw's action, Detroit's Angus had his agents track down fast and powerful young outfielder Sam Crawford of Brush's Cincinnati team. Crawford, who was only twenty-one years old when he led the National League in home runs the previous season with sixteen, proved to be an easy mark. A country boy from the small town of Wahoo, Nebraska, he worked as a barber before becoming a professional baseball player, and he already was making more money than he thought possible. The Tigers offered him a substantial raise as well as one hundred dollars advance money to sign for 1903–04, and Crawford jumped at it. When Reds president Garry Herrmann confronted him about his deed, a frightened Crawford backed down and signed yet another contract to stay with Cincinnati.

In Pittsburgh, Barney Dreyfuss was tipped off that Ban Johnson himself was coming to town on a player raid, so Barney and some of his men staked out the lobby of the hotel the night of the American League president's arrival. But while they were watching the main entrance, Ban and his accomplices escaped detection by taking the service elevator up to the room where the meeting was to take place. Waiting for them was Pirates catcher Jack "Peach Pie" O'Connor, who had signed on as an American League agent and then recruited six of his teammates to hear Johnson's offer. That night, Johnson got third baseman "Wee Tommy" Leach, a personal favorite of Dreyfuss, to sign his name to an American League contract. When the affair came to light, O'Connor was suspended from the team and a tearful Leach returned an uncashed thousand-dollar check to Johnson and begged Dreyfuss for forgiveness.

At the height of the hostilities, the final phase of the McGraw-Freedman-Brush scheme was enacted when John Brush sold his majority ownership of the Reds and headed to New York to take over control of the Giants.

On the afternoon of August 12, 1902, Andrew Freedman summoned reporters to his office to announce that Brush had assumed control of the team and would take the title of managing director.

"While I will remain the president of the club," said Freedman, "I will turn the inside affairs of the business over to Mr. Brush, as I have little or no time to give to baseball, while Mr. Brush will be able to devote practically all his time to the game."

That same afternoon, Brush held a long conference with McGraw. When he emerged from the meeting, Brush told the writers present the Giants were going to make every effort to strengthen the team by acquiring the best players money could buy.

"New York is the greatest baseball city in the world," he said, "and she is entitled to the best team that can be gotten together. From now on, my efforts will be directed toward building up the New York team into a pennant winner, and I think we will succeed."

The Giants' new owner then dispatched McGraw on a recruiting trip to the West. His instructions were to sign the best of Ban Johnson's stars he could land, regardless of the cost.

• • •

In Washington, Ed Delahanty was pressed into duty at first base, where in one game he stood arguing a call while a runner scored all the way from second base. Another time, he needlessly chased a batter from first base back toward home plate, allowing a runner to advance all the way from first to third.

Del's friend Harry Wolverton became so disenchanted with Washington he left town and went back to Philadelphia, where he patched up his differences with Colonel Rogers and rejoined the Phillies.

The Senators fell into the second division, and a losing atmosphere gripped the ball club. To break the monotony, the players resorted to pranks and horseplay. Two of them, Happy Jack Townsend and Case Patten, carried around a pair of white mice as pets. They stored the rodents in their pockets and on occasion would create an uproar by turning them loose in a crowded hotel lobby or dining room to "investigate" the premises. On one long train ride to St. Louis, Patten's mouse happened to take residence in third baseman Bill Coughlin's clothes. Although he was one of the toughest ballplayers in the league, Coughlin, a Pennsylvania coal miner known as "Scranton Bill," had a deathly fear of rodents. It was only after he had gotten fully dressed that he discovered the mouse on his body, and he let out a blood-curdling scream as he began jumping up and down and ripping off his clothes. Another time, someone put a rat in Coughlin's glove, prompting a similar reaction on the ballfield.

The Senators arrived in Detroit for Labor Day weekend, and they were joined on the bench by former Phillies slugger Big Sam Thompson, who lived nearby. Late in the game, Delahanty stepped to the plate, and Thompson pointed out to the distant left-field fence, behind which were some railroad tracks.

"Del ought to put the ball over there," said Thompson. "He used to do it."

"He hasn't forgotten how," answered Jimmy Ryan, the veteran Washington outfielder.

Ryan had just finished speaking when Del hit a drive with such force it took one bounce and disappeared over the left-field fence. The story in the *Detroit News* claimed that after the ball cleared the wall it "caught up with a passenger train on the way to Toledo, and there have been no reports since."

The fans cheered each hit Delahanty got that season as he battled his old roommate, Larry Lajoie, for the American League batting honors. The race ended amid much confusion and debate, and the outcome would not become known until Ban Johnson released the official league figures in December. At that time, Del was proclaimed the American League batting king with an average of .376, compared to the .366 mark credited to Lajoie. Ed Delahanty still was the "King of Batters." He had won batting championships in both the American and National leagues, a feat no player has matched since.

• • •

Late that season, a man went on a drunken rampage in a west side Chicago saloon, shooting a bartender and clubbing a policeman over the head with his gun before fleeing. The incident would prove to have a profound effect on the American League pennant race.

The man's name was Virgil "Ned" Garvin, and he was one of the best pitchers on Charlie Comiskey's Chicago White Sox. When sober, Garvin, a lanky Texan, was a kind and gentle man. But, in the words of one newspaperman, "Whiskey sets him wild and those Texas ideas of shooting, cutting and burning come over him." The outburst at the saloon marked Garvin's third attempt at killing in the previous two years, and Comiskey had reached the end of his patience. When Garvin appeared at the team's offices the next day, Comiskey began screaming and picked up a tin can, which he hurled at the pitcher's head. A frightened Garvin ducked out the door just ahead of the can, which went crashing into the hallway. That marked the end of Garvin's career in Chicago, as well as the White Sox's hopes to repeat as American League champions.

There were other events which also played a crucial role in determining the outcome of the 1902 season. It was Colonel Rogers's bad luck that not only were his legal maneuvers unsuccessful, they ultimately aided the crosstown rivals of the Phillies. Whenever American League teams came to Philadelphia to play the Athletics, they had to leave behind such valuable performers as Larry Lajoie, Elmer Flick, and Bill Bernhard of Cleveland; Red Donahue of St. Louis; Ed McFarland of Chicago, and Big Ed Delahanty, Al Orth, and Jack Townsend of Washington. As a result, Connie Mack's team won forty of its final forty-eight games at Philadelphia's Columbia Park for an overall record of fifty-six victories and only seventeen defeats on its home grounds. That was good enough to enable the Mackmen to claim the city's first baseball championship since the old Athletics won the American Association title nineteen years earlier.

In the National League, Pittsburgh finished an incredible 27½ games ahead of its nearest rival, Brooklyn. Attendance fell to 1.7 million, well below the American League total of 2.2 million. The old league was hurting. Its eight teams employed an unusually high total of 240 players, with Chicago trying ten men at third base, Cincinnati ten left fielders, and New York twenty right fielders.

A weak-hitting Cincinnati infielder named George Magoon got sick and had to check into a sanitarium after playing only forty-two games. To his surprise, the team not only paid his salary in full it even picked up his bill for his stay in the hospital.

When Magoon went to thank the Reds president Garry

Herrmann for such generous treatment, he was asked what his salary was for the next season. Magoon told him, and Herrmann replied, "I don't think that you are getting enough money, so we'll just add five hundred dollars to that amount." Dumbfounded, Magoon said he was willing to live up to his contract at the terms agreed. But Herrmann insisted, so the player signed a new deal.

"I guess a man won't work his best for people who treat you that way?" marveled Magoon as he left the office.

Everywhere there was money being thrown around as the two leagues fought to sign players. Salaries were up by more than 25 percent. Players were taking advance money for signing with one team, then turning around and signing the next contract offered them. The joke was, "A contract is an imaginary agreement between two parties, each of whom thinks the other believes it's binding."

The owners preached about the evils of contract breaking and talked about right and wrong, all the while making fantastic offers to convince players from the rival league to break their pacts and sign with them.

Cleveland secretary Davis Hawley summed it up the best. "The magnate here digs into his inside pocket," he noted, "brings out one thousand dollars in crisp new bills and tells the player that money is his in return for his signature. What is the poor boy to do? What would the average boy do?"

• • •

Ban Johnson had proved himself a master at turning defeat into victory. He had survived the unfavorable ruling in the Larry Lajoie case by engineering the deal which sent the ballplayer to Cleveland, thus bolstering one of his weaker teams. The American League leader was equally as determined to work John McGraw's defection and the Baltimore sabotage to his advantage.

Johnson already had made known his intentions of invading

the New York market. His problem of which team to place there had been solved by the failure of the Baltimore franchise. The last-place Orioles, unable to remain competitive in the wake of the departure of McGraw and the team's other top players, had been a failure both on the field and at the box office. It was the excuse he needed to abandon the Baltimore market.

But before Johnson could proceed with his plans to move the franchise to New York, the team needed to sign a drawing card. The player Johnson targeted was Brooklyn's five-foot, four-inch outfielder Wee Willie Keeler, who not only was one of the game's top stars but also lived in New York. A two-time National League batting champion and a master of bat control, it was Keeler who had coined the phrase "Hit 'em where they ain't" while playing for the old Orioles. He once hit safely in a record forty-four consecutive games, and like all the old Orioles, Keeler was a tough competitor. Once, he tore up his arm by shoving it through a fence to make a game-saving catch.

When repeated efforts to sign Keeler failed, Chicago's Clark Griffith, who was to be the manager of the New York Americans, enlisted the aid of Boston's Jimmy Collins. The two men arranged a meeting with Keeler, at which time they presented the little outfielder with a $10,000 contract to jump leagues. Keeler, who had begun his career playing for $1.50 per game, was staggered by the offer, but he said he needed to give the matter more thought.

The meeting was about to end when Collins turned to Griffith with apparent disgust.

"Don't depend on Willie, Griff. Get another man or your right field will be shy a star."

Taking his cue, Griffith declared he was confident that Collins was wrong about Keeler.

"I'll bet one hundred dollars that Keeler won't sign the contract you have in your pocket," Collins insisted.

Griffith turned to Keeler and winked knowingly. "His one hundred dollars is easy."

Keeler took the bait. He called Collins back, and both men posted one hundred dollars with Griffith. The deadline for the signing was set for March 1, 1903.

A few weeks later, Keeler was passing through Chicago with a barnstorming team when Griffith called on him at his hotel. During their conversation, Griff pulled out his wallet in search of an old newspaper clipping for Willie to read. When he returned the clipping to the wallet, Griffith held up two one-hundred-dollar bills to show Keeler.

"These are the stakes on that bet you made with Collins," said Griff.

"They'll both belong to me soon," answered Keeler.

"Come on over to Johnson's office and earn them. The contract is there."

Keeler needed no more prodding. Later that afternoon, he was in the office of the American League president, where he signed his name to the contract with the New York Americans. When he did, he was handed two thousand dollars in advance money plus the pair of hundred-dollar bills.

As soon as Keeler departed, Johnson drew up a one-hundred dollar check to be mailed to Collins back in Boston. The American League president placed the money in an envelope and turned to Griffith with a smile on his face.

"If we lose a few more bets like this," he said smugly, "there won't be any National League."

• • •

In New York, John McGraw was under no illusions as to the enormity of the task that faced him. The ball club he had inherited showed some improvement under his leadership, winning twenty-five games while losing thirty-eight, but still had finished last in the National League. Even the ravaged

Philadelphia ball club had managed to win eight more games than New York.

McGraw needed desperately to bring in some ballplayers, and he was running out of time to get them. He had spent much of the latter part of the season in pursuit of various American League stars, but just how well he had fared was a matter of debate.

McGraw had signed Kid Elberfeld of the Tigers in July, but since then the diminutive shortstop had signed another pact with Detroit and indicated he planned to stay put.

The Giants manager spent a lot of time in St. Louis unsuccessfully negotiating with Jesse Burkett, a three-time National League batting champion who had jumped to the rival league. Next, McGraw tried to sign Larry Lajoie but was turned down. He also attempted to get Elmer Flick, third baseman Bill Bradley, and outfielder Jack McCarthy of Cleveland, but none would make the jump. Neither would St. Louis shortstop Bobby Wallace. And the overtures to the former Phillies drew a stiff rebuke from Colonel Rogers, who threatened to take to court any team, either American or National, which tampered with his players.

To make matters worse, while McGraw was crisscrossing the country in search of players, the American League managed to sign away two of his top stars. Christy Mathewson and Frank Bowerman not only signed agreements to play with the St. Louis Browns in 1903, they each accepted five hundred dollars in advance money.

After much talking, McGraw finally convinced the two players to renege on their deals and stay put with the Giants.

Despite these well-publicized setbacks, McGraw remained as cocky as ever in the fall of 1902. He claimed to have signed several top stars, although he refused to reveal their names to lessen the danger of losing them.

"We are going to have a good team," he boasted to newsmen. "There is no doubt about that, for I have picked the players carefully and have taken only men I know can make good.

"Who are they? Well, just now I can't say, but there will be many new men here. When I came here, I found many things about the team I did not like, but what mistakes had been made were not made by me, and, of course, I don't want to knock any other person's efforts. There were some good players and some bad ones. There will be no bad ones on the new team."

. . .

Gambling was a way of life for many ballplayers. They played poker on their long train rides, shot craps in their hotel rooms, and placed wagers on just about any type of contest.

The great Cap Anson was famous for his annual wagers on his Chicago ball club to win the pennant. In 1897 alone, he bet a total of $2,000 on his team to finish first. Although he lost that money, he had cleaned up the year before by betting heavily on Republican William McKinley to win the presidential election. And while a major stockholder in the Giants, Eddie Talcott one year offered to bet anyone $250 to $500 that his team would finish among the top three in the standings.

But for Delahanty and many other ballplayers, the favorite source of wagering was the horse track. Del was a prominent horse player and his appetite for betting the races was well known throughout baseball. "Next to a base hit," wrote Paul Eaton in *Sporting Life*, "Dell likes a straight tip, with a big killing as a chaser."

Cincinnati writer Ren Mulford dubbed Delahanty the "ranking chief" of the "horsey boys." And there were plenty of horsey boys in baseball, so many that it often was said it was easier to get a ballplayer to talk about horses than ball games.

Even the magnates liked to bet the ponies. In Pittsburgh, Pirates secretary Harry Pulliam went so far as to arrange for a messenger boy to arrive at the office each morning with tips from "a friend" on that day's races. One day, Pulliam was tipped off to a sixty-to-one longshot named Tom Middleton. Not liking the odds, Pulliam declined to bet on the horse, and much to his chagrin it came home a winner. For months afterward, Pulliam's colleagues kidded him about his failure to cash in on the tip.

Delahanty had become a heavy bettor in the latter part of the 1890s, and he liked to brag he had discovered a "system" which could not lose. William Weart of Philadelphia was one of those who was privy to Del's methods. "You paid the tipping bureau so much for their information," explained Weart, "then you made your bet, and next you collected your money—that is, to hear Delahanty tell about it."

Frequently, Del managed to stay ahead of the bookmakers. And once he got on a hot streak, he knew how to make the most of it. Said Washington's Bill Coughlin, "He has the reputation of being very crafty once he has the best of it."

But horse players, like ballplayers, were prone to slumps. And in the fall of 1902, Del encountered one of his worst runs of bad luck ever at the racetrack.

He left Washington after the baseball season with a six-hundred-dollar advance on his 1903 salary but lost most of the money at the New York tracks. With his bankroll running out, Del was forced to contact Senators president Fred Postal by telephone to request another loan. Delahanty was one of his favorites, so Postal obliged by mailing him a check for one thousand dollars.

Compounding Delahanty's problems, rumors were circulating about his intentions for 1903. The talk had begun during the season, and Del had become the target of much abuse around the league. The Boston fans had been particularly vocal, harassing him with such taunts as "How much are they offering you to jump?" and "Gimme your old job, Del!"

When the season ended, a story broke that Delahanty and

Washington pitcher Watty Lee had signed with the Phillies. Another report claimed the big slugger was boasting he would play in New York in 1903 for "the fattest salary ever given to a ballplayer."

Delahanty's friends dismissed such tales and pointed to Big Ed's frequent and vocal denunciations of the National League and its magnates. Del was particularly critical of Giants owner John T. Brush, and while in St. Louis several newspapermen had overheard him declare that under no circumstances would he return to the National League.

But the National Leaguers would not give up. In October, Phillies manager Billy Shettsline tracked down Delahanty on a train ride to New York and handed him a packet containing three thousand dollars and a two-year contract with the figures left blank. To get the money, all Del had to do was fill in the numbers and sign the contract. The Washington writers reported that not only did Delahanty reject the offer, he got off at the next stop and wired Washington manager Tom Loftus to inform him what had happened. In his message, Big Ed assured his manager the Senators had treated him on the square and he intended to stick with them.

In New York, a newspaperman found Delahanty at Gravesend racetrack, and again the ballplayer proclaimed he would stick with Washington. "Any talk to the contrary is bosh," said Ed.

A few weeks later, Delahanty returned to Washington for the horse-race season at Benning amid more rumors that he was planning to jump. Eugene Cochrane, one of the directors of the Washington ball club, called on him, and the two men had a heart-to-heart talk. When it came time to part, Del looked Cochrane in the eye and assured him he would fulfill his Washington contract.

But once the Benning meet got underway, Del's bankroll continued to dwindle. And with it, so did his resolve.

• • •

John McGraw arrived in Washington that November feeling lucky. He went to the Benning racetrack, and there he spotted many of his old friends. There was the volatile Joe Kelley, the former Oriole now managing the Cincinnati ball club. Recently, McGraw and Kelley had been on the outs, but now they had patched up their differences. Another visitor to the track was McGraw's one-time friend Wilbert Robinson, who had completed the season as the Baltimore manager. Ned Hanlon, the former Orioles manager now with Brooklyn, also showed up for the races.

With Hanlon was Brooklyn's Charlie Ebbets, who left town a few days later in good humor after getting much of the bookies' money. His mood would be spoiled when he arrived back in Brooklyn to learn his star outfielder, Willie Keeler, had jumped to the American League. "Baseball contracts these days seem to be worthless, players breaking them at will," fumed Ebbets.

McGraw reveled in the atmosphere of the racetrack, and he was as skilled a judge of horses as he was of ballplayers. He was what was commonly known as a railbird, or one who stood on the lawn and inspected the horses as they made their preliminary gallops on the track. His friends liked to tell of the time McGraw was engaged in this activity at a track in New York when he spotted a horse named Cottage Maid. Impressed by the horse, he went to tip off his friend Louis Snell, a well-known bookmaker.

Trying to be discreet, McGraw tugged at Snell's arm and whispered the information to him. "Louis, bet on Cottage Maid. She will win to a certainty."

"What makes you think so, Mac?" asked Snell.

McGraw could barely keep his voice down, he was so excited. "Because I never saw a horse warm up so well and race with such freedom. If she don't win, I'll never claim to be a judge of a race horse again."

"Well, I guess you are right for once, Mac. I think she will win. I own her, you know."

"What?" shouted McGraw. "You own her!"

Snell broke out laughing, and McGraw stood there staring at him incredulously. Finally, Muggsy was able to speak again.

"Well, the tip goes anyhow. She will win all right."

Sure enough, Cottage Maid won handily, rewarding both McGraw and Snell.

But it was not the horses which commanded McGraw's attention at Benning. He was in town to see his old friend Ed Delahanty and to keep tabs on his fortunes at the track. McGraw had been in contact with Del since running into him at the track in New York, but recent events had added to the importance of signing the big slugger. St. Louis outfielder Jesse Burkett not only had backed out on an apparent agreement to jump to the Giants, the word was he had made off with some advance money from John Brush in the process. McGraw now was desperate to land Delahanty to fill out his outfield in New York.

The Giants manager went about his business discreetly, taking care not to be seen in the company of Delahanty and waiting for the chance to make his move. When it came, McGraw was ready.

One day, the two men met in private and McGraw made his pitch. Later statements in the Washington papers indicated that Delahanty, who had been losing heavily at the track, was in a state of desperation over his financial setbacks. Del himself later would admit that McGraw offered him a seven-thousand-dollar salary, which the Giants manager said was his limit. Del refused and countered with a demand for ten thousand dollars. McGraw passed on that figure.

Eventually, the two men compromised on what was believed to be a three-year deal that initially would be reported as worth eight thousand dollars a season and later given as six thousand dollars a year. Reportedly, Del did not sign the contract until he was in New Orleans a few weeks later, but it eventually became clear the deal was struck in Washington. At the time, McGraw gave him an advance of three thousand dollars.

Besides the advance money, Delahanty insisted on one other thing. He wanted a provision in the contract that he would receive his salary "whether he plays ball or not, whether he is enjoined or not and whether he is injured or not."

The deal was to be kept secret, so when Del left town with his wife and child for the races at New Orleans he continued to publicly deny the increasing rumors of his defection.

Privately, however, Del confided to close friends how he had outsmarted the baseball magnates.

"I have no reason to fear the American League," he boasted, "and I have been assured by McGraw that Colonel Rogers will not enjoin me from playing with a National League club other than Philadelphia. That is all cut and dried.

"While I hate to cut loose from so good a fellow as Tom Loftus at Washington, I am anxious to help New York beat out the Pittsburghs and Cincinnatis for the 1903 pennant."

The way Del saw it, he could not lose.

"Suppose I am enjoined from playing," he said. "My salary goes on just the same, so I am hooked up pretty well."

Meanwhile, McGraw quietly slipped out of Washington and returned to New York. As it turned out, he had been the big winner at the racetrack after all.

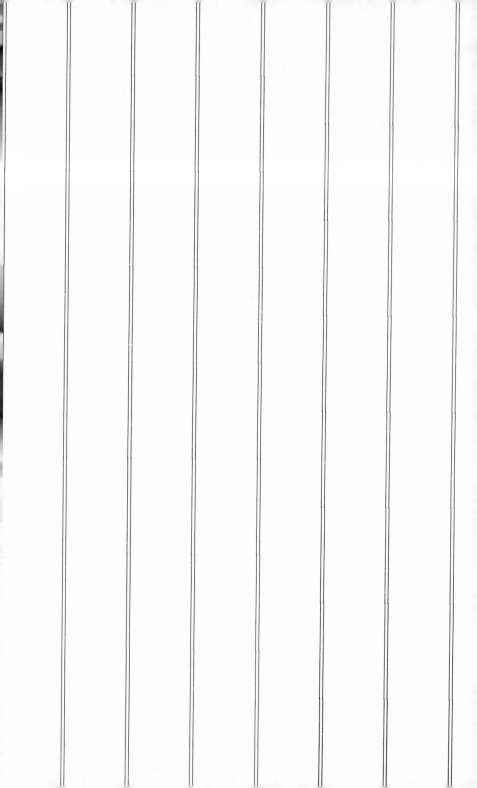

IV
THE PEACE
CONFERENCE

WHENEVER I GO TO A BASEBALL MEETING, I NEVER FOR-
GET TO CHECK MY MONEY AND VALUABLES AT THE
HOTEL OFFICE BEFORE ENTERING THE SESSION
CHAMBER.

FERDINAND ABELL

On a fall afternoon in 1902, Ban Johnson raised his shotgun and took aim at a flock of birds flying overhead. The gun fired, but to Johnson's dismay the birds continued their flight unharmed.

A few minutes later, Johnson, normally a crack shot, fired again. Once more, he missed. He shot a third time and again failed to hit his target. As he continued to fire with the same results, he grew more and more perplexed.

His hunting companions watched with amusement. Among them was Johnson's close friend Charlie Comiskey, owner of the Chicago White Sox. They were on an expedition to the woods of Wisconsin, near the northern Michigan border. Johnson had purchased a new shotgun for the trip, and he proudly showed it off to the others on the train ride north from Chicago. They all took turns admiring the gun, which had been made especially for the American League president. Then, as a prank, someone substituted blank cartridges for the live shells.

Everyone knew how Johnson prided himself on being a great hunter. The joke was that "Beebee," as Comiskey liked to call his friend, would tie an animal to a tree to shoot it or buy some fish off an Indian if that was what it took to keep from coming back empty-handed.

The hunters rode an old buckboard from the train station to the camp, about forty miles away, and Johnson was given the front seat, which allowed him the best chance to shoot game along the way. The woods were thick with birds that day, but each time Ban shot he missed. In exasperation, he claimed the gun was wrong. It had been misshaped and its stock shortened, Johnson insisted.

"You're a rotten shot, so don't alibi!" someone shouted gleefully. Someone else suggested Ban had been drinking too much whisky, making his aim unsteady.

The next morning, Johnson went out early to fire the gun.

He saw a bird on the ground and he fired one barrel. The bird walked away. He shot the other barrel, and the bird flew off unharmed.

Johnson turned to his guide, who was trying to keep a straight face.

"Henry, put a piece of paper on that tree."

The guide did as he was told, and Johnson took aim and fired. The paper remained untouched. He walked up to it and shot from close range. Still there was nothing.

"Henry, lend me your knife," he said.

Johnson cut open several shells and inspected them. His face became filled with rage. He stalked back to the camp, packed his bags, and ordered a buckboard to take him back to the station. His only words were, "I didn't think Commy would do that to me."

Things were never the same between the two men after that.

• • •

That December, the American League president embarked on a hunting trip of a different type. This time, Johnson was headed to New York in search of a site for a ballpark for the new team he proposed to put in that city. He was accompanied by his right-hand man, Charles Somers.

While Johnson and Somers were scouting the city, the National League magnates also were in town for their annual meeting. It was a bitter and acrimonious affair, marked by a successful revolt against New York's John Brush, who for the past year had controlled the league through a three-man commission which he headed. With Pittsburgh's Barney Dreyfuss and Philadelphia's Colonel John Rogers leading the opposition to what had come to be known as "Brush-ism," the National League magnates elected thirty-two-year-old Pittsburgh secretary Harry Pulliam as their new president. Having broken Brush's control of the organization, the other owners were free to undertake a bold initiative.

On the evening of December 11, Johnson and Somers were dining at the Criterion Hotel when they spotted three men approaching their table. They were National League magnates Garry Herrmann of Cincinnati, Frank de Haas Robison of St. Louis, and James Hart of Chicago. Johnson knew immediately the purpose of their visit.

The National Leaguers had come to see if peace terms could be arranged between the two leagues. Johnson told them he would meet with them the next day to give his reply.

The next morning, Johnson informed the three-man National League committee he would welcome peace talks. He proposed the two sides meet on or about January 5 to discuss the settlement.

As the men shook hands, Johnson could not help but reflect on the irony of the situation. Just two years earlier, he had sought an audience with the National League owners and had been told they would not send for him until "hell froze over."

As Chicago writer Cy Sanborn wryly noted: "Since that time there have been no cablegrams from the lower regions to the effect that his Satanic Majesty was learning to skate, yet . . . the old leaguers were falling over each other to get to Johnson."

• • •

As the New Year approached, and with it the long-awaited peace conference, baseball was in a state of confusion and turmoil. The National League still was wracked by bitter in-fighting and factionalism. There was confusion over what would be done with the numerous players who had signed contracts with more than one team. Among the contract jumpers, there was fear over punitive measures aimed at them as Ban Johnson argued for more than their banishment from the game. "Such a man should be sent to prison," said the American League president. "The public will never trust them, and they will do the game harm if they are allowed to remain." There were rumors flying about Johnson's proposed move into New York, and there was uncertainty over the future of the American League franchises in Washington and Detroit as well as Baltimore.

With feelings already on edge and the future of the game uncertain, baseball was rocked by another bombshell in mid-December 1902. In New Orleans, where his losses at the racetrack were mounting, Ed Delahanty finally confirmed the rumors that he was jumping to the New York Giants. The contract already was signed, Del told a reporter for the *New Orleans Times Picayune*, and John McGraw was en route to the southern city to meet the newest addition to his team.

When asked why he had made the jump to New York, Delahanty had a simple reply.

"Well, I'm a star player and am getting well along in years," he said. "I can't always make good money, and I'm a fool if I don't get all I can while the graft lasts."

The fallout from the news threatened the already shaky prospects for a peaceful settlement between the two leagues. Philadelphia's Colonel Rogers angrily reiterated his claim to Delahanty and issued an appeal to the National League board of directors to prevent the player from joining the Giants. 'I will fight the Delahanty case to the finish," vowed the Colonel. From New York, John Brush responded that he "would keep Delahanty [even] if it broke up the peace plans with the American League."

In Washington, there was outrage not only over Delahanty's defection but also over his deception of the public. The ballplayer had repeatedly assured the local fans of his intentions to return there and all the while he had been continuing his negotiations with the New York team.

The *Washington Post* labeled Delahanty "the human grasshopper" for his jumping tactics, and John Luitich warned in the *Sporting News*, "Trouble in large packages is in store for the big fellow."

• • •

Ban Johnson arrived in Cincinnati on the morning of Friday, January 9, 1903, on an overnight train from Chicago. With him were American League magnates Charles Somers of Cleveland, Charlie Comiskey of Chicago, and Henry Killilea of Boston, who, along with Johnson, composed the league's four-man committee to the peace conference. There also were some reporters in the traveling party, and they had joked with Johnson that his proposed arming of the special car with a Hotchkiss gun was unnecessary. Ban laughed and suggested that the car be christened the White Dove.

"For this trip at least," he added with a smile.

The American League president had reason to be in such good spirits. It had taken weeks of intense negotiations just to set the ground rules and agree upon a site and date for the peace conference. As recently as two days earlier, it appeared the proposed meeting might collapse, but a last-minute settlement had allowed the talks to become a reality.

The main sticking point had been Johnson's insistence that the committees from both leagues be given full power to reach an agreement. Johnson had no problem getting such a mandate for his committee, but the National Leaguers were deeply divided over the issue. New York's John Brush, turned down in his bid to get on the National League committee, refused to allow others to bargain away any of his disputed players, specifically Ed Delahanty. Philadelphia's Colonel John Rogers also insisted upon having his property rights protected, and Brush as well as Brooklyn's Charles Ebbets were opposed to allowing the American League to establish a team in New York.

Johnson was unwavering in his demand. He set a deadline of January 15 for talks to begin. Then he made an exaggerated show of preparing for a hunting trip to Missouri with his friend Comiskey. He reported to his office at the Fisher

Building in Chicago each day but dismissed all talk of baseball. Instead, he and Comiskey, who were back on speaking terms, swapped tales of their hunting prowess.

With the prospects for peace rapidly dwindling, the National Leaguers finally gave in. On Wednesday, January 7, Johnson received a letter from Cincinnati Reds president Garry Herrmann agreeing to the conference at a date of the American League president's choosing. Johnson wasted no time wiring Herrmann the peace conference would begin that Friday in Cincinnati.

For Johnson, it would be a triumphant return to the city where he had gotten his start in baseball.

• • •

It had been more than a decade earlier that Ban Johnson had first attracted attention as a baseball writer for the *Cincinnati Commercial-Gazette*. Tim Murnane, a former ballplayer who had become a prominent newspaperman, recalled the young Johnson "booming the Reds and coaching from the press box."

It was at that time that Johnson first met August "Garry" Herrmann, a city official. Herrmann, a gregarious sort, took a liking to the young writer and the two maintained their friendship over the years.

After Johnson went off to make his mark as a baseball executive, Herrmann remained an active force in local politics and a close ally of Cincinnati mayor Julius Fleischmann. It was through his connections with Fleischmann that Herrmann got into baseball. When Julius Fleischmann and his brother, Max, bought out John Brush as majority owners of the Cincinnati Reds in 1902, they sold Herrmann a small block of the club and named him president.

Although a newcomer to the game, Herrmann was well suited for the job. He courted the other owners and executives as well as the baseball writers by dispatching a voluminous amount of correspondence and entertaining them at lavish parties which featured his homemade German foods. Herrmann further endeared himself to the writers by presenting them with gifts of his special sausage, and he courted various civic groups by generously distributing ballpark passes.

The baseball owners quickly came to like Herrmann. More important, they also came to trust him. In political circles, Herrmann was known as "the man whose word is as good as his bond," and he gained a similar reputation among his new associates. As a result, it was Garry Herrmann who stepped forward as baseball's peacemaker that winter.

It was Herrmann and not newly elected National League president Harry Pulliam who conducted the negotiations with Ban Johnson over the ground rules of the peace conference. "He has been prominently before the public in Cincinnati for years," said Johnson, "has a splendid record and through him I believe the way may be found for a meeting under reasonable conditions."

At the same time, Herrmann also was able to act as a mediator among the deeply divided National League owners. In order to meet Johnson's demands that the peace committee be given full authority to reach an agreement, Herrmann worked out a compromise that appeared to appease the dissident National League owners. Any time the committee was in doubt as to its authority to act on a matter involving a team's property rights, a designated representative would contact the appropriate owner for instructions.

Finally, Herrmann, along with Pulliam, the league president, and owners Frank de Haas Robison of St. Louis and James Hart of Chicago, prepared to meet the American Leaguers.

Ban Johnson's committee arrived at the meetings with the solid backing of the other American League owners. As a further sign of unity it was agreed among the four delegates to back the Detroit team as strongly as possible in all player disputes.

By contrast, the National League committee had only the reluctant support of its colleagues. Years of feuding and double-dealing had made the National League owners suspicious and distrustful of each other, as Herrmann had learned early on.

There was a popular story that at his first National League meeting, Herrmann was spotted by Charles Comiskey wandering the corridors of the hotel. Comiskey asked what was wrong, and Herrmann replied that someone had stolen his watch.

"What did you expect?" asked Comiskey. "You just came out of a National League meeting, didn't you?"

• • •

Garry Herrmann stood in a meeting room of Cincinnati's St. Nicholas Hotel and happily greeted the other delegates to the peace conference. Herrmann's good cheer helped set the others at ease, and there was a mood of cautious optimism as the baseball men got down to business.

The two sides outlined the matters to be resolved, and it was determined that territorial rights and player contracts were to be the primary topics. Initially, there were few problems. The delegates agreed the two leagues would respect each other's contracts, eliminating any more jumping by the players. The merger of the two leagues into one twelve-team or sixteen-team circuit was dismissed, and the territorial rights of the two organizations were agreed upon. The American League was given the right to put a team in New York but agreed not to place a franchise in Pittsburgh, as had been contemplated.

Herrmann emerged from the room to update reporters on the proceedings and he announced cheerfully, "We are all on good terms and both sides are expressing candid opinions."

Next to him, Comiskey nodded his head in agreement.

"I like the way Mr. Herrmann talks in the meeting," said Comiskey. "He tells what he thinks and doesn't waste much time about it, either."

The trouble began the next morning. It came time to decide how to divide up the contract jumpers and other disputed players, and as the delegates began reviewing the names on the list an air of tension began to grip the room. In all, there were sixteen players who fell into this category, but the hottest arguments centered on four men. They were Ed Delahanty, George Davis, Kid Elberfeld, and "Wild Bill" Donovan.

By chance, three of these players were claimed by the New York National League club. Delahanty had contracts with both New York and Washington. George Davis, a star shortstop, had been under contract with the Chicago Americans before jumping to New York. Elberfeld, also a shortstop, had signed with the Giants in midseason and then turned around and re-signed with Detroit of the American League. The fourth player, Donovan, was being fought over by Detroit and Brooklyn.

At the mention of Delahanty, Ban Johnson stood and launched an assault on the actions of the ballplayer. The American League president wanted to make an example of the slugger by blacklisting him from baseball for his contract jumping. By the time Johnson finished talking, feelings against Delahanty were running so high that seven of the eight delegates were ready to throw him out of the game.

Only one man spoke up for Delahanty. In a rare break of unity among the American Leaguers, Charlie Comiskey took the floor and argued that to take such action would be making a scapegoat of the ballplayer.

"Usually, when a player signs a second contract," pointed out Comiskey, "it is done after a man of influence has convinced him that his original contract is not binding, that the organization to which he is bound is on the verge of bankruptcy and in no position to fulfill his obligations, and that the signing of the new contract is the only thing that will keep him in the game."

It was a noble gesture on Comiskey's part, but he had other reasons for his actions. He knew if Delahanty were blacklisted, the same punishment might be given his player, George Davis.

But Johnson was adamant. He urged the delegates to blacklist not only "contract jumpers" such as Delahanty and Davis but also the owners and agents involved in such deals. As Johnson later proclaimed publicly, New York's John Brush and John McGraw would have been punished equally with the players.

The debate raged for two hours. Only the staunch opposition of Comiskey saved Delahanty from banishment. Finally, the National Leaguers present came to realize the impact such an action would have on one of their fellow owners, Brush, and they backed off. The move for the blacklist was defeated.

Next came discussions on each of the disputed players, and there were more angry words and heated exchanges. At the height of the arguing, Herrmann startled the delegates by rising from his seat and walking toward the door. Before leaving, he turned and urged the others to take some time to cool off, then he stalked out.

The ploy had the intended effect. When the talks resumed, Herrmann announced he was withdrawing his claim to "Wahoo Sam" Crawford, his powerful young outfielder who had just slugged a league-leading twenty-three triples. Although Crawford had re-signed with the Reds after signing a contract with Detroit, Herrmann was willing to surrender the player to the American League as a gesture of peace.

Pittsburgh's Barney Dreyfuss, who was present at the conference although he was not on the National League committee, followed suit by offering to give up outfielder Jimmy Sebring, also claimed by Detroit.

The gesture was warmly received by Ban Johnson.

"That's the proper spirit," he said, adding that he was satisfied that Sebring belonged to Pittsburgh and the American League could not accept such a sacrifice by Dreyfuss.

That set the tone for the remainder of the session. The owners agreed to set 1902 as the base season for settling the contract disputes. All players who jumped prior to that season were allowed to remain with their clubs. Those jumping after the season began were to be returned to their old teams provided those clubs could validate their claims. Any other cases not clearly covered by these guidelines would be settled as fairly as possible.

As the delegates went down the list of players, there was much bargaining and even a few arbitrary decisions. Pitcher Vic Willis, for example, had not signed with the Boston Nationals but he was awarded to that club rather than Detroit.

The American League could well afford the concession, as Detroit emerged as one of the clear winners of the proceedings. In addition to gaining Crawford from Cincinnati, it also was awarded Kid Elberfeld, who had signed first with New York, and Wild Bill Donovan, whom Brooklyn claimed it had signed to a two-year deal.

But when Ed Delahanty's name came up for discussion, there were more harsh words. Ban Johnson had given Washington his assurance he would not surrender its star player to the other league, and he made clear his intentions to keep that pledge. After considerable debate, the National Leaguers agreed to return Delahanty to Washington provided third baseman Tommy Leach was given back to Pittsburgh at the expense of the American League club to be placed in New York. Johnson accepted the offer but only after Pittsburgh awarded infielder Wid Conroy to the New York Americans to prevent that team from being without a third baseman.

George Davis, the other player singled out by Johnson for

his contract jumping, also was returned to the American League. He went to Comiskey's Chicago Americans rather than the New York Giants.

The final scorecard of players showed the Americans with a 9–7 advantage, but of more importance was the breakdown of the names. Brooklyn and New York, the two National League clubs which had held out against the peace talks, had suffered the most. Brooklyn lost its claims to both Wild Bill Donovan and Wee Willie Keeler. New York lost Ed Delahanty, George Davis, Kid Elberfeld, and speedy outfielder Davey Fultz, and also faced the prospect of having its territory invaded by the American League. The Giants' only solace was the retention of pitcher Christy Mathewson and catcher Frank Bowerman in the face of claims by the St. Louis Americans.

That evening, Garry Herrmann stepped outside the conference room with a typewritten document in his hand. On it was the rough draft of the agreement between the two leagues. Even the magnates appeared surprised by what had transpired. In just fifteen hours, they had worked out an agreement that would prove to bring "rock-ribbed stability" to the game.

After two years of bitter and costly warfare, peace had broken out in baseball.

• • •

There was a story Harry Pulliam liked to tell about his new position as National League president. It concerned his predecessor in the office, Nick Young, who had held the position for seventeen years.

One day, Young had taken a pleasure trip to Pittsburgh to see a ball game. No sooner had he settled in his seat than a dispute broke out on the field. Someone hurled the ball over the fence, then players from both teams rushed the umpire and began shoving him around. Immediately, a group of reporters descended upon Young and demanded to know what he proposed to do about such disgraceful conduct.

Pulliam, who was sitting next to the league president, never would forget Young's response.

"With a look of pain," recalled Pulliam, "Uncle Nick side-stepped all their questions by murmuring: 'I've got such a headache. I'm sorry I came.'"

After just a few weeks in the office, Pulliam came to know all too well the meaning of Young's words.

The euphoria of the peace conference soon gave way to the bickering and infighting which had marked National League politics over the years. John Brush of New York was the first to express his displeasure over the terms of the agreement. The Brooklyn and Philadelphia clubs also registered complaints, and there were reports of grumblings from Boston.

Pulliam had scheduled what had been dubbed the "Amen Meeting" in Cincinnati on January 19 to ratify the treaty, but three days before it got underway he was hit with his first setback as league president. Papers were served on him notifying him that Brush had obtained a temporary injunction restraining him from ratifying the action of the joint peace committee.

In Philadelphia, Colonel Rogers was outraged. His troubles of the past year had convinced him to get out of baseball, and a Philadelphia group headed by broker James Potter was willing to buy the team for two hundred thousand dollars in a deal orchestrated by Barney Dreyfuss. The sale had been expected to be completed within a matter of days, but now it was being blocked by Brush's legal proceedings.

That set the stage for yet another stormy National League meeting. For three days, the National League magnates aired their differences and lashed out at each other. Colonel Rogers refused to attend, but he did send Pulliam a letter to read on his behalf. In it, Rogers again stated his claim on Ed Delahanty and protested the action of the New York club in signing the player.

Whenever there was a vote taken on ratification of the

treaty, it came out either 6–2 or 6–0, depending on whether the New York and Brooklyn clubs voted nay or abstained.

It was Garry Herrmann who finally broke the impasse by threatening to move his team to the American League if the treaty was not approved. He also got the owners to agree to compensate Brooklyn for the loss of pitcher Wild Bill Donovan. Brush was won over by assurances that the agreement only gave the American League the right to place a team in the borough of Manhattan and nowhere else in New York. Confident that Andrew Freedman's Tammany Hall connections could prevent the Americans from finding suitable grounds in Manhattan, Brush at last gave his reluctant approval.

Once the final two holdouts fell into line, the owners were able to give unanimous endorsement to the treaty. One by one, they placed their names to the document. When it came time for Brush to sign, he scrawled his signature in the appropriate space and then looked over at Herrmann.

"You may make me eat that agreement," said Brush, "but you can't make me say that I like it."

The other magnates burst out laughing, and even Brush joined in the merriment.

• • •

That January, a young man sat in his room at the Occidental Hotel in San Francisco, crying as he wrote a letter.

"Dearest Martha," he began. "With tears streaming from my eyes I pen these few lines to you, the dearest and sweetest little girl in the whole world. The act I am about to commit is simply terrible, but I can not help it, dearie. I am to blame—nobody else—so I am going to face it as rigid as I have many other wrong acts."

He had identified himself as "George Murray of New York" when he signed the guest register, but that was not his real name. He was George "Win" Mercer, the clever pitcher whose dark good looks and charming ways had made him a favorite first in Washington and more recently in Detroit.

Mercer had arrived in California with a traveling team of baseball stars. It had been an ill-fated journey. Mercer had started the trip in good spirits, fresh from winning fifteen games for a weak Detroit ball club and being rewarded with a promotion to manager of the team. Only twenty-eight years old, his future looked bright.

But things soon turned sour. One of the ballplayers, Willie Keeler, fractured his left collarbone. Catcher Mike Kahoe was knocked out of action with a split finger, and infielder Jimmy Williams also injured himself. Mercer became bothered with a pulmonary problem which did not respond to treatment, and he began to brood over this. He also received word that his brother was suffering from consumption, and Mercer feared the disease would strike him, too.

The ballplayer fell into one of his frequent bouts of depression. At such times, he always followed a familiar pattern of behavior. Gambling was Mercer's tonic, and the greater the risk playing the horses or shooting dice the greater the cure. "Consummate nerve was always in evidence in his play," a *Washington Post* reporter once noted, "and the excitement was strangely enough a sedative for his exaggerated blues."

But Mercer's luck took another turn for the worse. He began to lose heavily at the track, and he became even more despondent. Mercer's heavy gambling losses led him to more serious trouble. As treasurer of the team, he handled all the players' money on the trip. It later would be reported that he borrowed cash from the treasury to place more bets in an effort to get even again, and eventually ran up what was reputed to be an eight-thousand-dollar debt.

On Monday, January 12, 1903, two days after baseball's peace agreement was reached in Cincinnati, Mercer had another losing afternoon at the horse track in Oakland. He returned to the Langham Hotel, where the all-stars were quartered, and gathered his belongings without saying a word to anyone. From there, he went across the bay to San Francisco and took out the room at the Occidental.

He wrote four letters. One was to his mother and one to his sweetheart. Another was to the proprietor of the hotel. The last was to one of the men in the traveling party, Morris "Tip" O'Neill. It listed the bills due the various people in the traveling party and instructed Morris there were two sacks of money in the hotel safe and sixty-two dollars in Mercer's trousers.

Mercer also offered some advice. "A word to friends," he warned. "Beware of women and a game of chance."

In closing, he wrote: "Well, dear pal, with tears in my eyes, I say good-bye forever. May everyone connected with our trip forgive me. I wanted to do right. Please forgive me, dear friends. Win."

Mercer arranged the letters neatly on the desk. Next, he attached a rubber tube to a gas jet. He turned on the gas and placed the tube in his mouth. Minutes later, Win Mercer, the idol of thousands, lapsed into unconsciousness and never woke up.

• • •

In New Orleans, Ed Delahanty continued his nomadic existence. He frequented the horse tracks by day and escorted his young wife around town at night.

One day in January, he returned to the hotel where he lived and found a telegram waiting for him. It was from Ban Johnson, notifying Del of the peace agreement and informing him he must return to the American League.

Del seemed to take the news philosophically. He promptly wired his acquiescence and resigned himself to the fact he would not be able to play in New York.

Shortly afterward, a friend from Cleveland visited him and asked what his plans were for the coming season.

"I suppose I'll have to go back to the Washington club," said Del, "but that is not a cause of complaint from me for I was treated well there. And I guess if I deliver the goods I'll have no trouble.

"A ballplayer's standing is dependent on what he does on the ballfield, and I propose to do my best for Loftus. If I have good luck in batting, I'll fare all right."

Delahanty claimed to have no regrets. He simply had been looking after his own interests.

"I left to better myself," he said, "not because I was dissatisfied or was anxious to be on Brush's payroll, or be under McGraw's management. I wanted the money and got it."

But whether Del would be able to keep the money soon became a matter of contention. He received word from Ban Johnson that not only would he not be allowed to play ball for the Giants, he also must pay back the advance money he received from the National League team.

Del protested that his New York contract called for him to receive his pay whether or not "injunctions or unforeseen debarments" prevented him from playing with the club.

"I'll play with Washington again," he vowed, "but the New York advance money is in my kicks to stay."

When Johnson continued to insist upon such payment, Del changed his mind about returning to Washington. He began to tell reporters that if he could not play in New York he would give up the game. Such claims were met by widespread skepticism, but many of Delahanty's friends took the threats seriously. It was not so much a matter of principle as economics, noted the *Washington Post*. Delahanty's salary with Washington was forty-five hundred dollars, and he already had received a six-hundred-dollar advance on that amount. That left only thirty-nine hundred dollars. To earn that money, he first would have to reimburse New York the reported four-thousand-dollar advance he had received from that club. That meant Del would lose a hundred dollars playing ball for Washington. Even the *Post* noted he "would be a fool to play here at a loss."

As the debate raged, Del continued to have his good days and his bad days at the racetrack in New York. In his letters to friends, he claimed the good ones outweighed the bad ones and that he was making money "playing the runners." Not everyone believed him. There were increasing reports of frequent setbacks at the track and mounting losses. It was said that on one day alone, Delahanty lost a staggering four thousand dollars betting the horses. Word around the track was that Del had become a "plunger"—a reckless bettor who tried to cover his losses with more and more rash bets.

And finally, there came the day the ballplayer was so sure he had hit on a sure thing he put up $1,000 against $150 that his horse would finish first or second. The horse failed to place, and Del lost his money.

"When his friends heard that," reported William G. Weart in the *Philadelphia Press*, "they knew his race track fever was hopeless."

• • •

Back in New York, John Montgomery Ward greeted a visitor to his law office in the Wall Street district. The former ballplayer was forty-two years old, but he remained a fashionably handsome man with distinctive blue eyes and a moustache that curved stylishly upward.

In the eight years since the former brotherhood leader had retired from baseball, his life had continued to be an unbroken string of successes. He had opened a law practice, and by the turn of the century had become one of New York's leading attorneys, with an estimated annual income of ten thousand dollars. He took up the game of golf as a hobby and soon ranked among the top ten amateur players in the country. He

Charles Comiskey, president of the Chicago White Sox. *(National Baseball Library, Cooperstown, New York)*

John McGraw in 1899, when he was player-manager for the Baltimore Orioles. *(The Sporting News)*

John McGraw (right), manager of the New York
Giants, and his star pitcher, Christy Mathewson.

(National Baseball Library, Cooperstown, New York)

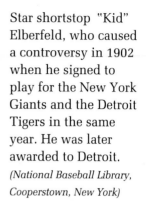

Star shortstop "Kid" Elberfeld, who caused a controversy in 1902 when he signed to play for the New York Giants and the Detroit Tigers in the same year. He was later awarded to Detroit.

(National Baseball Library, Cooperstown, New York)

Shortstop George Davis, who held out in a contract dispute for almost two years until he was cleared to play for the New York Giants.

(The Sporting News)

John Montgomery Ward, one of the most versatile players the
game of baseball has ever seen. He went on to become a lawyer
and represented such players as George Davis in their contract
disputes. *(The Sporting News)*

went on a hunting trip to Scandinavia, and he brought back a polar bear.

Ward also maintained an active interest in baseball, and was a frequent visitor to the ballpark as well as various league meetings. Fittingly, his greatest courtroom triumph came in one of baseball's most celebrated legal battles. The case involved former infielder Fred "Unzer Fritz" Pfeffer, who had been suspended without pay by New York owner Andrew Freedman in 1896. Pfeffer hired Ward as his attorney and filed suit against the team, claiming breach of contract. The lengthy court fight finally ended with a jury awarding the ballplayer the full amount of $737.

That victory had been especially satisfying to Ward, for it had been Freedman who had fired him as New York manager eight years earlier. The case also brought Ward a lot of business from ballplayers in need of legal help.

Among those players was George Davis, who had replaced Ward as manager of the Giants and now had arrived at his law office a few weeks after baseball's peace conference in 1903. Davis brought with him two contracts for the lawyer to inspect. One had been drawn up by Ward, the other had not.

Ward took the documents and read them over carefully. When he finished, he thought for a few minutes before giving his reply.

"George," he said simply, "you have gotten yourself into a bad box."

• • •

George Davis was one of baseball's most controversial and mysterious figures. He had arrived in New York in 1893, when Giants manager John Montgomery Ward had traded the popular Buck Ewing to Cleveland for the young shortstop. Although Ward was roundly criticized for the deal, Davis had proved to be an immediate sensation. He batted over .300 nine years in a row, stole as many as sixty-five bases in a season, and anchored the New York defense from his shortstop position.

Davis also was an innovative player, introducing the technique of standing in front of a mirror and taking cuts at an imaginary ball in order to detect flaws in his swing. Articulate and well spoken, he even wrote a series of newspaper articles giving pointers on how to play baseball.

With his intelligence and baseball skills as well as his leadership abilities, Davis seemed a natural choice to succeed Ward as manager of the Giants in 1895. The young ballplayer even had a heroic quality about him, once gaining much acclaim for stopping on his way to the ballpark and climbing into a burning apartment building to save two women and a small child, carrying them out one by one.

But Davis was a strange man, and many players believed he could not be trusted. One popular tale about him concerned the time he was a young boy growing up in Cohoes, New York. He hung around with some tough street kids, and he shocked his family with the coarse language he learned from them. George was five years old when his uncle came over from Albany one day to talk to him about his behavior.

"George," said the old man, "I have been told that you are in the habit of swearing a good deal of late. Is this true?"

"Uncle Joe, it is a ——— lie!" blurted out George just before he burst into tears.

Davis never enjoyed much success during two brief stints in charge of the team, and the second time he was named to the position he was accused of getting the job by undermining the authority of Buck Ewing, who had returned to New York as manager.

After guiding the Giants to a seventh-place finish in 1901, his only full season as a manager, Davis had worn out his welcome in New York. That winter, Clark Griffith of the Chicago White Sox arrived in the city on a player hunt and was told by the Giants office the team would not bid on Davis's services. Acting on this assurance, Griffith signed Davis to a two-year deal with a four-thousand-dollar salary, making him the highest-paid shortstop in the game.

That contract was drawn up by John Montgomery Ward, who assured Davis it was an iron-clad pact.

"If this contract can be broken," boasted Ward, "any contract ever made could be set aside."

Although his batting average slipped one point below the .300 mark in 1902, Davis enjoyed a solid season in the American League, stealing thirty-one bases and fielding brilliantly. White Sox owner Charles Comiskey was so impressed with Davis's solid play and leadership abilities he planned to make the shortstop his manager to replace Griffith, who was in line to lead the new American League team in New York.

Those plans were wrecked in the fall of 1902 when John McGraw, who was desperate for an infielder after failing to acquire either Larry Lajoie or Kid Elberfeld, convinced Davis to jump back to the Giants. According to Davis, he returned to New York only because McGraw informed him the reserve clause in his old Giants contract still was in effect and the team was going to enforce it.

If Davis had any doubts about the validity of McGraw's claims, they were put to rest by the new two-year deal the Giants were willing to give him. He was offered a boost in salary to sixty-three hundred dollars, with twenty-seven hundred dollars of that in advance money. As an added incentive, the Giants agreed to pay for any legal problems he might have as a result of the contract. Davis also would receive seventy-five dollars per month in the winter and, like Ed Delahanty, he was promised he would continue to be paid by the team even if legal problems prevented him from playing ball.

The signing prompted a furious outburst by Comiskey.

"Why, his own lawyer drew up his contract so tight that I couldn't break it with a ton of dynamite," thundered the White Sox owner. "I don't think he can, either."

To show he meant business, Comiskey got an injunction preventing Davis from playing with New York. Later, Chicago's claim to the player was validated by the peace conference.

But Davis was not willing to surrender so easily, especially after being told he must repay the Giants his advance money before he would be allowed to play ball. Armed with his New York and Chicago contracts, he again sought out Ward for legal counsel.

There would be conflicting accounts of just what advice Ward gave his client. Although he had drawn up the Chicago contract, Ward claimed he was unaware of the reserve clause in Davis's previous contract with New York.

"Either contract is enforceable," Ward told his client.

Furthermore, added Ward, while Davis could not be enjoined from playing in New York he might be prevented from playing in any other city and held financially responsible for violating his Chicago contract.

There also was a problem with the clause in Davis's New York contract guaranteeing payment even if he were unable to play for that team. Ward informed Davis he would have to report to the New York club before he could receive any pay from it.

As the lawyer characterized it, Davis "was between two horns of a dilemma."

Ward later would testify he told Davis he should settle his financial matters with the New York club in order to play for Chicago.

However, the ballplayer's actions after he left Ward's office indicated otherwise. Davis immediately went to John McGraw and, according to the Giants manager, informed him he would not return to Chicago and that on his lawyer's instructions was holding the New York club responsible for his salary and legal costs as specified in his contract with the team.

That put George Davis in open defiance of the peace

agreement. And once again, John Montgomery Ward was involved in a challenge to the baseball establishment.

But there was an ironic twist to this confrontation. This time, Ward found himself supporting the validity of the reserve clause. He also received his $250 in legal fees for representing Davis from the New York ball club. Paying the bill was Giants owner John Brush, the architect of the old classification plan which had led to the Brotherhood War.

• • •

That March, ballplayers across the country began the annual ritual of packing their bags for the trek south to the various training camps.

The White Sox arrived at Birmingham, Alabama, and owner Charles Comiskey admitted he had all but abandoned hope that George Davis would join the team at its camp in nearby Mobile. Lee Tannehill would move to shortstop and Nixey Callahan would both manage the team and play third base.

John McGraw stopped over in Washington on his way south, and he was asked about the rumor he was willing to trade Christy Mathewson to the Senators for Ed Delahanty. A look of shock came over the New York manager's face.

"What!" he said incredulously. "I would not give Mathewson for a team of Delahantys."

What he would do, said McGraw, was give Washington the pick of his pitchers, barring Mathewson, and an outfielder or catcher, plus six hundred dollars for the slugger. It was unlikely Delahanty would return to Washington anyway, claimed McGraw, who pointed out the player still would owe the Senators one hundred dollars at the end of the season.

"He would be a fool to play here at a loss when he could draw a New York salary doing nothing," said McGraw.

The next day, the Giants checked into their hotel in Savannah, Georgia, and there was a telegram waiting for McGraw. It was from George Davis, requesting permission to practice with the team at his own expense. McGraw immediately wired back his approval.

In New York, ground was being broken for construction of the new American League ballpark. Adding to the excitement of the event was a story making the rounds that Delahanty was about to be transferred to the New York Americans in exchange for outfielder Lefty Davis and cash.

That same day, National League president Harry Pulliam received a check for thirteen hundred dollars, to be turned over to the Cincinnati club as payment for the money it had advanced outfielder Sam Crawford, now with Detroit. The check was signed by Detroit president Sam Angus, who had made good the amount owed by his new player.

After delivering the money to Cincinnati's Garry Herrmann, Pulliam went to New York to confer with Ban Johnson. The two league presidents emerged from their meeting to announce that if Ed Delahanty and George Davis did not report to their clubs as assigned by the peace conference, they would be blacklisted from baseball.

"The American League has no intention of allowing any person, be he a player, manager, or a club owner, to violate the peace agreement in any way," proclaimed Johnson.

The American League president also stressed that the player himself must pay back the advance money to the Giants before he could suit up. No team would be allowed to make good the debt, as Detroit had done for Sam Crawford.

Elsewhere in New York, Hector Clemes, a stockholder in the Washington baseball club, showed some visitors around his well-furnished apartment in the Criterion Hotel. In one room, there was a newspaper photograph of Ed Delahanty pinned to the wall. One of the guests paused to ask about the status of the player.

"Yes, Delahanty will play in Washington or he will not play ball at all next season," said Clemes. "What I admire most about the American League is its determination to put down contract jumpers."

The visitor saw some marks on the clipping and he stepped forward for a closer inspection. It was then that he noticed someone had added to the picture a hand-written inscription. It called for the shooting of all contract jumpers before summer.

• • •

From Cleveland, the Delahanty brothers joined in the migration of ballplayers to their respective clubs. Tom left his job at a local saloon and headed to Denver, where he served as manager of the Western League team. Joe went the opposite direction, to Worcester, Massachusetts, of the Eastern League. So did Frank, only twenty years old as he departed for Syracuse of the New York State League. Jim, who had played briefly for the Giants in 1902, caught a train south to join Little Rock of the Southern League.

Only Big Ed stayed put, growing more restless each day at his winter quarters in New Orleans. He dispatched letters to his many friends among the newspaper writers and the ballplayers vowing never to return to Washington and proclaiming that if he could not play in New York he would play nowhere. Few people took such threats seriously, especially after Del sent word to Washington to ship his uniform and bats to him so he could practice with the clubs training in New Orleans.

He corresponded with John McGraw, and in reply he received assurances from the New York manager he would be paid by the Giants if he would refuse to play for his American League club.

Del claimed to have made money betting the horses that winter, but in March he confided to friends that the ponies had been "hitting him" rather hard the past week. On St.

Patrick's Day, he had another bad afternoon at the track, dropping $150 on the handicap. That evening, he ran into his old friend, Cleveland manager Bill Armour, and told him he planned to report to the Giants' camp in Savannah. Armour talked him out of taking such action, and after much discussion Delahanty indicated he might return to Washington. But first, insisted Del, the ball club would have to pay the Giants for the four thousand dollars advance money he had received.

That day and the next, telegrams arrived from manager Clark Griffith of the New York Americans, who was anxious to secure Delahanty's services for his team. Del responded by wiring Senators president Fred Postal requesting a meeting with manager Tom Loftus in Washington.

Del then sent his wife and child back to their home in Philadelphia and bought himself a train ticket to Washington, with a stopover in Atlanta to confer with Griffith. Delahanty departed New Orleans on Saturday evening, March 21, still hopeful his journey might take him to New York after all.

But there was trouble along the way. In Georgia, his train was brought to an unexpected stop outside Atlanta. Word came back that a wreck was blocking the railway lines ahead, and traffic would be held up indefinitely. Del stepped outside and looked helplessly down the tracks. There was nothing for him to do but sit and wait, his plans once more derailed.

• • •

Spring training meant different things to different managers. In Savannah, John McGraw's Giants put on their uniforms each morning and ran five miles from their hotel to the ballpark. At the end of the day, they ran back. In between, McGraw drove them relentlessly, not only teaching them new skills but instilling in them the hustle and spirit of the old Orioles. One day, he was running with his men when his bad knee buckled on him, convincing him his days as an effective ballplayer were over. But McGraw was a driven man. The next day, when the run to the practice field began, he was there to lead the way.

In Washington, the Senators reported to the practice field and tossed the ball around the wet grounds and entertained themselves by batting against an odd contraption that jokingly was referred to as the team's "dummy twirler." The device was a "pitching cannon" which shot baseballs toward the plate with varying degrees of speed and movement, and while everyone agreed it was "the invention of a genius," the players who batted off the machine were skeptical it was of much practical benefit. When not toying with this new gimmick, the Washington players tried as best they could to work out the stiffness in their joints by running in the damp and cold. Of the sixteen major-league teams, only the Senators were too cheap, or too poor, to travel to the South for training.

Tom Loftus, the manager of the Senators, laughed and joked with his players. He was forty-six years old, a good-natured, easygoing man who was considered one of the great "kidders" of the game. One of the many stories the players liked to tell about him was the time he was managing Cincinnati of the National League in 1891 and he called over outfielder Long John Reilly and second baseman Bid McPhee prior to the start of a game.

"You'll have the sun in your eyes this afternoon, John," Loftus told Reilly, "but I'll lend you a pair of smoked glasses. Then you might get a chest protector. Let the flies hit that and Bid will get them as they bounce back."

And in 1901, Loftus created a sensation as manager of the Chicago Nationals when he ended that club's longstanding practice of riding in open carriages and transported them to the ballpark in carryalls. "Some of the old-timers were staggered at first," joked Loftus, "but I put blinkers on them and backed them in."

Loftus's popularity with his players also stemmed from the free rein he gave them and the lack of discipline he imposed.

An illustration of his managerial style was provided the time he sat at the back of the grandstands reading a newspaper while his players practiced on the field below.

But Loftus could be stern when the occasion demanded. Once, team president Fred Postal came down out of the stands and was about to join the players on the bench during a game when Loftus stopped him short.

"You're all right in your place, Fred, but not here."

Postal obediently retreated to the stands. "I guess Tom was right," he said meekly.

• • •

Ed Delahanty finally arrived in Washington on Tuesday afternoon, March 24. A handful of reporters waited on the platform to greet the big slugger as he stepped off the train. He was noticeably overweight and his tone was subdued as he stopped to talk with them.

"I have two contracts for this season," said Del, "and the one I like the better seems hard to fulfill. The powers that be in the two leagues have decreed that I must report to the Washington club, and here I am."

The next day, Delahanty sat down with Tom Loftus for the first time since the end of the past season. The meeting was brief and resolved nothing. Del said he would play in Washington but he would not repay the advance money to New York. Loftus insisted the ball club would not make the payment for him.

To prove he meant business, the manager would not even let Delahanty play in the team's practice games. While Del passed his time at the local racetrack betting the horses, the Washington outfielders struggled to get in shape for the upcoming season.

Jimmy Ryan, who had broken in as a left-handed shortstop with Cap Anson's White Stockings eighteen years earlier, jogged about slowly in center field. He was forty years old and prone to charley horses. Kip Selbach, a stocky German who was a champion bowler in the off-season, discovered a knot in his shoulder when he tried to throw the ball. He feared the underhand delivery used in bowling had given him a dead arm. "I lay it all to bowling and would advise all ball players to quit the alleys if they want to preserve their arms," warned Selbach. Ducky Holmes, a thirty-four-year-old castoff signed by Loftus as a replacement for Delahanty, impressed no one his first few days in camp. The writers branded him a has-been and claimed he had a "glass arm."

A week passed, and the players began grumbling openly about the treatment of Delahanty.

"Loftus will make the mistake of his life if he lets the big fellow slip through his mitt," said third baseman Scranton Bill Coughlin. "Delahanty is the idol of a big majority of players and was very popular with the Washington men last season."

Boileryard Clarke, the Washington catcher, backed up that sentiment. "Del is popular with the players, and I am sure if he plays up to his old-time form the patrons of the game will soon forgive a man who desired to take advantage of an offer that insured him twenty-four thousand dollars for three years' work."

Loftus said little about the matter other than to reiterate that Delahanty "must straighten out the tangle in which he finds himself."

On Saturday, April 11, with the season only two weeks away, a contrite Delahanty finally showed up at his manager's room asking to talk.

"I'm ready to square up with New York," said Del.

Loftus waved him in, and the two aired their differences in a lengthy meeting. Delahanty said he believed he had been held out of the exhibition games because the manager did not want him on the team. Loftus assured Del that money was all that stood between them. The ballplayer said nothing for a few minutes, then admitted he was unable to repay the money owed even if he was willing to do so. After much wrangling, the two men finally worked out a solution. The Washington ball club would pay the four thousand dollars to the Giants, then get the money back from Delahanty by deducting half that amount from his salary in 1903 and half in 1904.

The two men shook hands on the deal and left the room smiling. Outside, they ran into a waiting newspaper reporter.

"I wish to say to the Washington public that Delahanty is not as bad as pictured," Loftus told the writer. "I know he took advantage of the war to get more money, but when I requested him to report he came on without a murmur."

The reporter asked Delahanty if he had anything to say to the Washington fans. Del thought for a moment before giving his answer.

"I will try to please my former friends here," he said, "and if any of them feel sore against me, I will attempt to make them forget all about it with that trusty bat of mine."

After six months of turmoil, the King of Batters was back, an aging ballplayer hoping for one last hurrah.

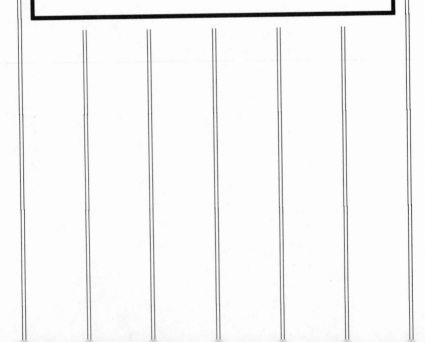

V
LAST
BATS

A bottle of ale or beer with the evening meal has a very soothing effect on the nerves. Baseball makes such demands on the nervous energies that most men really need something quieting after a hard-fought struggle.

JOHN MONTGOMERY WARD

Opening Day 1903 arrived and the players in both leagues donned their new uniforms, rode in special carriages to the ballparks, and marched onto the playing fields behind brass bands playing such favorites as "The Washington Post March" and "Columbia, the Gem of the Ocean." At Philadelphia, Ban Johnson presided over the ceremonies as the American League championship pennant was raised over the ballpark. In Cleveland, the fans voted to rename their team in honor of their great second baseman, Napoleon Lajoie. The newly named Naps arrived in Detroit and found the pitching mound shaved down to ground level so as to handicap their pitchers, the tallest in the league. In Boston, five-foot-eight-inch George Winter of the Puritans delivered the first pitch of the new season from atop a mound built up so high it resembled "the breastworks on a battlefield." In Chicago, the former ballplayer Billy Sunday was ordained as an evangelist of the Presbyterian Church on the same day his old team opened play against St. Louis. The Philadelphia Phillies started out under new ownership, with Colonel Rogers and Al Reach selling out to the local group headed by James Potter.

In Washington, two buses of enthusiastic rooters equipped with brass and vocal trumpets joined the parade of ballplayers riding down Pennsylvania Avenue behind Haley's band. At the ballpark, the band played marching songs, the players lined up on the field, and politicians made speeches. On one side of the diamond stood the Senators. On the other were the members of the New York team, the new American League franchise, making its inaugural appearance. Loud cheers greeted the home-team players as they were honored with presents, and Ed Delahanty stepped to home plate to be given a gigantic horseshoe made of roses. There were so many spectators they filled the grandstand and the bleachers, then spilled out onto the field, lined up so deep many of them could not even see the action.

The Senators wore new white uniforms with dark blue collars and cuffs and a stripe down each leg, and white caps with vertical blue stripes. A large "W" was emblazoned on the left chest of each jersey. Not even all the fancy trimmings could hide the extra weight carried by Delahanty, but he set himself right with the fans by belting two drives into the bleachers during practice.

Washington had no mayor to throw out the first ball of the season, so District Commissioner West, dubbed "Mayor West," stood in a special box behind the catcher and made the ceremonial delivery. Umpire Tommy Connolly took the ball and turned it over to Smiling Al Orth, whose nineteen victories the year before had earned him the honor of working the opener. His pitching opponent was New York's "Happy Jack" Chesbro, who had gained his nickname because of the sunny disposition he displayed while working in a mental institution in Middletown, New York, nine years earlier.

They were two of the game's shrewdest pitchers. Orth relied on control and cunning to fool the batters, throwing the ball so softly Ossee Schreckengost of the Athletics once reached across the plate and disdainfully caught a pitch bare-handed. "Can't you throw any harder than that?" Schreckengost taunted the pitcher. Chesbro was best known for his "wet ball." His reputation for slobbering all over the ball was such that when he was pitching for the Pirates, the Phillies once scooped up some horse manure from the road and smeared it on all the game balls. When Chesbro went to the pitching box and smelled the ball handed to him, the Philadelphia players laughed and called out, "You're not going to lick those balls, are you?" Chesbro yelled back, "Listen, I'll do it to win a game."

Through four innings, Orth and Chesbro battled on even terms. In the fifth, with the score tied, 1–1, the Senators got a man in scoring position, and Delahanty stepped to the plate swinging his long, heavy bat. Chesbro delivered another one of his wet pitches, and Del tore into it, sending a scorching shot into left field for a base hit. The run scored easily, giving Washington the lead, and Del was given another sustained ovation.

Orth made the run stand up, and four innings later Washington had a 3–1 victory. That afternoon, Del left the ballpark happy to be back in favor with the fans.

• • •

For John McGraw, the new season began with a new friend-ship. That spring, the aloof young pitcher Christy Mathewson showed up in Savannah, Georgia, with his new bride, Jane. They were a handsome couple. Mathewson, six feet two inches and two hundred pounds, had broad shoulders, blond hair, blue eyes, and a clean-shaven face. He was the All-American boy who neither smoked nor drank nor cursed. His wife was a pretty woman, with dark brown hair and gray eyes. While McGraw and Mathewson toiled at the ballpark each day during training camp, their wives spent their time together, inspecting the shops of the town and strolling through the parks where the spring azaleas were budding. The two women became friends, as did their husbands. When it came time to travel north for the season, the two couples decided to live together.

They moved into a furnished, ground-floor apartment only one block from Central Park. There were seven rooms, and the rent was fifty dollars a month. McGraw paid the rent and the gas bill, and Matty bought the food. It was the beginning of a lifelong friendship. McGraw, the tough little manager, was thirty years old at the time. Mathewson, his star pitcher, was twenty-two.

The rebuilt team was beginning to take shape under McGraw. Roger Bresnahan batted leadoff and played all three outfield positions as well as catcher, first base, and third base. Sam Mertes, who returned to the National League after two years with the Chicago Americans, and George Browne, a young outfielder who came over from Philadelphia, provided the power at the plate. Billy Gilbert, a shortstop in Baltimore, moved over to second base. Iron Man McGinnity and Christy Mathewson almost formed a two-man pitching staff.

There was a famous New York fire brigade known as the Big Six, which had a reputation for being the city's most dependable. One day, newspaperman Sam Crane filed his story on the Giants and noted, "Mathewson is certainly the 'Big Six' of the pitchers." That gave birth to one of baseball's most famous nicknames and added to the mystique that was beginning to surround the Giants.

The team practiced hard at all times, even in pregame workouts. Hobbled by his bad knee, McGraw stationed himself at first base for a workout prior to the third game of the season, against Brooklyn. He fielded a throw from second by Bresnahan and was getting ready to peg the ball home when he heard a shout of warning. He turned to the outfield and was hit flush in the face by a ball inadvertently thrown in his direction by Dummy Taylor.

The force of the throw knocked McGraw to the ground, and he lay there groaning in pain as blood poured from his nose and mouth. An ambulance was summoned to take him to the hospital, where the bleeding finally was stopped and tubes inserted into his nostrils.

The doctors patched him up, and McGraw returned to the ballpark that same day. Although in great discomfort, he watched the final innings of a 5–5 tie from the stands. McGraw's Giants were tough, but no one was tougher than Muggsy himself.

• • •

Ban Johnson traveled to Washington on Friday, April 24, to see his fledgling New York team, and he brought with him stage comedians DeWolf Hopper and Digby Dell.

Hopper was one of the most popular entertainers in the

country as well as one of the most rabid baseball fans. Fifteen years earlier, when Ed Delahanty was just breaking in with Philadelphia, Hopper was appearing in a show at Wallack's Theatre on Broadway. One day, he learned Cap Anson's White Stockings and the New York Giants would be in the audience as special guests of the management.

As a tribute to the ballplayers, the young comedian decided to recite a poem that recently had appeared in a San Francisco newspaper. Its title was "Casey at the Bat," by a little-known writer named Ernest Thayer. Hopper delivered his reading, and when the mighty Casey struck out, the ballplayers in the audience were on their feet shouting with enthusiasm. The poem became Hopper's most famous act, and soon "Casey" was being performed at theaters all over the country.

Hopper and Dell drew a lot of attention to themselves that day by pulling for New York, but their rooting was to no avail. Delahanty banged out three hits, and the Senators won the ball game, 7–1.

That same day, Secretary H. H. Farrell of the National Association of Baseball Leagues was handed a telegram from President Sexton of the Western League. He was stunned as he read the contents of the message.

"Delahanty, of Washington, accepted terms with Denver and wants to report there now. Shall I permit deal to go through or stop it? Answer quick."

Farrell immediately wired the Western League president ordering him to stop the transaction by whatever means necessary. "We should not embarrass the decision of the major leagues in this their most important case," he stated, "nor deprive the Washington club and the American League of one of its most valuable assets—Player Delahanty."

When word of the proposed deal leaked out, it prompted the predictable response. Delahanty was caught in the center of another controversy, accused of double-dealing less than one week into the season.

Del was furious, and he stormed around his hotel the next morning raging at the injustice. It was all a misunderstanding, he told anyone who would listen, and he had the evidence to prove it.

Del's proof was a telegram he had received just the night before from Mr. Packard of Denver, offering him a four-thousand-dollar salary to join his team. Although he had inquired about playing ball in the West a month earlier, Del since had resolved his problems with the Senators.

"When I made a settlement with Manager Loftus," he said, "I had no more idea of deserting the Washington club than I have of jumping off the Washington Monument."

Delahanty claimed to be hurt by the allegations, which once more had put a black mark on his reputation.

"It puts me in a bad light before the public just after I had fixed up things to play here and try to do good work."

At the ballpark Saturday afternoon, Del flailed angrily at the ball and made four outs in four trips to the plate. His only consolation came in the final inning of an 11–1 defeat. He charged in on a shallow fly by John Ganzel and just as the ball was about to fall in safely for a hit, Del stabbed out with his right hand and made a bare-handed catch. The bleachers fans gave him a loud cheer, and for the first time all day a smile crossed Del's face.

• • •

The season brought with it the usual optimism in Washington. There were two victories in four games against New York, followed by two more triumphs in three tries against Boston. To their astonishment, the Senators found themselves perched in second place in the standings. The final game with the Puritans ended, and the players packed their belongings in their hand-held grips, loaded their equipment into large trunks, and boarded the horse-drawn carryalls which transported them to the train station. They left town

April 29 and headed north to New York, the first stop on a monthlong road trip.

At New York, there were more bands, more parades, and more speeches awaiting them. This time, there was special cause for celebration. April 30, 1903, marked the arrival of the American League in New York, and the christening of the new Hilltop Park, also known as Highlander Park.

Ban Johnson himself led the parade to the flagpole, marching alongside team president Joseph Gordon while the band played "Yankee Doodle." Gordon was tall and lean, a stately looking man with white hair and a neatly trimmed white moustache. He was a coal merchant, and his name gave rise to his ball club's identity. The most famous regiment in the British Army at the time was the Gordon Highlanders. The New York ballpark was located in the Highlands area of Manhattan. Thus, the team became "Gordon's Highlanders."

In a box close to the Highlanders' bench sat two other prominent men. They were the real powers behind the ball club, with Gordon merely serving as the front man. One was Frank Farrell, a short and stocky man known as the "pool-room king of Manhattan." He was said to be the biggest illegal bookmaker in the city, operating hundreds of pool rooms and gambling halls through his syndicate. When Farrell first had approached Ban Johnson about buying the new American League franchise, he handed over a twenty-five-thousand-dollar check as a sign of good faith.

"If I don't put this ball club across, keep it," he told Johnson.

"That's a pretty big forfeit, Mr. Farrell," said Johnson.

Joe Vila, the sportswriter who had arranged the meeting, looked at the American League president and smiled. "He bets that much on a race, Ban."

Farrell served as vice president of the team, but he preferred to remain in the background. He always sought to keep his name out of newspapers, and he was so adept at doing so it was joked that he was "John Doe himself."

Next to Farrell sat his longtime ally, Captain William "Big Bill" Devery of the New York police. Their association dated back to the time Farrell ran a saloon at Sixth Avenue and Thirtieth Street and Devery was the captain of the precinct house half a block away. The two men became close friends, and coincidentally Farrell's establishment never had any trouble from the police.

Devery, a big man with a huge stomach, also liked to keep a low profile, but this was not easy for a person of his size and reputation. The New York press labeled him the most corrupt policeman in the city's history, and even the staid *New York Times* called him a "vulgar wretch" who was "unfitted for any useful vocation, trusted by no one with anything at risk, and lacking every moral and mental quality which would recommend him to public confidence."

Although he owned a substantial amount of stock in the team, Devery preferred to keep his holdings secret. A reporter approached him during the opening day ceremonies to ask about his investment, but Devery modestly dismissed any such notion.

"Me a backer?" he exclaimed with surprise. "I only wished I did own some stock in a baseball club. I'm a poor man and don't own stock in anything."

The very thought of such a preposterous idea seemed to amuse Devery. "What would I do with a ball team? Me pitch with a stomach like this? Not on your life."

On the field, the band played "Columbia, the Gem of the Ocean," and Farrell and Devery along with the other spectators present stood and sang. There were exactly 16,243 people in that crowd, a tabulation made possible by the automatic counting devices attached to the turnstiles.

The field itself was uneven and rocky, and a rope had been stretched across the outfield to mark the outer boundaries. No one present seemed to mind. Just six weeks earlier, the site had consisted of rocks, trees, and some swampland. When

Johnson had expressed his intention the year before of placing a team in New York, he had been warned he never would get the land he needed. Andrew Freedman of the Giants still had his Tammany Hall connections, and he was determined to block any move the American League made. "No matter where you go," Johnson was told, "the city will decide to run a streetcar over second base."

Freedman and his supporters had proceeded to conduct a block-by-block search of Manhattan in an effort to buy up any site large enough for a ballpark. They started at the Battery and worked northward, but when they got to the Highlands they gave up because they were certain the ground there was too rugged.

But Johnson and his backers outsmarted Freedman. They acquired a lot in the Highlands, and in a matter of weeks somehow managed to blow up and haul off thirty thousand square feet of rock and wood and replace it with soft soil from the excavation site of a subway tunnel. "We had to use so much dynamite that if unleashed at exactly the same second it would have blown up half of New York," said Johnson.

Meanwhile, Farrell and Devery used their own political clout to fend off every attempt by Freedman to sabotage the project.

Incredibly, the American Leaguers managed to pull it off. Work on the wooden grandstands did not even begin until five days before the first game was to be played, but when the ball club arrived in town for the first time everything appeared to be in place.

Jack Chesbro delivered the first pitch in the new ballpark, and Washington's Clyde "Rabbit" Robinson, a tiny shortstop, slammed a drive into right field. Wee Willie Keeler, wearing a pair of blue glasses to shield his eyes from the sun, turned and raced back in pursuit of the ball. Suddenly, he pulled up short. In front of him was a gully that still cut across the field, a reminder of the team's rocky beginnings. Keeler barely avoided falling into it.

That proved to be only a temporary setback for the Highlanders, who also were being referred to as the Hilltoppers, the Porch Climbers, or, in deference to their ownership, the Burglars. With Chesbro pitching masterfully and Keeler knocking out two hits, walking twice, and scoring three runs, the New Yorkers opened their ballpark in style with a 6–2 victory.

In the grandstand that day, George Davis sat and watched the game unrecognized by the spectators around him. Afterward, he made his way to the clubhouse, where he joked and swapped stories with the other players.

Suddenly, the door opened and in walked Tim Murnane, the popular baseball writer. Spotting the holdout ballplayer, Murnane went over to question him. "When do you expect to be playing ball again?" asked the writer.

Davis looked up from the crowd of players and smiled. "I guess I will have all the ballplaying I can attend to before the season is over."

• • •

It was a troubled time for Ed Delahanty. In New York, a writer spotted him wandering down the street, appearing to be drunk. The two were old friends, having known each other for thirteen years, and the man gently persuaded Del to return to his hotel. He watched as the ballplayer tamely made his way home.

Word came from Philadelphia that his wife, Norine, was ill, so Del went to visit her on a Sunday, when there was no game. He rejoined the team in Boston, where the *Boston Herald* taunted him with a cartoon that showed him wearing a pained expression as he stood in front of some shivering fans in the bleachers. One of the fans was yelling, "Say, Del, lend us some of that four thousand dollars to burn—it's cold up here!"

He had batted forty-four times and made only ten hits for

a weak .227 average. Still, the old slugger attracted attention everywhere he went. Men crowded around him in hotel lobbies and boys tagged along after him on the street, calling out his name.

He made his first appearance on a ballfield in Philadelphia in two years, and the Quaker City fans greeted him with loud cheers and whistles. Del responded by lining a double off the center-field fence, driving a single into the outfield, and dropping a fly ball. There were eight Washington errors that game, and the Senators lost, 19–5.

A day later, Rube Waddell, a big left-hander for the Athletics, stood on the mound with a crazy smile on his face. Two years earlier, Waddell had pitched for Tom Loftus with the Chicago National League team. When the Rube failed to show up for a pitching assignment one day, Loftus found him marching at the head of a circus parade as it passed by the ballpark. That was the last the manager saw of his pitcher until the circus left town. Waddell's friends called him Eddie. He had an overpowering fastball, pinpoint control, and the best drop ball in the league.

Waddell watched Delahanty walk to the plate, then he turned and waved his outfielders back until they were standing up against the fence. His first pitch streaked toward home, and Del hit the ball so hard it shot straight down the left-field line and slammed off the fence with enough force to bounce all the way back to the infield. Big Ed hustled around the bases and slid into third for a triple, and the fans applauded his effort. It was just like the good old days in Philadelphia.

Delahanty hit another long fly ball to score a run, and the Senators led, 3–0. Connie Mack's team came right back at them. Ollie Pickering got on first base and decided to steal second. Five times he broke for the bag, and five times the batter fouled off the pitch. Although growing weary from the wasted sprints, Pickering would not give up. On the sixth pitch, he made another dash to second, and this time he made it safely. Three runs in the Philadelphia fourth tied the score, and two more the next inning put the Mackmen ahead to stay.

The mood of the Washington players turned ugly. They had lost six times in seven tries on the road trip and now resided in last place in the standings. The newspapers accused them of "stupid playing."

Base runners got picked off base and ran so slowly they were accused of having "lead in their shoes." The substitute players neglected to go on the base lines and serve as coaches. The players performed listlessly and never argued with opponents or umpires. "I have a very ladylike team," complained Loftus. The pitching was terrible, and injuries began to take their toll. Shortstop Charlie Moran had to be sent home with a bad leg. Infielder Gene DeMontreville pulled a charley horse and could not play. Shortstop Rabbit Robinson wrenched an ankle. "Silent Joe" Martin, a rookie who had nothing to say unless spoken to first, was pressed into duty at second base. Al Orth filled in at shortstop, and his pitching suffered as a result of the double duty.

Loftus became angry and held his men up to ridicule. He jokingly proposed a footrace featuring Delahanty and the other plodders on the team—catcher Boileryard Clarke and first baseman Scoops Carey. Someone added that if such a contest were staged the disabled players should also be included. "It would be interesting to see which one could finish first in that bunch of base-runners," the *Washington Post* noted sarcastically.

On Saturday, Case Patten gave up nineteen hits, and the Senators again were beaten by the Athletics, 13–11. A fly ball fell between Jimmy Ryan in center field and Kip Selbach in right, and the two players shouted at each other, arguing over who should have made the play. Ryan complained to Loftus he had no faith in Selbach in right field. In turn, Selbach said he was uncomfortable in the position and wanted to play left field, where Delahanty resided. Ducky Holmes, who had joined the team in anticipation of replacing Delahanty, was angry over his role as a reserve.

From Philadelphia, the ball club embarked on the long train ride west. In St. Louis, Del slugged five hits in fifteen at-bats but the extra weight he was carrying plus a sore leg he favored caused him to hurt his back. He sat on the bench and brooded in Chicago, where the losing continued. The *Washington Star* claimed he looked like a "fat man escaped from a circus."

In Cleveland, the Senators faced a skinny right-hander named Clarence Wright who threw the ball so hard he knocked off catcher Harry Bemis's mitt five times. The Senators managed only three hits, and in desperation Loftus sent Delahanty to the plate as a pinch hitter. Standing at the plate stiffly, the best Del could do was an easy groundout.

That was the last straw for Loftus. Shortly after the 9–1 defeat, he gave Delahanty a train ticket and sent him to the hot baths at Mount Clemens, Michigan, to get himself in playing shape. A few days later, DeMontreville joined Del at the Michigan spa.

For a week, the two ballplayers sat in the steam baths, soaking their sore muscles, with Del shedding his excess pounds as well. They rejoined the team at the end of May in Boston, the last leg of the long journey.

Delahanty met with Loftus in the manager's hotel room. Ed still was not in his old playing shape, but he appeared trimmer and he moved about better. Loftus, on the other hand, had aged greatly on the road trip. The Senators had won only six of twenty-three games, and the manager had become as tired and discouraged as his ballplayers. He greeted Del coolly and informed him he would be playing right field. Kip Selbach's frequent requests to be moved to left field had been granted, and Loftus planned to keep the stocky German there. Delahanty angrily replied he would not make the switch. He never had played right field during his sixteen-year career and he did not propose to begin doing so now. There were harsh words between the two men, and soon they were shouting at each other.

Finally, Del stormed out of the room, vowing he never would play right field. As he left, he heard Loftus yelling out the door after him, telling him he either would change positions or quit the team.

Later that afternoon, Secretary Hewitt arrived at Delahanty's room to confiscate his uniform and inform him the ball club would not purchase his transportation back to Washington. Once again, Del backed down.

The next day, Friday, May 29, Puritans pitcher Big Bill Dinneen stood atop the raised pitching mound in Boston and mowed down the seemingly inept Washington batters. Only one man gave Dinneen trouble in the 7–2 Boston victory. On his first time at bat in two weeks, Ed Delahanty lined out a clean single. In the sixth inning, he hit a towering home run, his first of the season. But not even the two hits plus a base on balls gave Del much satisfaction. Between at-bats, he sullenly stationed himself in right field, where he only half-heartedly chased down any balls hit his way.

• • •

There were many surprises in baseball that spring. In Chicago, owner Charlie Comiskey watched with satisfaction as his White Sox raced to the front of the American League with twelve victories in their first eighteen games. One day, his team won a one-run ball game and Comiskey rewarded the players by buying each of them a fifty-dollar suit.

Comiskey was forty-three years old, a statuesque man with a prominent nose and a stately head of hair which he combed straight back. Chicago writer Hugh E. Keough dubbed him "the Old Roman." Others called him baseball's odd genius. "Odd in his ways, in his speech and in his actions," wrote the *Washington Post*. "But his judgment has proved unerring."

The White Sox owner also was a troubled man, fearful that

he was the victim of a strange curse placed on him when he was a player years earlier. One day a ball he threw accidentally struck an old woman who was picking rags from a dump on the other end of the lot. Comiskey tried to apologize, but the woman was too angry to listen. Instead, she pointed a bony finger at him and in a raspy voice uttered the words, "May you live to see all your kith and kin die!" Comiskey did not believe in such spells, so he dismissed the incident. But in 1902, two of his younger brothers and his father all died within the space of a year. That November, another brother, Edward, was seriously injured in an accident.

To add to his personal tragedies, Comiskey lost the services of his manager, Clark Griffith, who went to the New York Americans, and his best player, George Davis, who refused to rejoin the White Sox after being ordered to do so by the peace treaty.

The old woman's threat began to haunt him. Was he really cursed? he wondered. Then the season began, and Comiskey's luck appeared to change. His weakened ball club played like a winner and moved to the top of the standings under the direction of Nixey Callahan, who not only managed the team but also pitched and played third base and the outfield.

And one day in mid-May, Comiskey received a telegram from Davis asking for money and a railway ticket in order to report to Chicago. The Old Roman was ecstatic. He made all the necessary arrangements and was about to dispatch the money to the holdout ballplayer when another telegram was delivered to his office. Once again, it was from Davis. Only this time, he was writing to state he had changed his mind and would not be joining the White Sox after all.

• • •

In New York, John T. Brush spent his lunch hours exercising his gaunt frame on a rowing machine in the corner of his office at the St. James Building. In the same building, Harry

Pulliam fired off a sternly worded letter to Giants outfielder Roger Bresnahan, warning him that his repeated ejections for his outbursts against the umpires would not be tolerated. The next such offense, stated Pulliam, would result in a suspension of thirty days.

George Davis passed the days working out with the Giants or hanging out at the racetrack, playing the ponies. He reached an agreement with Brush allowing him to keep his twenty-seven hundred dollars advance money and be paid half his salary to remain out of the game until he was cleared to play for the Giants. He had become baseball's man without a country. A writer for the *Washington Post* observed his dilemma and wrote, "George Davis wanders sadly about the New York grounds every day like a soul lost in the suburbs of Paradise."

The New York ball club could afford the luxury of paying the ballplayer not to play. The New York papers trumpeted the exploits of John McGraw's Giants with full-page pictures and glowing accounts of their victories. While the Giants were battling for the National League lead, Clark Griffith's Highlanders fell into the second division of the American League and were chastised by the press for their disappointing showing after a big buildup.

Brush would arrive at the Polo Grounds, and youngsters would crowd around his carriage cheering him and asking for passes. The Giants owner always sat in box 66, opposite first base, and not behind home plate because he did not want to be bothered by the net.

The defending champion Pirates came to town for a showdown with the Giants, and 31,500 fans paid their way into the Polo Grounds while another 5,000 gathered on the bluffs overlooking the field to watch the New York victory. It was baseball's biggest crowd since back in the 1880s at the old Polo Grounds.

In left field, where the fifty-cent seats and the bleachers joined, there was a flag marking the spot where Buck Ewing hit a legendary drive out of the park in 1890. In right field, another flag flew where "Silent Mike" Tiernan drove the ball over the fence and onto an adjoining lot. The markers were reminiscent of the old Giants, a team of sluggers. The new Giants of McGraw were a team of battlers.

The belligerent attitude of the ball club began at the top. Brush was the only National League owner who refused to allow free admission to league president Harry Pulliam and his guests. And when the Giants made their first trip of the season to Chicago, Brush bought a seat in the bleachers rather than sit with Cubs president James Hart.

On the field, McGraw fought for any advantage he could get. One of his targets was Pittsburgh's Honus "Hans" Wagner, the most feared batter in the league. Nicknamed "the Flying Dutchman," Wagner was a big, gangly-looking German with powerful arms and huge, meaty hands. Not only was he a strong hitter and a fast runner, he was an amazingly versatile performer. Wagner could play any position on the diamond, and he had such a powerful throwing arm that he once caught a one-hopper in left field and fired the ball to first base in time to beat the runner by ten feet.

But Wagner was a quiet, sensitive man who almost had been run out of the league before his career had begun. When he broke in with Louisville in 1897, the veterans on the club refused to let him take batting practice. His fifth day on the team, Wagner again was pushed aside by an older player, and the big rookie quietly walked back to the bench without putting up any resistance.

"Why didn't you take your cuts?" demanded manager Fred Clarke.

"They won't let me," answered Wagner.

Clarke, a scrappy man with a fierce moustache, spat out his reply. "Get back in that box or get off this ball club!"

Wagner obediently marched back to the plate, where the batter shot a stream of tobacco juice at his feet and asked what he thought he was doing. The rookie calmly cocked his bat and aimed it at the man's head.

"I'm going to hit at somethin' and I don't much give a damn what it is," said Wagner.

The startled player barely was able to duck in time to get out of the way. No one on the team ever challenged the Dutchman again.

But early in the 1903 season, McGraw singled out the Pirates star for a test of his own. He ordered his players to goad Wagner into a fight, which would result in his ejection and deprive Pittsburgh of its best player.

The Giants eagerly accepted the challenge, insulting the Dutchman with vile curses and ridiculing his looks and his family. Wagner refused to take the bait, quietly waiting to respond in his own manner.

He got his chance when pitcher Iron Man McGinnity had to cover first base on a ground ball. Wagner was approaching the bag at full speed when he appeared to trip, and in an apparent effort to break his fall he reached out and grabbed hold of McGinnity with his left arm. The next thing the pitcher knew he was being pulled to the ground, a powerful arm wrapped around him and crushing him against a rugged body. The two men landed hard, with Wagner falling on top of McGinnity and pinning him to the ground. As they lay there, Wagner discreetly brought up his right hand out of sight of the umpire and squeezed his fingers hard against his tormentor. The New York pitcher writhed in pain, trapped helplessly as the Dutchman looked down at him and grinned.

"Take it back," hissed Wagner.

McGinnity had no choice. He took it back.

• • •

Out west, Tigers manager Ed Barrow showed up at the St. Louis ballpark one morning on Memorial Day weekend and found his shortstop, Norman "Kid" Elberfeld, practicing with the Browns. Barrow was a thickset, muscular man who once floored former English heavyweight boxing champion Sandy Ferguson during a brawl in Boston. He marched onto the field and confronted St. Louis manager Jimmy McAleer, accusing him of tampering with his player, then turned his wrath on Elberfeld. The boyish-looking Elberfeld glared at his manager defiantly. Only five feet seven inches tall and 134 pounds, the "Tabasco Kid" backed down from no one.

Elberfeld was a mountain man from Tennessee. He was hot tempered, belligerent, and as rough as any player in the game. When his legs were slashed by a runner's spikes, he would pour whisky into the open wounds to keep out the infection and continue playing. Once, a runner he tagged out at second base was called safe and he angrily hurled the ball so far up the wire netting in front of the grandstand that two men were able to score. His rookie year with the Phillies in 1898, he smashed dishes to the floor to get the attention of waiters if the service in restaurants was too slow to suit him. The Philadelphia and Cincinnati ball clubs gave up on him as an incorrigible, but Phillies manager George Stallings liked the Kid's nerve. When Stallings went to Detroit as manager of the American League team in 1901, he signed Elberfeld and made him his shortstop.

There was little Elberfeld could not do on a ballfield. He was a skilled hitter, a speedy base runner, and a flashy fielder. He was a natural left-hander, but when he broke his left arm as a youngster he taught himself how to throw with his right hand. He put his ambidexterity to good use, occasionally roaming far behind second base and shedding his glove to make a left-handed pickup and throw all in one motion.

But from the time Barrow took over as manager of Detroit in the spring of 1903, he clashed with his shortstop. Elberfeld had been led to believe he would be named captain of the ball club. Instead, Barrow gave the position to second baseman Heinie Smith. Elberfeld demanded to be traded and began the season in a sulk. He ranked among the league leaders in batting with an average around .400, but he also made costly errors at critical times and displayed an ugly disposition. Barrow criticized the player for his careless habits and his recalcitrant attitude. In turn, Elberfeld talked to John McGraw of the Giants and then McAleer of the Browns about joining their ball clubs.

The Tigers arrived home from St. Louis on June 1, a Monday. The Browns came with them, the two teams forced to keep each other's company for eight uneasy days thanks to a schedule maker who put them in Detroit for four games, St. Louis for one more plus a postponement, and back to Detroit for yet two more games.

That afternoon, a sidearm offering from Jack Powell of the Browns sailed inside on Elberfeld, and the Kid fell to the ground in an exaggerated motion, howling that he had been struck by the pitch. Umpire James Hassett disagreed and ordered him to resume his position at the plate. The Kid's face turned red with anger. He tossed his bat aside in disgust, walked slowly back to the bench, and took a long drink of water before casually returning to the plate.

In the ninth inning, Elberfeld kicked at the ground around his shortstop position and waited for the game to end. Mike Kahoe took his lead off first base, where he had arrived thanks to Sam Crawford's muff of his fly ball. There was one out, and the Tigers led, 6–4. Pitcher Wild Bill Donovan fired the ball toward the plate, and Bill Friel poked a soft liner toward shortstop. Kahoe already was sprinting for second, and all Elberfeld had to do was catch the ball and toss it to first base for a game-ending double play. Instead, the ball hit off his mitt and fell to the ground. Elberfeld reached down for the ball but somehow overran it. Kahoe slid safely into second and Friel made it to first. Ed Barrow stood next to the Detroit bench fuming over his shortstop's play.

Bobby Wallace followed with a base hit to load the bases

and "Honest John" Anderson, a big Norwegian, sent another hit into the outfield to score two runs and tie the game. A fly ball by Barry McCormick allowed Wallace to dash home with the third run of the inning. St. Louis won the ball game, 7–6.

When Elberfeld reached the clubhouse, Barrow was waiting for him. In three of the six games against the Browns, Elberfeld had made a muff, fumble, or wild throw at a critical point. Barrow accused him of "throwing down" the team. Elberfeld just laughed at his manager. He boasted he had been negotiating with the Browns as well as another team about buying out his contract. He brazenly offered to pay the Detroit ball club a thousand dollars for his release, proclaiming that another team would reimburse him that amount. Barrow refused. The only way Elberfeld could stay in baseball, roared his manager, would be to allow himself to be traded elsewhere. The Kid said he would play only for the Browns or Giants or he would play for no one.

The next day, the Detroit ball club dispatched a statement announcing that shortstop Norman Elberfeld was given an indefinite suspension and a two-hundred-dollar fine for "laxity of training habits and the deliberate throwing of three games during the St. Louis series."

Elberfeld returned to his quarters in Detroit, where he began packing his belongings and making arrangements for his family to return to his home on Lookout Mountain in Tennessee. There he owned some cattle, which ranged freely on the mountain, their ownership identified only by the brands they bore. Once, another mountaineer had accused Elberfeld of stealing one of his calves, which had a brand that was faded and indistinguishable. The dispute ended up in court, and the other man was awarded the calf. But Elberfeld got the last laugh. A few weeks later, the calf fell ill and died. Many of the residents of the mountain suspected it had been poisoned. But no one openly accused Elberfeld. He was not a man to be crossed.

• • •

That same Memorial Day weekend, Athletics pitcher Rube Waddell entertained himself by attending the Eagles' carnival in Philadelphia. There were trapeze artists, high-wire performers, clowns, dancing dogs, great white stallions, and wild animals of all sorts. There also happened to be a brave barber, who offered a free shave to any man daring enough to crawl in the lion's cage with him to have his face manicured among the king of beasts.

The Rube could not believe his luck. The next day, a Saturday, he was to pitch against a New York right-hander by the name of Barney Wolfe. What better way to prepare to subdue a Wolfe, thought Waddell, than to face a lion.

The crowd cheered as the famous pitcher came down out of the stands, pushed his way through the bars, and sat in a chair in the middle of the cage. The barber stood next to him with his razor, and the lion tamer cracked his whip to keep the beasts at bay.

Waddell leaned back in the chair and made himself comfortable, even propping his heels on the footrest. The barber proceeded to administer the shave, and to add to the excitement a lion occasionally leaped over his feet.

But this was not enough to satisfy Rube. Pretending to be annoyed at the lions' antics, he pulled out a toy pistol and fired blanks at the animals. The spectators roared their approval. Waddell acknowledged the cheers and then walked over to stroke the head of one of the beasts. It was a stunt even the lion tamer himself did not dare to perform, but he was too afraid to protest. When the Rube finally left the cage, he did so to thunderous applause.

Properly warmed up, he went out the next day and tamed Wolfe and the New Yorkers.

At noon on Monday, June 1, the train carrying the Athletics pulled into the Washington station. Only two hours remained before he was to pitch against the Senators, but Waddell was in no hurry to get to the ballpark. First, he wanted to see the famous Washington Monument. With him was his constant companion, Charley Dryden, the Philadelphia sportswriter who had been appointed his "keeper" by Connie Mack. It was Dryden's job to keep the Rube out of trouble and on hand for his pitching assignments.

The two men arrived at the monument and stared up in amazement. It was 555 feet, ⅝ inches high and had 898 steps leading to the top.

"Charley, I want to see if it's real," said the Rube.

Waddell walked up and touched the structure. A security man nearby watched him suspiciously. The Rube ran his hand over the smooth surface, then put his mouth on it and tried to take a bite. That was all it took to bring the guard running. There was an automatic twenty-dollar fine for such actions, he informed Waddell. Only Dryden's persuasiveness and good humor got the Rube off the hook.

"He has rubber teeth," Dryden explained to the officer.

Shortly afterward, Waddell strolled onto the field at the Washington ballpark and beat the Senators, 1–0, on a two-hitter, laughing and smiling all the while.

• • •

There were forest fires in New England that June, and the smoke drifted southward all the way to Washington. There it hung over the city in a great pall. A funeral procession passed the Washington ballpark, and the horse-drawn hearse pulled up near the fence next to the scoreboard. The undertaker got out wearing a large silk hat and paused to look out across the playing field at the game in progress. In the press area, a writer watched him and noted wryly that upon seeing the Senators the undertaker could not decide which one to load first.

A fly ball drifted out to right field, and Ed Delahanty looked up into the blue haze and hesitated just long enough for the ball to fall safely for a base hit. Two more drives were hit in his direction that inning, and he loafed on both of them and they too went for hits. The visiting St. Louis Browns scored six runs in that one inning, and the Senators were beaten, 9–1. It was Washington's eighth loss in a row. Sitting in the clubhouse afterward, Del did not seem to care. He fingered the new yellow bat which had been given him by Socks Seybold of the Athletics. Del had used the club to hit two doubles that day, giving him eight hits in twenty-six at-bats since rejoining the team. The newspapers made mention of the fact that his batting average finally was above the .300 mark. Behind his back, the other players talked less about Big Ed's hitting than his fielding. They still laughed about the play where he caught a fly and was so slow getting rid of the ball a runner scored all the way from second base.

The next day, Del made two more hits. He was beginning to hit like the Delahanty of old, but the Senators lost again.

On June 6, Tom Loftus sat on the bench in a rumpled suit and frowned as he waited for play to begin. As his team continued to lose, there was increasing discontent among the Washington players and fans. Most of their unhappiness was directed at the manager. The players grumbled openly about his leadership, and the fans shouted down at him from the stands, questioning his judgment.

Loftus was an old-time baseball man. A quarter of a century earlier, in 1878, he had managed and played second base for the Peoria Reds, a famous ball club that featured the great underhand pitcher Old Hoss Radbourn as well as future major-league stars Bill and Jack Gleason and Jack Rowe. Loftus was only twenty-one years old at the time. The next year, he was captain of a Dubuque team that included a rising young star named Charlie Comiskey.

Loftus appeared in only nine games as a player in the National League and American Association, but he became a respected manager. He guided clubs in the old Union Association and the American Association and also served stints at the head of the Cleveland, Cincinnati, and Chicago National League clubs before arriving in Washington. Along the way, he earned a reputation as an expert on the rules and an astute businessman. In the winters, he ran a saloon and operated a hotel in his hometown of Dubuque, Iowa. The writers called him "the Sage of Dubuque." His first year in Washington, in 1902, the Senators turned a profit. Fred Postal, the president of the team, was so pleased he rewarded Loftus a 25 percent share of the ball club.

Hector Clemes, the Senators stockholder from New York, sat next to Loftus on the Washington bench for the final game of the series with the Browns. On the field, Watty Lee, a young left-hander, fired his final warmup pitch to the catcher, and umpire Jack Sheridan called for play to begin. Jesse Burkett, the cocky little St. Louis outfielder, made his way to the plate carrying an oversized, barrel-shaped bat.

Burkett was a product of the old Cleveland Spiders, a loud, abusive player who would show up at the park early and smuggle boys under the gate to pitch to him so he could practice his hitting. He had won three batting titles but he was best known for his hot temper and his frequent fights. Once, he was thrown out of both games of a doubleheader in Louisville, escorted off the field through a police cordon, and fined two hundred dollars for inciting a riot. In St. Louis, the rooting section in right field was dubbed "Burkettville" in his honor. The other ballplayers called him "the Crab" for his sour disposition. He had a loud, needling voice, and he specialized in taunting opponents and enemy fans.

Burkett was about to take his position at bat when he spotted Loftus talking to his fellow stockholder sitting next to him. That was too inviting a target for Butkett to pass up. He stepped back and turned toward the stands as if he had an important announcement to make.

"It's all a great bluff Loftus is making about being Postal's partner!" Burkett called out in a voice loud enough to be heard all over the ballpark. "He wouldn't be smiling on that bench if he had stock in the club! His money's all right, win or lose!"

Loftus sat there too stunned to respond, his face turning red as he heard the fans laughing and jeering in response to the taunt.

A moment later, Burkett lined a shot into the outfield for a hit. Reaching first base, he called out derisively, "Cherries are ripe!"

The Senators got the best of it that day, winning 10–0 as Lee tossed a five-hitter and Delahanty banged out two more doubles and a single. But afterward, Loftus was in no mood to celebrate the end of his team's nine-game losing streak. He confronted St. Louis manager Jimmy McAleer and angrily complained about Burkett's insulting remarks. Loftus was an owner as well as manager, he informed McAleer, and he would not tolerate such disrespect from a ballplayer. McAleer just laughed at him.

• • •

When he arrived in Washington the first Sunday in June, Larry Lajoie brought with him a small boy. They marched up to the front desk at the Ebbit House, and the men and women in the crowded lobby turned and stared at the famous ballplayer and his traveling companion. Lajoie carried a black grip. The boy had a large suitcase. On its side was painted, "Petie Power, Mascot." He was an orphan, and Lajoie had taken him under his wing. The boy was made the mascot of the Cleveland team and once school was out he even was allowed to travel with the players. He idolized Lajoie, as did most Clevelanders.

On Monday, June 7, the Frenchman stood on the sideline of the Washington ballpark next to his one-time roommate, Ed Delahanty. The Cleveland ballplayer had endured his own hardships during recent months. That winter, he had fallen ill with what at first was diagnosed as pneumonia. Later, Lajoie learned he actually was suffering from pleurisy, a painful inflammation of the membrane lining the lungs. It was feared he would not be able to play at all that season, but on opening day the Frenchman had recovered sufficiently to see action. Like Delahanty, he struggled with his batting in the early weeks of the season, hitting a weak .200 into May, and he also spent time at the many hot baths in Mount Clemens. But slowly, Lajoie began to regain his strength and with it his batting prowess. In Washington, he visited with Delahanty and laughed about reports of his demise.

"The newspapers have had me quite ill for a long time now," said Lajoie, "but as you see, I am looking pretty good for an invalid. I felt the effect of my illness for a long while afterward, but I am well and strong now and playing just as good baseball as I ever did."

The Cleveland ballplayers wore blue uniforms with white trimmings. It was said the team was the prettiest in the league. It certainly was the biggest, with huge, strapping six-footers such as Lajoie, Clarence Wright, Earl Moore, Piano Legs Hickman, Bill Bradley, Ed Walker, and Addie Joss.

There also was a tiny outfielder, Harry Bay, who was barely bigger than Petie Powers but so fleet he was known as "Deerfoot." He was the first man up for the Naps, and he caught hold of one of Smiling Al Orth's slowballs and sent it on a line over first base. The ball carried deep into right field, where it landed by the clothesline that was hung out near the clubhouse. Delahanty plodded over from his position, chased down the ball, and finally pegged it back to the infield. While he did, "Deerfoot" Harry Bay fled all the way around the bases for a home run.

The Naps won that day, 6–2. They won again the next day, 8–6, and matched that score the following afternoon. In the three games, Del made seven hits and Lajoie six. Afterward,

the Cleveland ballplayers loudly packed their bags and prepared to depart town. It was June 10, a date Larry Lajoie
would not forget. His teammates were headed to Philadelphia
for their next game. He and Strawberry Bill Bernhard were
scheduled to take a separate train to Boston, still forced to
avoid Philadelphia because they remained in contempt of the
Pennsylvania court. And then a telegram arrived from
Philadelphia, informing the two players that Judges Ralston
and Davis had cleared the contempt charges. Judge Ralston
still believed the ballplayers deserved to be punished, but
since the baseball leagues had proclaimed peace he said he
was willing to drop the matter.

The next day, a weekday crowd of more than seven thousand turned out in Philadelphia to cheer Lajoie as he doubled
and fielded flawlessly in a 3–2 Naps victory. King Napoleon
left the field a happy man. For him, the long and troublesome
legal ordeal was over.

• • •

June 10 also marked a turning point for Clark Griffith of the
New York Highlanders. The Old Fox spent the day in Detroit,
apart from his ball club on an urgent mission.

It had been imperative that the American League field a
strong team its first year in New York, but so far Ban Johnson's
invaders had failed miserably. While McGraw's surprising
Giants were battling for the National League lead, Griffith's
high-priced Highlanders were languishing in seventh place in
the American League. Highlanders president Joseph Gordon
responded by issuing Griffith an ultimatum: He had one last
chance to place the team on "the road to victory." If he failed
he would be replaced as manager. In desperation, Griffith
began casting about for a ballplayer who would not only
strengthen his team but also help him steal some headlines
from McGraw.

Griff's first choice was Ed Delahanty. Despite all his problems, Del still was a potent hitter and one of the top attractions in the game. Because of Delahanty, the lowly Senators had outdrawn all the other Eastern teams on their recent road trip to the West.

Griffith had tried without success to get the slugger during his contract dispute with the Washington ball club, and in early June, he made another bid to bring Delahanty to New York. Griff contacted Washington manager Tom Loftus, whose unhappiness with Delahanty was well known, and expressed his interest in a trade. The two sides began working out a deal, with the principals involved being Delahanty and first baseman Scoops Carey of the Senators and second baseman Jimmy Williams and first baseman John Ganzel of the Highlanders.

At one point, Loftus was ready to agree to a trade, and word of the proposed deal leaked into the press. When Delahanty found out about it, his spirits soared. As it turned out, he perked up too much for his own good. He went on a batting tear, knocking out eleven hits in twenty at-bats against St. Louis and Cleveland, and Loftus backed off on the trade. Griff tried to keep the deal alive by offering Ganzel, a slick fielder but mediocre hitter, straight up for Delahanty. Loftus wired his reply: "You are crazy."

But Griffith had other options to pursue. While his ball club was at home to play Cleveland, he traveled to Philadelphia to talk to Detroit's Ed Barrow about suspended shortstop Kid Elberfeld. Barrow wasted no time informing the New York manager he already had received several attractive offers for Elberfeld.

Garry Herrmann of Cincinnati was willing to pay four thousand dollars for the shortstop. Charlie Comiskey of the White Stockings was offering to swap George Davis in an exchange of holdout shortstops. The Boston Americans were willing to trade their shortstop, Freddy Parent, in a one-for-one deal.

Griffith put in his bid by offering Ernie Courtney, a utility infielder, and a couple of bench-warmers. Barrow laughed at the proposal. He had his own offer to make. In exchange for Elberfeld, he wanted third baseman Wid Conroy and outfielder Davey Fultz, both proven hitters. Detroit newsman B. F. Wright jokingly reported that upon hearing this proposal, Griffith fainted.

Actually, Griff's reaction was to leave for Detroit to deal directly with Tigers president Sam Angus, a Detroit insurance man and railroad contractor. A loyal American Leaguer, Angus proved to be much more receptive to Griffith's plight. In an effort to help strengthen the New York team, he agreed to accept veteran shortstop Herman Long, thirty-four years old, and Courtney in exchange for Elberfeld.

Griffith barely could contain his excitement as he left Angus's office. For a very small price, he had just acquired the drawing card his team so desperately needed.

• • •

Kid Elberfeld put on a New York Highlanders uniform for the first time Saturday, June 13, three days after the trade. There were puddles of water around Highlander Park, and the grass still was damp and soggy from the steady rains which had fallen all morning. On the visitors' bench across the way were Elberfeld's former Detroit teammates. The Kid spotted Ed Barrow and waved contemptuously at him.

There could not have been a better setting for Elberfeld's debut with his new team. Just one day earlier, he had agreed to terms with the Highlanders. By chance, the Tigers happened to arrive in town at the same time he did. The weather held down the size of the crowd, but the twenty-one hundred fans who did show up were loud and boisterous. The first time Elberfeld stepped to the plate, loud cheers drowned out the few scattered catcalls and jeers. The Kid failed to get a hit, but later he laid down a sacrifice bunt and cleanly fielded both balls hit his way.

The two teams battled into the bottom of the ninth inning tied 2–2 when New York's Jack Chesbro worked his pitching opponent, Jack Deering, for a base on balls. Lefty Davis sacrificed Chesbro to second, bringing up Wee Willie Keeler with only one out. First base was open, and the Tigers had to decide whether to walk the hard-hitting Keeler rather than give him a chance to win the game. Elberfeld, the next man up, was praying they would. He wanted a chance to deliver the winning hit against his old team. Instead, Barrow elected to pitch to Keeler. The Detroit manager was more afraid of Elberfeld than a two-time batting champion.

Keeler ripped a long drive into the outfield, and when the ball fell safely and began rolling toward the fence Chesbro took off running. He arrived at home plate with the run that gave the Highlanders a 3–2 victory, and there waiting to greet him was his new teammate, Elberfeld.

The New York rooters tossed their derbies high in the air in celebration, and Clark Griffith raced onto the field clapping his hands. Suddenly, things were looking up for the Highlanders. They had won three games in a row, and there was talk of overtaking first-place Boston, just 7½ games ahead of them.

• • •

On laundry day in Washington, outfielder Ducky Holmes drew washer duty. He sat on a stool in the clubhouse, surrounded by the piles of sweaty and soiled uniforms. In front of him was a large tub, a washer board, and a wringer. There were many extra chores a ballplayer was required to perform to earn his keep. Laundry duty was the worst.

Holmes was a short, stocky man whose nickname came from his usual walk. He had been a conductor on a railroad before becoming a ballplayer, and since breaking in with the old Louisville club of the National League in 1895 he had remained on the go. In eight years, he had played for six different teams. Ducky was a dependable hitter and a fast runner, but he was best known for a controversial and highly publicized run-in he had with Giants owner Andrew Freedman.

It happened in 1898, the year after Holmes was turned loose by the Giants. Ducky was playing for Baltimore after starting the season with St. Louis, and in a game at the Polo Grounds he struck out with the bases loaded. Walking back to the bench, he was taunted by the New York rooters.

"Hey, Ducky!" one of them yelled. "You're a lobster! That's why you don't play for New York anymore!"

Holmes yelled back his reply loud enough for everyone to hear. "But I'm glad I don't have to work for no Sheeny no more!"

Freedman, who was Jewish, was enraged by the remark. He jumped out of his box seat and tried to get onto the field to have the ballplayer arrested. Instead, he found his path blocked by several Orioles armed with bats. Freedman ordered umpire Tom Lynch to remove Holmes from the game, and when Lynch refused to do so the Giants owner demanded an apology from the player. Holmes responded by spitting at him. During the showdown, fans began streaming onto the field in anticipation of a fight. Lynch tried to get Freedman to return to his seat and order the field cleared, but when the owner stood his ground the umpire had no choice but to forfeit the game to the Orioles. An indignant Freedman retaliated by making a grandiose show of refunding the spectators their money, refusing to pay the Orioles their share of the gate receipts and demanding that Holmes be suspended for his "insulting language . . . to the Jewish race and the Hebrew patrons of the game." The National League board of directors tried to appease Freedman by suspending Holmes for the remainder of the season, but when the ballplayer took his case to court the directors quickly backed down and reinstated him. As a result, Ducky became a hero to the other players in the league.

Arriving in Washington in 1903, Holmes remained as out-spoken as ever. He had signed with Tom Loftus on the promise he would replace Ed Delahanty in the outfield, only to be relegated to a reserve role when Del returned to the ball club. Holmes was unhappy with his status and he voiced his complaints loudly and frequently. And as the Senators continued to lose game after game, Ducky found plenty of sympathetic listeners among the Washington fans and writers. They called for Loftus to shake up his lineup and give Holmes a chance in an effort to break the team's losing ways. But during the first two weeks in June, the only action Ducky got was in the laundry room.

The White Sox followed the Naps into Washington, and Holmes finally made it into a ball game. He went in to replace Delahanty as a base runner in the eighth inning and scored to cap a four-run rally which got Washington even with Chicago. The next inning, the White Sox scored five runs to win easily, 11–6. That made it four losses in a row for the Senators and thirteen in their past fourteen games.

The next day, Holmes was back on the bench watching as Smiling Al Orth baffled the White Sox with his slowball and the Senators knocked out thirteen hits for a 10–0 victory. When Orth retired the final batter for a rare victory, the fourteen hundred fans raced onto the field to join the Washington players in their celebration.

Afterward, no one was happier than Ducky Holmes. That afternoon, Loftus informed the ballplayer he had been sold to Charlie Comiskey's team. When the White Sox left town, Ducky went with them, leaving the dirty laundry behind.

• • •

John McGraw's Giants returned to New York from their western trip and walked into a freshly painted and refurnished clubhouse on June 18. It was John Brush's way of welcoming his team home. Despite all the predictions of their imminent demise out west, the Giants had managed to hold on to first place in the National League race. Brush boldly predicted that if his team kept winning, someday there would be a crowd of fifty thousand in the Polo Grounds. It seemed a preposterous notion. That was almost twice as many people as had ever attended a single baseball game.

That afternoon, Christy Mathewson threw a pitch wide of the plate to walk Chicago's Jimmy Slagle with the bases loaded. Outfielder Dirty Dick Harley, the former American Leaguer who had ripped open McGraw's knee in Baltimore a year earlier, taunted the New York manager as he jogged home from third base with the only run of the ball game. Matty, who had won thirteen of his previous fifteen decisions, pounded the ball into his mitt in disgust.

The Chicago ball club also was undergoing a transformation. It still was referred to by its old nicknames "Colts" or "Orphans," but more and more it was becoming known as the "Cubs." It had a new identity on the field, also. Manager Frank Selee, who had won five pennants with Boston in the 1890s, had moved husky catcher Frank Chance to first base and discovered a flashy young shortstop in Joe Tinker. At second base, he added a frail-looking kid by the name of Johnny Evers. The names Tinker, Evers, and Chance soon would become part of baseball lore.

Two years earlier, with Tom Loftus as manager, Chicago had finished one game out of last place. In June 1903, Selee had the Cubs in third place. Their victory over the first-place Giants left them just a game and a half behind the leaders.

Afterward, McGraw sat in front of his locker and slowly peeled off his uniform. He received word that Pittsburgh had won again that afternoon, beating Boston, 7–2, to move into a virtual tie for first place with New York. The news was greeted with silence in the Giants clubhouse. The Pirates were on one of the most incredible streaks in baseball history. The defending champs had won twelve games in a row, the first six of them by shutouts, starting with a 7–0 victory over the Giants two weeks earlier. The Pittsburgh pitchers had hurled fifty-seven scoreless innings in a row during that stretch. It seemed the Pirates might never lose again.

The New York players weren't the only ones feeling the pressures of the tightening pennant race. At the club's headquarters in the St. James Building earlier that day, team president John Brush summoned secretary Fred Knowles to his office. The Giants president was in a combative mood. The western trip had exposed the weakness of his ball club in the infield, and the recent surge by the Pirates had only aggravated the problem. Meanwhile, George Davis was playing shortstop for a semipro team in Rhode Island and continuing to draw his pay from the Giants. It was a situation Brush was determined to correct.

Assisted by Knowles, the Giants president drew up a strongly worded protest to be sent to National League president Harry Pulliam. The complaint centered on the trade of Kid Elberfeld to the New York Americans.

Brush began by expressing his surprise at the Elberfeld transaction. He went on to review the situation in baseball the past year and state that his club had suffered more than any other in the recent peace agreement by allowing an American League team to enter the city.

"In return," wrote Brush, "it was certainly entitled to know the exact playing strength of the rival club in New York City."

Furthermore, maintained the Giants president, since Elberfeld was under contract to the New York National League club for 1903, the team could have taken out an injunction preventing the shortstop from playing with the American League. It did not, said Brush, in the spirit of peace. Therefore, the transfer of Elberfeld to the New York Americans was a "violation of the 'peace agreement.'"

Then Brush delivered the punch line. Because of the Elberfeld deal, Brush demanded that Pulliam remove the league's restrictions on George Davis playing for the Giants.

Brush affixed his signature to the document and handed it to Knowles to be delivered to the National League president. Since Pulliam shared headquarters space in the same building with Brush, the Giants secretary did not have far to go.

The next day, it rained hard in New York, forcing the postponement of the Giants' game with the Cubs. A visitor to Brush's office found the old man seated on his rowing machine doing his daily exercises. Brush nodded to the man, then glanced out the window at the downpour.

"For the first time in my baseball experience," he joked, "I feel the need of knowing how to row."

In Boston that day, the Pirates routed the Beaneaters, 12–2, to move past the Giants into first place. The Pittsburgh winning streak now was at thirteen games, just four short of the National League record.

• • •

Winning streaks also were the talk of the day in the American League. The Highlanders won six in a row before being stopped, 7–0, on a rain-soaked field in Detroit. The Athletics took a five-game winning streak to Chicago, where they battled into the bottom of the ninth inning tied 1–1. The White Sox got two men on base, and newcomer Ducky Holmes hit a ball so far over Ollie Pickering's head the Philadelphia right fielder took one glance at it and started walking off the field. When W. A. Phelon, Jr., filed his report for *Sporting Life* a week later, he claimed the ball still hadn't come down. It was one of the longest drives ever hit at South Side Park, but under the rules Holmes only got credit for a single since the winning run scored from third base on the play.

In Washington, Ed Delahanty lined a shot into center field to send Kip Selbach and Jimmy Ryan racing home with the winning runs in a 2–1 triumph over Detroit. A day later, Happy Jack Townsend found his speedballs and curves going just where he aimed them, and he held the Tigers to four hits, beating them, 5–1. Suddenly, the Senators had a modest three-game winning streak. When rain washed out the following game with Detroit holding a 7–1 lead in the second inning, keeping the Washington streak intact, Tom Loftus began to wonder if his team's luck was changing.

Rain still was falling when the Washington ballplayers gathered at the train station that evening. It was June 17, a Wednesday, and the Senators were leaving for St. Louis, the first stop on a two-week trip that would take them to the four western cities in the league.

Del showed up wearing an expensive blue suit and a silk tie highlighted by a large diamond pin. Del liked to dress well and he liked to sport flashy jewelry, but never had his teammates seen him looking so prosperous. He had a diamond ring on each hand. In his pocket was a handsome gold watch that had been presented to him years before by his followers in Philadelphia. One observer admired all the diamonds he was wearing and surmised Delahanty had on fifteen hundred dollars' worth of "sparklers."

An old friend stopped to talk to him, and Ed assured the man his financial troubles were over. "I'm solvent again," he boasted.

Once the train ride began, many of Del's teammates learned otherwise. The diamonds Delahanty had with him—about two thousand dollars' worth—were not recent purchases after all. They belonged to a Washington jeweler, who had given them to Del to try to sell to his teammates while on the trip.

The train lurched westward, and the players smoked large cigars and played poker. Scranton Bill Coughlin stopped by to look over Del's assortment of rings, pins, and other trinkets set with diamonds, and walked away proudly wearing a diamond ring. If you like it, Del told Coughlin, you can purchase it when we return to Washington. Rabbit Robinson was given a gold watch to try out.

Robinson was a newcomer to the team, a twenty-one-year-old kid out of West Virginia. He liked Delahanty. Unlike many of the older ballplayers, Del had a reputation for treating rookies and other youngsters on the square. Robinson found him to be good-natured, modest, and generous. Most of all, Del was kind to the young players.

But there was a darker side to Delahanty's personality which sometimes came into evidence. On those occasions when he indulged too heavily in liquor, he would become despondent and quarrelsome.

The journey to St. Louis continued that night and into the next day. Along the way, Del began drinking shots of whisky. His mood turned morose, and he began talking of death. He confided to his friends that before leaving Washington he had purchased an insurance policy on his life, with Norine and the baby designated as beneficiaries. It was a twenty-four-hour policy, which meant it would be in effect only for one day.

No one paid much attention to such talk. Everyone on the team knew about Delahanty's problems. His contract squabble had left him in debt, and the word among the players was that Del also had domestic troubles. He was said to be jealous of his wife, and this often led him to drink heavily when he was away from home. Many of the players who knew Norine dismissed such stories. They knew her to be a devoted, kind, and dutiful wife.

There were other rumors about Delahanty's strange behavior in recent weeks. It was said that on one occasion he turned on the gas in his room in Washington in an attempt to kill himself.

But those closest to Del disregarded such tales. They recalled the time a couple of years earlier when a group of players had been sitting in a Philadelphia hotel lobby talking about a man who had committed suicide by drowning himself. Delahanty listened to the views of the others for a while and then piped up with his own thoughts on the subject.

"No one but a coward would ever drown himself," said Del.

• • •

Red Donahue, a pitcher for the Browns, was caught drinking a bottle of beer in the St. Louis clubhouse and fined one hundred dollars by manager Jimmy McAleer. Still angry over the fine, the red-headed pitcher sat at the end of the bench and watched sullenly as the Browns played the Senators in the first game of the series in St. Louis on Friday, June 20. The first time he saw Ed Delahanty jog lazily onto the field, he was shocked at the condition of his old friend.

A big right-hander, Donahue had played four seasons with Del in Philadelphia and had pitched against him after the two jumped to the American League in 1902. Often, the two men had talked of their plans to retire from the game and become business proprietors. Del bought some land in Cleveland and talked of opening a saloon someday. Donahue carefully saved his money, also planning to buy a saloon or perhaps a hotel back in Philadelphia.

Delahanty hit one single in three at-bats for the Senators, but it seemed to Donahue there was something wrong with his former teammate. He ran the bases poorly and dropped the only ball hit to him in right field. The Browns won, 4–0, for their first victory in two weeks, and afterward Donahue remarked to one of his teammates that Delahanty was playing only a "half-hearted" game. The other player nodded his agreement. The word around the ballpark was that Del had been drinking and was in no shape for baseball.

There were others in the Washington traveling party whose activities led to the same suspicions. On Saturday, manager Tom Loftus seemed unsteady as he handed umpire Tommy Connolly his lineup card before the game. Connolly and St.

Louis manager Jimmy McAleer both concluded that Loftus was drunk, but neither man said anything about it.

It was an uncomfortably hot day, and Loftus fanned himself as he sat on the Washington bench beneath a canopy cover. Next to him was his young son, who was serving as the team's mascot on the road trip. The Senators failed to score in the top of the first inning, and Smiling Al Orth went to the pitcher's box to toss his warmup pitches to catcher Boileryard Clarke. Jesse Burkett prepared to bat for the Browns, and he was greeted by the usual taunts from the Washington players. The difference this time was that the normally reserved Loftus, who still was smarting from Burkett's remarks about him in Washington, joined in the banter.

"Strike the son of a bitch out!" Loftus called to his pitcher.

Burkett turned to the Washington manager to yell back his reply. "Nice language, that! I'll have you put out of the grounds!"

The St. Louis batter appealed to the umpire for relief from the attacks on his heritage. Ordinarily, Connolly would have put a stop to such language immediately. But Loftus normally conducted himself in an orderly manner, and the umpire did not want to embarrass him in his current condition. So this time, Connolly did no more than promise Burkett he would not allow a repetition of such language. That seemed to satisfy Burkett, who stepped back into the batter's box.

Suddenly, there was another, louder taunt from the Washington bench. This one concerned Pebbly Jack Glasscock, Burkett's brother-in-law and the former ballplayer who had sold out the brotherhood more than a decade earlier. The heckler claimed that Glasscock was in fact Burkett's father.

The insult caused Burkett to snap to attention.

"What's that?" he shouted.

Even the Washington players seemed caught off guard by the remark. Orth paused on the pitching rubber, and Clarke looked up from his catching position to see how Burkett might respond. The answer came quickly enough.

Burkett threw down his bat and sprinted toward the Washington bench. He got there so fast Loftus barely had time to rise before the first two blows from Burkett's fists crashed into his face. The Washington manager staggered backward and fell in a great heap, blood streaming from his nose. He struggled to his feet and lunged toward his attacker. When he did, Burkett broke free from some players trying to restrain him and renewed his assault. Several ladies in the crowd screamed at the sight of the blood as the two men clinched and rolled on the ground kicking and swinging. The police rushed onto the field to break up the fight, but Burkett was in such a frenzy he managed to throw one policeman off his back and punch Loftus again before he finally was pulled away.

Both men were ordered from the field by Connolly. Burkett walked off defiantly as cheers and hisses rained down on him from the stands. Loftus, bloodied and dazed, was jeered loudly as he was escorted to the private office of Browns president Robert Lee Hedges.

Loftus bathed his face and regained his composure, then returned to the grandstand to watch the remainder of the game. As he sat there, his friends came to express their regrets and to check on his condition.

"This fellow Burkett is bughouse and has been ever since he has been in baseball," Loftus told them, "but I never thought he was nutty enough to make a break like this."

The others listened sympathetically and nodded their heads in agreement, but when they left many of them were convinced the Washington manager had been drinking and had been at fault.

"Loftus was in liquor and made a display of himself," Hedges complained to acquaintances.

On the field, the Browns led, 3–2, and had two runners on

base in the eighth inning. Charlie Hemphill pushed a bunt in front of the plate, and Al Orth scooped up the ball and pegged it to first base. It should have been a routine play, but somehow the ball ripped through the upraised mitt of first baseman Scoops Carey and hit him flush in the nose. He went down as if he had been shot, his nose badly broken and pouring out blood. The Washington players watched glumly as the popular first baseman was helped off the field and taken to the St. Louis clubhouse for medical treatment.

Jesse Burkett was sitting on a stool inside the clubhouse when he looked up to see Carey brought into the room and placed on an old wooden table. Burkett had seen lots of baseball injuries in his fourteen seasons, and he offered to assist Dr. Starkloff in dressing the player's wounds.

Carey was in great pain, but Burkett managed to comfort him while the doctor went about his work. The two men were concentrating on their tasks when they heard the door open and someone enter. It was Loftus, who had come to check on his injured player. Spotting Burkett, the Washington manager began cursing him and challenging him to renew their fight. His tone was so threatening Dr. Starkloff feared another outbreak of violence and rushed from the room for help. Burkett coolly continued to apply ice to Carey's wound and did not even look up as he answered the Washington manager.

"I'm done with you as long as you let me alone. But, Tom, don't ever make another break like you did this afternoon."

Loftus refused to back down and again tried to goad Burkett into a fight. Finally, St. Louis pitcher Jack Powell and a policeman arrived to calm the Washington manager and lead him from the room.

But the day was not yet complete for Loftus. He saw his Senators wipe out a three-run deficit by scoring four runs in the top of the ninth only to turn around and give up two runs in the bottom of the inning to lose, 7–6.

Later, he received word that Ban Johnson had acted quickly

to punish all the parties involved in the brawl. Umpire Tommy Connolly was censured for ignoring Burkett's appeal for protection against the verbal abuse. Burkett was fined fifty dollars for striking Loftus. And Loftus was suspended for five days for provoking the assault.

The joke around the league was that Loftus actually was being rewarded, not punished. After all, he would not have to see his team play its next five games.

• • •

From St. Louis, the Washington ball club traveled to Chicago, where the Senators encountered more misfortune. Catcher Lew Drill was hit in the head by a pitched ball and forced to the sidelines. Another pitch struck Jimmy Ryan in the hand, knocking him out of the lineup, also.

Meanwhile, Ed Delahanty continued his troubling behavior. He purchased another twenty-four-hour insurance policy the day the team departed St. Louis. He remained despondent and withdrawn. When the game was rained out the first day in Chicago, one newspaper reported that Delahanty spent the day "indisposed." On the field, he played with so little enthusiasm observers were led to question his motives.

"Reports from the West indicate that Delahanty is not trying to do his best," read an item in the *Washington Post*. "His fielding at times is rather suspicious."

There was only one area where Del remained above reproach. When he stepped to the plate, he still was as fearsome a batter as there was in the league. He hit a single in a 7–2 Washington loss at Chicago. The next day, he singled for one of only three Washington hits in a 4–1 loss to the White Sox. That marked fifteen consecutive games in which Del had hit safely, with twenty-five hits in fifty-eight at-bats.

Not even the hitting streak could improve Ed's mood. When the Senators departed Chicago for the next stop on their trip, he purchased another twenty-four-hour insurance policy.

• • •

The rains that plagued the Northeast finally broke on Thursday, June 25. In Philadelphia, catcher Frank Roth splashed across the soggy turf only to muff a foul pop hit by Jimmy Sebring of the Pirates with two outs in the tenth inning. Given a reprieve, Sebring lined a triple into the corner to break up a tie game as Pittsburgh gained its fifteenth consecutive victory. In the second game of the doubleheader, the Pirates finally were beaten, 5–1. It was their first loss in more than three weeks.

At the Polo Grounds that day, Billy Lauder committed two errors at third base and Charlie Babb botched a grounder at shortstop as the Giants were beaten twice by the Reds, 5–0 and 11–2. The unhappy New York fans shouted at John McGraw to put himself in the game. McGraw ignored their pleas and watched angrily as the Cincinnati batters hit one grounder after another past the shaky Giants infielders.

Elsewhere in New York, Harry Pulliam read over a lengthy statement he had prepared in response to the protest filed by John Brush. The thirty-three-year-old Pulliam had a reputation for fairness and honesty, traits which did not always endear him to others in baseball. Three months after he had been elected secretary of the Pittsburgh club in 1899, Pulliam received a complaint from a fan who claimed to have torn his overcoat on a nail in the grandstand. Pulliam told the man to buy a new coat and send the bill to the ball club. When Pirates president W. W. Kerr learned of Pulliam's actions, he had him fired. Pulliam got his job back when Barney Dreyfuss gained control of the club from Kerr in a power struggle, but the young executive never forgot how quickly a baseball magnate could turn on those who served him.

Pulliam knew the move he was about to take would touch off a storm of protest, but he told friends he was acting with a clear conscience. He was granting the Giants permission to suit up George Davis in defiance of the peace agreement.

Pulliam based his decision on Brush's claim that the Giants had priority of title by contract to Norman Elberfeld and George Davis. Those two players, as well as Ed Delahanty, had been surrendered to the American League in the interests of peace, but Brush maintained his club's rights to those three players "were not prejudiced by the Cincinnati Agreement." Pulliam agreed, and cited as proof of this position that when attempts were made to trade Davis and Delahanty to the New York American League club, Johnson had agreed with the National League president that such action was a breach of faith and he blocked the transactions.

Since Elberfeld occupied a similar position to Davis's and Delahanty's, it therefore was a violation of "the spirit if not the letter" of the peace accords to allow him to be transferred to the New York Americans.

In conclusion, wrote Pulliam, "I am constrained, after most careful consideration of the matter, to allow the said New York Club to exercise its legal rights and make such disposition of the services of George Davis as they are legally advised that they can do."

Pulliam dispatched the letter to Johnson along with the other owners in the two leagues, then returned to his office to ride out the storm. Down the hallway, George Davis already was in the Giants headquarters meeting with McGraw and Brush. McGraw was so anxious to get his new shortstop into action, he immediately appointed him captain of the team.

• • •

In Cleveland that day, a slender six-foot pitcher for the Naps tipped his cap to the League Park crowd, revealing his dark wavy hair and handsome face. His name was Earl Moore, but when he signed a hotel register he always identified himself by the self-proclaimed title, "Earl Moore, S.E.I.B." The initials, he explained, stood for "Steam Engine in Boots."

He threw the ball in a sidearm, or "crossfire," motion and two years earlier had been credited with the American League's first no-hit game. His popularity in Cleveland was such that cigars and babies had been named after him.

On this day, Moore retired the first nine Washington batters he faced and even struck out the great Ed Delahanty. The Naps led, 4–0, by the time Charlie Moran walked to lead off the fourth inning for the Senators. There was a wild pitch, enabling Moran to race to second base, but Kip Selbach was retired for the first out of the inning.

The next batter was Delahanty. He stepped to the plate and assumed his majestic pose, his arms raised and his big yellow bat held high over his head. Del glanced down to see catcher Fred Abbott flashing his finger signs to the pitcher, and he laughed. Ed was a master at picking up signals, often enabling him to know exactly what pitch was coming. Moore took his windup, stepped to the side, and twisted his body to hurl his crossfire pitch toward home. Del timed his swing perfectly and lined a shot into the outfield for a single, advancing Moran to third base.

It was the 2,597th hit of Delahanty's big-league career, a total then exceeded only by Cap Anson. No one gave much thought to it at the time, especially in light of Moore's shutout pitching and Cleveland's 4–0 victory, but that was to be Del's last hit.

• • •

That afternoon, Ban Johnson was doing some paperwork in his Chicago office when he was handed the letter from Harry Pulliam. Johnson almost shot straight out of his chair when he read the paper. A few minutes later, Charlie Comiskey arrived at the office. He already was aware of the letter, having read a copy in the Chicago newspapers. Johnson was furious, not just over Pulliam's action but also over the way he handled the affair.

"I don't care a rap for what Pulliam said," raged Johnson, "but if he had to say it, it seems to me that he should have had enough consideration for me to have sent me a copy of the letter before making it public. I am going to treat Pulliam in kind, and when I have prepared my reply it will be promptly given to the public."

There were some newspapermen outside his office, and Johnson went out to issue an angry denunciation of the National League president.

"Pulliam is weak, and John T. Brush, taking advantage of this, has placed him under his influence," Johnson said scornfully.

True to his word, Ban did not even bother to send Pulliam a reply to his directive. Instead, Johnson sent a telegram to Cincinnati president Garry Herrmann stating his position on the matter.

"Pulliam's decision in Davis case unwarranted and absurd," wired Johnson. "No restrictions were placed on clubs in the matter of awarded players. Subject not even discussed at peace conference. Think it duty of National League to promptly nullify Pulliam's action."

Herrmann, who also was caught off guard by Pulliam's letter, did not need much prodding. Neither he nor Chicago's James Hart and St. Louis's Frank de Haas Robinson, the other members of the National League peace commission, had been consulted by Pulliam before his decision. Herrmann felt betrayed by his league president, and he entered a vigorous protest, claiming the Davis ruling was grossly unfair. He also issued a public rebuke of Pulliam.

"He is in the wrong, and the New York National League Club management is wrong," Herrmann told his Cincinnati writers. "The idea of Mr. Pulliam, an employee of eight club owners, doing as he has done is ridiculous. I won't stand for it, even if I go broke."

Robinson and Hart also lined up in opposition to Pulliam's ruling, once again leaving the National League owners publicly divided.

In Chicago, Johnson conferred with Comiskey and indicated he would delay action in the matter, waiting to see if the Giants were indeed allowed to play George Davis. But Johnson did not plan to remain idle for long. He leaked word to the press that if the conditions of the Cincinnati agreement were not restored, his league was ready to resume the war with the Nationals and concentrate its attacks on the New York and Pittsburgh clubs.

That evening, all talk of pennant races in baseball was overshadowed by talk of war. It appeared the long-sought peace agreement was not even going to last for one season.

• • •

At the intersection of Thirty-third and Broadway in New York, a man wearing a suit and wide-brimmed hat leaned against a street post reading a morning newspaper while waiting on a streetcar. The headlines that Friday morning, June 26, were full of dire predictions of the resumption of the baseball wars.

"New War Clouds Darken Horizon," read one headline, beneath which was a subhead stating, "The Miserable Davis Case Likely to Cause a New Conflict." In the text of the story, New York writer W. H. Rankin glumly noted, "Ominous clouds are gathering on the base ball horizon."

The man was Fred Clarke, the famous manager of the National League champion Pittsburgh Pirates. He read the details of the George Davis case and Harry Pulliam's letters with special interest, then folded up the paper and tucked it under his arm. With him were two of his Pittsburgh players, shortstop Hans Wagner and pitcher Deacon Phillippe, and team secretary Locke. They had arrived in New York the previous night, and now were en route to the Polo Grounds for a show-down with the second-place Giants.

Clarke had just put away his newspaper when he looked up to see Fred Knowles walking up. The New York secretary gave Clarke a friendly slap on the back and asked how he was doing.

"I'm an in-and-outer, Fred," answered Clarke. "One day I feel good, the next I'm bad. This is one of my off days."

Knowles smiled playfully. "Don't wish you any hard luck, but I would like to see you out of the game for some days."

Clarke smiled at the remark as he and the others boarded their streetcar. Wagner might be Pittsburgh's greatest perfor-mer, but Clarke was the driving force behind its success.

A star outfielder and batter, Clarke also was a shrewd man-ager and one of the most fearless competitors in the game. He got his first baseball job through a want ad in the *Sporting News*, and broke into the National League with Louisville in 1894. The team didn't have a uniform for him, so Clark had to borrow one that was several sizes too large. He stepped onto the field with his pants legs rolled up about a foot each, and the fans ridiculed him with the nickname "Pants." His teammates scoffed at the undersized bat he brought with him. "Pitchers will saw that thing off in your hands," they claimed. Clarke said nothing, instead silencing his critics with a record five hits that first game.

Three years later, he became manager of the Louisville club at age twenty-four and responded to the challenge with a .390 batting average. The club later merged with Pittsburgh, and Clarke led the Pirates to back-to-back titles in 1901 and 1902. He was a tough competitor, and he never hesitated to use his fists to enforce his authority. When pitcher Jesse Tannehill balked at pitching out of turn one day, Clarke beat him up.

The streetcar arrived at their destination, and Clarke and

his companions hopped off and began walking toward the Polo Grounds. The New York ballpark was one of the few that provided dressing quarters for the visiting teams, so the Pittsburgh ballplayers still were in their civilian clothes as they entered the gate.

Inside, they spotted Giants pitcher Iron Man Joe McGinnity standing by a wall.

Clarke nodded his head in recognition. "Hello, Joe, how's the arm?"

"All right, Fred. Never better."

McGinnity casually fell into step behind the Pittsburghers. Ahead, Frank Bowerman and Roger Bresnahan of the Giants appeared out of the shadows.

"Why, how are you, Fred old boy?" Bowerman called out cheerfully.

Bowerman, one of the New York catchers, normally was a rude and surly man. His sour disposition was such that he once raced a woman to grab the last empty stool on a ferry boat, then had the woman arrested for assault when she slapped his face in anger.

But on this occasion, he was all smiles as he held out his hand in a show of greeting to Clarke.

"Say, Fred, I want to speak to you a moment."

"Sure thing," answered Clarke.

Bowerman led the way down a corridor, while McGinnity and Bresnahan casually lagged behind. The other Pittsburgh players paid no mind as they headed the opposite direction toward the visitors' clubhouse.

At the end of the hallway was a small, freshly painted room. The two men walked in, and Clarke heard the door shut behind him. Suddenly, Bowerman wheeled around to face him.

"Fred, did you tell Warner I could not catch for him?" Bowerman asked angrily.

Clarke thought for a moment, trying to recall a remark he had made earlier to Jack Warner, another catcher for the Giants.

"I don't remember, Frank. Maybe I did tell him that. You know you said it."

Still unsuspecting, Clarke had both hands at his side. In one of them was the newspaper he had been reading. He never saw the swing coming until Bowerman's fist crashed into his jaw, knocking him to the ground. Quickly, Bowerman pounced on his victim, pinning him down with his knees while pummeling him in the face with his fists.

Outside, Pirates secretary Locke heard the commotion and realized what was happening. Frantically, he rushed toward the door, but Bresnahan roughly shoved him away. Locke turned and raced off to get Knowles.

One newspaperman who witnessed the ensuing confusion claimed Knowles was so unnerved by what was happening he "was rubbing his hands and squawking like an old maid whose hen roost had been robbed."

After a few minutes, a policeman arrived, but even he had trouble getting past the New York ballplayers guarding the door.

"Let them fight," growled Bresnahan.

The other Pirates never even realized what was happening. They were sitting around on the visitors' bench when Clarke walked up, his clothes disheveled and his hat crumpled. His face was covered with mud and scratches, and one eye was swollen. In his hand, he still was holding his newspaper.

"What happened to you?" someone asked.

Clarke refused to answer at first before reluctantly admitting, "I was suckered."

Recounting what happened, Clarke could not help but remember what Knowles had told him earlier that morning. Apparently, the Giants secretary was not the only one on the New York ball club who wanted to see Clarke out of action.

• • •

It would take more than a beaten and swollen face to keep Fred Clarke from playing a ball game. At four o'clock that afternoon, the Pittsburgh outfielder had a bat in his hand and eagerly awaited his first trip to the plate as the third batter in the lineup. On the mound, Christy Mathewson prepared to throw his first pitch to Pirates leadoff batter Jimmy Sebring. Catcher Frank Bowerman squatted behind the plate, his knuckles still scraped and cut from the morning's activities.

But it was not Bowerman or Clarke or even Matty who commanded the attention of the nearly ten thousand spectators on hand at the Polo Grounds that Friday afternoon. At shortstop, George Davis pounded his fielder's mitt and leaned forward in the crouch that had become so familiar to New York fans over the nine seasons he had been a fixture at the position.

The previous week, Davis had been playing for the Woonsocket Gyms semipro team in Rhode Island. Now, his long exile from the major leagues was over. For the first time in almost two years, George Davis was back in a New York uniform.

There had been some concern that his playing would be protested by the Pirates. The Cincinnati ball club already had let it be known it would refuse to take the field if Davis were allowed to suit up against it. Chicago and St. Louis also stood in opposition to the ruling by Harry Pulliam. Brooklyn, Boston, and Philadelphia had aligned themselves with New York on the matter. Only Pittsburgh's Barney Dreyfuss refused to take sides, leaving him holding the balance of power in the dispute. Dreyfuss wisely chose to take no action against Davis until he had the opportunity to confer with Pulliam.

The fans cheered every move Davis made. He fielded two grounders cleanly and made one putout at second base. He batted four times and hit one single.

Meanwhile, Matty continued his amazing mastery over the Pirates. He gave up eight hits and walked two batters, but with men on base he was almost unhittable. The Giants built an eight-run lead, then Matty coasted to an 8–2 decision. It marked Mathewson's fourth victory over the champions and his fourteenth overall, the most in the league.

The Giants now had won forty games, the same number as the Pirates. With Davis in the lineup, all the talk of a championship in New York no longer seemed so improbable.

. . .

That same Friday, Ed Delahanty picked up a copy of the *Cleveland Press* and saw across the top of the front page a bold headline proclaiming, "Base Ball War Is On Again."

Below this startling announcement were subheads which added, "Brush and Dreyfuss Are Arranging for a Raid on the American League, 'Tis Said," and "The Davis Incident Merely the Opening Gun of the Fight to Come."

The ensuing story stated "there is not much reason to doubt" the war between the two major leagues would be renewed.

Just the night before, Delahanty had taken one of his teammates to the family house on Phelps Street for a dinner of corned beef and cabbage, or "Irish turkey" as the ballplayers liked to call it. Ed had been in good spirits then, but the story in the newspaper changed all that. He became extremely agitated, and he paced around the hotel telling anyone who would listen, "The peace agreement has gone to smash!" He told several of his teammates he was going to join the New York National League club. They tried to calm him, reminding him the Senators had a ball game that afternoon, but Delahanty no longer cared. He was more concerned with finding a drink.

Elsewhere in the hotel, the Washington ballplayers gathered in small groups in the lobby or their rooms to talk about the prospects for renewed hostilities between the two leagues and what it might mean to them.

Jimmy Ryan scoffed at the talk of baseball wars and legal battles. Ryan had played eighteen seasons in the big leagues, and he claimed most of those years he had not even bothered to sign a contract.

"I put in several seasons at Chicago without putting my

autograph to any paper," he boasted. "As long as you play good ball they want you, and when you don't they let you out.

"All I want to know is what I'm going to get, and when I give my word I'll keep it. I never found any club that did not fulfill its promise to me."

Kip Selbach had his own tales to recount. One of them concerned John McGraw, who two years earlier had persuaded Selbach to leave the New York Giants to join the Baltimore Orioles of the fledgling American League.

"McGraw talked me into signing, giving me a great line on the new league's possibilities," recalled Selbach. "Then I'll be darned if he didn't jump back himself to the Giants."

It was ladies' day at the ballpark that afternoon, and a lively crowd of almost three thousand was on hand. Many of the fans had come to see Delahanty, but he was mysteriously absent. The newspaper writers reported only that he "was under the weather." Without him, the Senators managed only three singles and were beaten, 1–0.

There was a doubleheader the next day, a Saturday, and again Delahanty was missing. Once again, his absence was reported as due to illness, but the ballplayers knew better. Del was loose on a drinking spree.

On the field that day, each team won one game, and the Cleveland players screamed and howled that every close call by umpire Silk O'Laughlin went against them. And every time they disputed one of his decisions, O'Laughlin would taunt the Clevelanders with the reply, "What are you going to do about it?"

• • •

So many fans swarmed into the Polo Grounds that Saturday, they overran the reinforced squad of policemen on duty at the ballpark. A frantic call to police headquarters resulted in the dispatch of an extra two hundred men to try to handle the crowd. There were people packed into every corner of the ballpark. Reporter W. M. Rankin watched them squeeze into the grandstand and the open seats and remarked to a colleague that breathing room could not be had at any price. There were more than thirty-two thousand fans in all, the largest crowd ever to witness a baseball game in New York. And that did not count those who climbed the trees outside or lined Coogan's Bluff to peer down at the action below.

Fred Clarke of the Pirates gained a measure of revenge that day, hitting a tremendous drive off Iron Man McGinnity and racing all the way to third base for a triple. He scored on a hit by Honus Wagner, and the run proved to be the turning point in a 4–2 Pittsburgh victory.

George Davis, looking out of shape from his long layoff, made five outs in five at-bats and committed one error.

On the field, the showdown for first place went to the Pirates. But at the ticket office, the Giants were becoming the big winners in baseball.

• • •

The trip from Cleveland to Detroit provided the Washington ballplayers a welcome relief from the drudgery of train travel. For this leg of the western journey, the team would travel across Lake Erie by steamboat.

That Saturday evening, shortly before the boat was to depart, Ed Delahanty finally reappeared at the hotel where the Senators were quartered. His hands trembled and he raved incoherently; he appeared to be suffering from delirium tremens. At times, he seemed to be hallucinating, and once he pulled out a large knife and threatened to kill himself.

Reporter Paul Eaton observed Delahanty's behavior in Cleveland and logged the following entry in his journal: "Del proceeded to do a sensational tank act, and was soon filled with enthusiasm, and he doesn't take his with sugar in it, either, as was shown by his making several scenes and threatening other players and himself with a knife."

It was up to Del's roommate, Jimmy Ryan, to calm the raging

ballplayer and persuade him to accompany the team to Detroit. Ryan assured his friend that the night on the boat would do him good and perhaps in a couple of days he would be in condition to play ball again.

It was a warm night, and the ride across the lake was a pleasant one. Some of the players passed the time in the smoking room, while others played cards or slept. Delahanty stood on the deck and stared out across the dark waters of Lake Erie. Del always had enjoyed the water, and his friends claimed he could have been a champion swimmer had he not been a ballplayer. When he played in Philadelphia, Del and his Phillies roommate, Billy Hallman, spent much of their free time on swims in the Delaware River or the Atlantic Ocean. "There were but few men in the country who were as much at home in the water as he was," Hallman recalled. "I have seen him do all kinds of tricks in the Atlantic Ocean even when it was at its worst."

It seemed that all too soon the boat docked at Detroit and the command "All ashore!" was given. It was Sunday morning, June 28. The team went straight to the Griswold House, one of Senators owner Fred Postal's two hotels in the city, and immediately marched into the dining area for breakfast.

The weary ballplayers presented quite a sight. Delahanty was pale and unshaven. Jimmy Ryan's right hand still was black-and-blue from being hit by a pitched ball in Chicago. Catcher Lew Drill had only been out of the hospital a couple of days since his beaning in Chicago, and one observer said his head "looked like a pumpkin." Bill Coughlin had hurt his right hand the day before, and it was swollen to twice its size. A few players limped from sore or sprained ankles.

All conversation in the room stopped, and the other diners stared at the ballplayers in amazement. Ryan smiled back at them and raised his bandaged hand in the air in a mock show of triumph.

"Hail to the war survivors!" he shouted.

VI

THE

BRIDGE

He had the blues,
So he quaffed some booze
And turned up dead
In just necktie and shoes.

Buffalo Courier-Express

Jack Deering awoke Sunday morning, June 28, in Detroit and set off from his home on Leverett Street to attend the services at a nearby church. It was a pleasant summer day, and the young Detroit pitcher thought about that afternoon's ballgame as he walked down the street. Sunday ball was illegal in Michigan, but the Tigers circumvented the rule by playing their games across the state line in Toledo, Ohio. It did not matter to Deering, a rookie, where the game was played. That day, he would have the opportunity to face Connie Mack's Athletics, who would conclude their series with the Tigers and depart for Cleveland afterward.

When the services ended, Deering had just enough time to catch the train to Toledo for the game. But a terrible thing happened to the ballplayer. He became violently ill outside the church, and had to be taken home and put to bed on a doctor's orders. Deering's failure to arrive in Toledo with the other players was a great mystery. Tigers manager Ed Barrow had a carriage sent to the depot to meet the next train and rush the pitcher to the ballpark in time for the game, but it returned empty.

Although disgusted by the turn of events, Barrow was not concerned about Deering's absence. As the Detroit manager knew, it was not the first time a ballplayer had simply disappeared.

• • •

That same morning, a man by the name of John R. Robinson of Saginaw, Michigan, showed up at the Oriental Hotel in Detroit to call on his friend Andy Coakley of the Athletics. Coakley was a college man, and while attending Holy Cross the year before had pitched for Connie Mack's team under the assumed name of Jack McAllister.

By chance, Robinson happened to run into several Washington players who also had stopped by the hotel to visit after their arrival in town. One of the Senators he had a chance to talk with was Ed Delahanty.

Robinson had heard of Del's recent troubles, but he looked him over and thought to himself that Ed was "in good health and a rational frame of mind."

Del mentioned that manager Tom Loftus had laid him off without pay "on account of overweight," an action which the ballplayer claimed was an injustice.

Robinson sympathized with the ballplayer, believing he had a legitimate complaint. Not only was Del's batting average of .333 the highest on the Washington team, it put him even with Larry Lajoie, the league's other great slugger. And Delahanty was on a hot streak, with twenty-six hits in his past sixty-two at-bats.

Robinson noticed one other thing about Delahanty. With a large diamond pin prominently displayed in his tie and "sparklers" on both hands, it seemed to Robinson that Del looked as prosperous as ever.

• • •

Not much had changed at the St. Clair Street fire station in Cleveland. There still was a baseball diamond on the lot next door, and the firemen still oversaw the games played there by the neighborhood kids.

Monday morning, June 29, there was the usual game going on, and the firemen watching rehashed the weekend's events in baseball. The talk turned to Ed Delahanty and how he had missed three of his team's games against the Naps. There were rumors about Del's drinking problems, but no one said anything bad about him, especially in front of the old captain. Big Ed still was a hero to the firemen.

Around the corner, a messenger arrived at the Delahanty house on Phelps Street to deliver a telegram. It was from a member of the Washington ball club in Detroit, urging Mrs. Delahanty to hurry to that city to help take care of Ed. He had resumed drinking to excess and had become delirious, the message stated.

Mrs. Delahanty, accompanied by Ed's younger brother, Will, and another woman, left later that day for Detroit. She wondered what might be done to save her oldest son from his troubles.

• • •

A heat wave gripped the upper midwest that Tuesday. In Cleveland, a man by the name of Frank Dubrow was driven so mad by the rising temperatures, he sprang from his bed in the morning and cried out, "I'm burning! I can't stand it any longer!" He ran from the house half-dressed and showed up at a nearby police station, where he begged the officers to shoot him. Instead, they locked him up for public intoxication. Elsewhere in the city, women passed out on streetcars and men collapsed on the sidewalks. The only sign of relief from the suffering came when the ice delivery men settled their one-week strike and began making their rounds again.

It also was a sweltering hot day in Detroit. At the ballpark that afternoon, Washington's Happy Jack Townsend was rocked for fifteen hits, four of them by Wahoo Sam Crawford, and the Senators were beaten, 8–0. Townsend, who had been dubbed "the Delaware Peach" the previous season, was taunted by the Tigers with his new nickname, "the Delaware Lemon." Boileryard Clarke, a catcher, was moved to first base for the Senators. Silent Joe Martin played third base. Charlie Moran, fresh out of Georgetown College in Washington, D.C., was the shortstop. Watty Lee, a pitcher, took over right field.

Elsewhere in town, a subdued Ed Delahanty sat across the table from a Catholic priest and prepared to sign his name to a hand-written document. Del had made many agreements before, but never had he signed such a pact as this. It was a "be good" pledge.

The priest smiled reassuringly. For about an hour, he had

counseled the wayward ballplayer and convinced him to alter his destructive behavior. Del had listened quietly, and at the urging of his mother had agreed to all the conditions on the document. He promised he would treat Washington manager Tom Loftus "on the square." He vowed "to leave the 'red-eye' alone." He admitted that it was his drinking that had prevented him from playing good baseball and he promised to reform.

Finally, Ed scrawled his signature across the bottom of the pledge, making it an official agreement. But it was just a contract, and sometimes those were broken.

On Wednesday afternoon, a man known as "Detroit Andy" roamed the grandstands at Bennett Park, hawking his scorecards and shouting advice to the Detroit players. His real name was Andrew Rudolph, and his devotion to baseball and the Tigers was such that during the season he neglected all else to spend his days at the ballpark. When "Detroit Andy" bid on the scorecard concession at the ballpark, pitcher George Mullin rewarded his loyalty by helping him secure it.

On the field, Jack Deering returned to the pitcher's box after his mysterious disappearance and was pounded for seven hits and four runs in just three innings of play. The Tigers were beaten by Smiling Al Orth and the Senators, 4–1, but "Detroit Andy" remained unshaken. Afterward, he showed up in the clubhouse, offering his services as an "assistant rubber" for any Detroit player in need of a massage.

Back at the Griswold House, all talk of that day's ballgame was overshadowed by the discovery that thieves had broken into the room of Tigers shortstop Herman Long and stolen all his jewelry. Among the valuables missing was a championship pin given him by the popular Boston fan "Hi Hi" Dixwell when the Beaneaters won the pennant in 1898.

A group of Washington players sat around the lobby, and one of them, outfielder Kip Selbach, watched as Ed Delahanty nervously walked back and forth across the room. Del reminded Selbach of a tiger pacing a cage.

It had been twenty-four hours since Ed had signed the pledge, and he desperately wanted a drink. A physician had advised him to stop by taking a little whisky each day until he had broken off for good, but this was not enough to satisfy Del's craving. Adding to his unsettled state of mind, the *Detroit Times* had carried a page-one article that morning, detailing his behavior in recent days. At the top of the page was a two-column picture of Del, and beneath was a headline which read, " 'Del,' Mighty Hitter, Signs Pledge." A smaller headline below added, "Big Fellow Decides to Cut Out the Booze." Seeing his problems spelled out on the front page of the newspaper only added to Del's distress. That evening, he slipped out without a word to his mother or his teammates and got drunk once again.

The ballplayers did not know what to make of Del's actions. Some were growing weary of his erratic behavior. Others feared for his safety. None of them knew what he might say or do next.

Thursday morning, Ed was back at the hotel, behaving rationally one moment and acting like a madman the next. He escorted his mother and her lady friend to the train depot and placed them on a car for a day trip to Mount Clemens. Mrs. Delahanty was so encouraged by her son's appearance and apparent good spirits, she asked if he might be able to play in that afternoon's ballgame.

"No," Ed said cheerfully, "I feel a great deal better, but not quite good enough to play. I'll be all right, though, when the team reaches Washington."

As the train left, Mrs. Delahanty turned to her friend and commented that Ed looked "happy as a lark."

Not long afterward, the door to Delahanty's hotel room burst open, and Washington pitcher Howard "Highball" Wilson raced out into the hallway, his eyes wide with fright. Big Ed chased after him, brandishing a large knife and shouting he was going to kill the tiny pitcher.

At some point during these confused days in Detroit, Del also wrote a letter to Norine and enclosed one of the accident policies, made payable to their daughter. In the letter, Ed informed his wife when his train would be arriving home. He also wrote that things looked so bad for him he hoped the train would jump off the tracks and "be dashed to pieces," and he along with it. But Del had not purchased any insurance since the team left Chicago for Cleveland, and the policies he had bought on the trip were only of the twenty-four-hour variety. None were in effect when he wrote his letter. On Tuesday, he wired Norine to meet him in Washington the following Friday, but the team was not scheduled to return there until Saturday morning.

Delahanty also repeatedly told acquaintances in Detroit that Harry Pulliam's actions in the George Davis case and the appearance of Davis in a Giants uniform were proof that the peace agreement had been broken. Del continued to believe he would be the next ballplayer to join John McGraw's team in New York.

Whatever Del's thoughts or plans, he had lapsed back into a remorseful and nervous state by the time the Senators prepared to leave for the ballpark on Thursday. His brother, Willie, climbed aboard the bus to accompany the team to the game, but Ed stayed behind.

One of the last Washington players to see Delahanty was Scranton Bill Coughlin, the third baseman. He stopped by Del's room that morning to return the diamond ring Ed had given him to wear on the trip. Del tried to convince him otherwise, but Coughlin insisted on giving the ring back. He said he didn't want to take a chance on losing it.

• • •

Highball Wilson recovered from his scare at the hands of Delahanty that morning to pitch his best game of the season Thursday afternoon. For eight innings, he shut down the Tigers without a run while his boss, Senators president Fred Postal, stood among the Detroit rooters and shouted out his encouragement.

"By gosh," Postal exclaimed as the undersized pitcher retired the Tigers in the eighth inning, "that shrimp is all right!"

But Detroit's George Mullin was even better. He held the Senators to only three hits, and the Tigers finally won, 1–0, on a bases-loaded single in the ninth inning.

That marked the end of the Senators' two-week western trip, during which the team had won only two games and lost eleven. "Mark that number," noted Washington writer John Luitich, referring to the unlucky total of thirteen games.

The members of the Washington traveling party wondered what more could go wrong. Since leaving home, manager Tom Loftus had been beaten up and suspended, Scoops Carey had broken his nose, Jimmy Ryan and Bill Coughlin had injured their hands, Lew Drill had been beaned, and Ed Delahanty had become indisposed.

The players got their answer back at the hotel. Delahanty had left without saying a word to anyone, leaving behind some of his personal belongings and his uniform, minus his baseball cap. He had not even bothered to leave his mother the money to pay her bill at the hotel, although the last time she saw him he had at least two hundred dollars in cash and about fifteen hundred dollars in diamonds on him.

With no trace of Ed's whereabouts, the ballplayers went to the train depot without him. There, they boarded an eastbound train which would take them to Philadelphia and then to Washington. No one noticed that all the team's baggage and baseball equipment was mistakenly loaded onto another train.

• • •

Michigan Central train No. 6, with a top speed approaching an incredible seventy-five miles per hour, hurtled along the railroad tracks on its overnight run from Detroit to New York City. It had begun its daily journey eastward across Ontario, Candada, at 2:45 P.M. Thursday, July 2, and was scheduled to pull into Grand Central Station Friday morning, one of 464 trains that arrived or departed the busy terminal each day.

In the Pullman sleeper car, a man wearing a tailored blue suit, silk tie, high-topped lace shoes, and a black derby lit a cigar and began puffing on it, blowing out great rings of smoke. The other passengers asked him to stop, but he refused. He continued to smoke, even though it was against the rules to do so on a sleeper when there was a buffet car attached, as was the case on train No. 6. It was not until the conductor was summoned that the man finally put out his cigar.

The conductor, whose name was John Cole, checked his watch and noted that the train was about twenty minutes outside St. Thomas. He left to continue his rounds, but a few minutes later heard the call bell ringing over and over, annoying the passengers. He was forced to cut the line to prevent it from being rung anymore.

Not long afterward, there was a crashing sound, and Cole rushed back to the Pullman car to discover the man in the blue suit had broken the glass case enclosing the axe that was provided for use in case of a fire. The man agreed to pay for the damages he had caused and said he would feel better if he could have a drink. Two glasses of whisky were brought to him, and he drank them both.

Cole knew the man had drunk at least five shots of whisky since boarding but he did not believe him to be drunk, merely despondent and in the mood to make mischief. He was holding a coupon ticket for Buffalo and New York, with a berth in the Pullman car Havana, and he had with him a dress suitcase and black leather satchel.

Forty-five minutes later, the mischief continued. This time, the unruly passenger placed his shoulder against a wood partition separating the compartments in the Pullman and attempted to push it down. Cole ordered him to stop, and the man obediently went over and sat down.

It was past ten o'clock at night when there was another commotion. A woman was asleep in an upper berth on the sleeper car when the troublemaker reached in and tried to pull her out by her ankles. This was more than the other passengers were willing to stand. An angry delegation sought out Conductor Cole and demanded he do something to protect them.

When Cole arrived on the scene, he was accompanied by several other trainmen, who were there to prevent any further trouble. This time, the conductor did not attempt to reason with the man. The train was halted at the small way station of Bridgeburg, on the Canadian side of the Niagara River just across the Buffalo, and the man in the blue suit was told he would have to get off. It was 10:45 P.M.

The other passengers watched as the man was gently but forcibly pushed down the aisle toward the exit. He offered no resistance as he went. Cole handed him his hat and pointed him toward the way station, reminding him not to make any trouble as he still was in Canada.

"I don't care whether I'm in Canada or dead," came the reply.

A few minutes later, Michigan Central No. 6 pulled away, leaving the man alone in a strange place in the middle of the night. Just across the river, in the same direction the train had disappeared, he could see the lights of Buffalo shining before him.

• • •

It was 10:55 P.M. when Sam Kingston walked out of the telegraph office on the Canadian side of the Niagara River.

Later, he would claim to have seen someone nearby in the dark, but if he did he paid the person no attention. Kingston, a rugged man about sixty years of age, was night guard for the International Bridge, a job that paid $1.74 a day.

He watched as Michigan Central No. 6 crossed the bridge on its way toward Buffalo. He waited seven or eight minutes, at which time a freight from the Black Rock section of Buffalo, on the American side, passed him heading west. Kingston then continued his rounds, slowly walking toward the center of the bridge, which extended to Squaw Island and across Black Rock Harbor to Buffalo. The river was about twenty feet below, with a current of about eight miles per hour as the water flowed out of Lake Erie toward Grand Island about ten miles to the north. There, the river turned westward for its descent over Niagara Falls and on to Lake Ontario.

It was a single-track railroad bridge with the tracks laid on wooden ties and iron sidebeams adjoining the ties but about six inches lower. There was no footwalk nor was there a railing, but the sidebeams were about a foot and a half wide. Kingston had just reached the third span when he was startled to see a man standing to the side of the tracks. It appeared to Kingston the man was leaning against a pillar and staring into the river below. The guard called out to the stranger and flashed his bull's-eye lantern in his face to get a better look at him.

This seemed to anger the man, who shouted back an angry threat at Kingston.

"Take that lantern away or I'll break your face!"

Kingston stepped back to stay out of the man's reach.

"Have you permission to be on this bridge?" he demanded.

Once again, the man reacted angrily.

"Take that light away or I'll knock your damned brains out!" he warned.

Or perhaps his words were: "If you don't take that light

away, I'll knock your block off," or "Keep away from me or I'll brain you!"

Kingston would not be able to recall for certain. But he did remember thinking the intruder was either drunk or crazy and had no right to be on the bridge. The next moment, the guard lunged forward as if to grab the man.

• • •

Thirty-five minutes after the passenger had been put off the train at Bridgeburg, the steamer *Ossian Bedell* was passing through the open draw on the International Bridge. It was 11:20 P.M., and no one on board heard the splash when a man came plummeting down from the bridge and landed in the water nearby. Nor did anyone on board hear his cries for help, which were drowned out by the noise of the boat's engines.

But standing on the bridge above, Sam Kingston could hear the man calling out from the water. He looked and about 150 feet away he caught a glimpse of a man's head in the river. The boat continued on its way and soon was gone. Kingston listened, but now there was only the sound of the water in the darkness below.

The guard picked up a hat that was lying on one of the ties, placed it on his head, and resumed his duties. He did not report the incident on the bridge until early the next morning.

The same Friday morning, another passenger train came up from the west and followed those same tracks across the International Bridge into Buffalo. On board were the members of the Washington Senators baseball team, returning from their road trip in the west. It was a hot and tiresome ride, and it was not likely that any of the players even noticed as they passed over the bridge where just a few hours earlier a man had fallen to his death.

• • •

It was the Fourth of July weekend, and a record number of visitors flocked to Niagara Falls. Conservative estimates placed the figure at fifteen thousand people. The trains and trolleys were packed, and the New York Central Railroad alone carried more than three thousand passengers to the falls. It was one of the "Seven Natural Wonders of the Modern World," actually a series of three waterfalls. The American Falls and Luna Falls were completely on the U.S. side, and the International Boundary ran through the center of Horseshoe Falls.

Two years earlier, a forty-three-year-old schoolmistress by the name of Mrs. Anna Edison Taylor got inside a specially-made barrel with a one-hundred-pound anvil in the bottom and was lowered into the river at Grass Island just above the falls. The barrel remained upright as it passed through the one-mile-long upper rapids, a descent of 51 feet, and was swept over Horseshoe Falls to crash into the churning waters 164 feet below. Incredibly, the woman emerged from her unlikely vessel seventeen minutes later, badly bruised and shaken but otherwise unharmed, the only person known to have survived a trip over the mighty waterfall.

At eight o'clock Friday morning, July 3, a tourist on the Gorge Road Railway car running out of Niagara, New York, had his field glasses trained on the whirlpool area beneath the falls at about the same point where rivermen had pulled Mrs. Taylor's barrel from the water following her historic journey. He spotted an object in the water and kept it in his sights for several minutes trying to make it out. To his surprise, it appeared to be the body of a man, bobbing facedown in some driftwood.

Twenty miles upriver, Chief Griffin of the Ontario police was in a boat with two assistants searching the waters around the International Bridge for the missing stranger from the train. Sam Kingston's report to the police stated that while crossing from Bridgeburg to Buffalo at about eleven o'clock

Friday night, he had encountered an unidentified man "leaning against one of the trusses of the third span of the bridge." According to the guard, he held up his lantern and this seemed to anger the man, who threatened him. Believing the man to be unarmed and drunk, Kingston said he ordered him to move on. Then there was a slight struggle between the two, after which the stranger ran toward the open draw. The next thing he knew, said Kingston, there had been a splash in the water and the man had disappeared.

When he found no sign of the man, Chief Griffin returned to shore, convinced the body had been carried far downstream by the current. There was no clue to the man's identity, but since it was believed he had come on a train from the west, officials from Michigan Central sent telegrams to St. Thomas and Detroit seeking information on travelers from those points. Based on Kingston's description that he "was well-dressed, smooth shaven, about forty years old, and weighed about 160 pounds," the police chief guessed the missing man was a delegate to the electrical engineers' convention in Niagara.

• • •

While Chief Griffin was attempting to learn the identity of the missing man, a reporter from the *Buffalo Evening News* found Sam Kingston at his home in Fort Erie. It was an easy house to find, as it was located just next to the Fort Erie racetrack.

By now, Kingston had been cautioned by bridge foreman Paul Colclough to modify what he said about the incident. Kingston repeated what he had told police about the incident on the bridge, but this time he added another detail to the story. When the stranger repeated his threat against the guard if he did not remove the lantern, Kingston noticed he was "the worse for liquor," so he grabbed the man by the collar to pull him down.

"Just then my foot caught between two ties, and I fell down," said Kingston. "Before I could get my foot out, the man was gone and I heard a splash."

The guard also added a simple explanation for the stranger's actions.

"It is the opinion of everybody I've talked to about the case," added Kingston, "that the man committed suicide and was thinking about it when I saw him first up against the side of the bridge."

The reporter paid no attention to the hat Kingston was wearing as he spoke. It was a black derby, size 7⅛, and the label on the inside identified it as coming from the Hub store on Pennsylvania Avenue in Washington, D.C.

• • •

Later that day, the authorities walked out on the International Bridge to reconstruct for themselves the events of the man's apparent death. Surveying the scene, C. J. Metcalf, assistant to Chief Griffin, observed that the draw of the bridge, where the man supposedly had run, was fully three spans away from where the guard had confronted him. Metcalf looked at the automatic gates protecting the draw and realized the man could not have reached there as claimed by the bridge guard.

The police spoke to Paul Colclough, the foreman of the bridge, and he provided another twist to the confrontation between his guard and the stranger. According to Colclough, Sam Kingston told him that when he held up his lantern he noticed the man had some kind of weapon in his hand. Perhaps it had been a stone or a club "or something of that sort," Colclough said.

Curiously, that same morning a bridge tender found a railroad hat wedged between two girders on the bridge. It turned out to be the hat worn by Sam Kingston.

When the hat was returned to him, Kingston explained that

in the confusion following the scuffle he must have grabbed the stranger's derby by mistake.

The police now had possession of the black derby, which offered them the only clue as to the stranger's identity.

• • •

In Chicago that Saturday morning, the Fourth of July, John McGraw watched as a deputy sheriff went from room to room at the Victoria Hotel in search of George Davis. The deputy had with him a writ of injunction obtained by American League president Ban Johnson the previous day, prohibiting Davis from playing at West Side Park.

In his search, the officer poked into the closets and back rooms. He even looked beneath the back stairs, where he was startled to find the hotel cat wearing an expensive new collar. The band was a gift from Giants secretary Fred Knowles from the team's previous trip to the city. On that occasion, Knowles left the hotel one evening and discovered he had lost a pocket-book containing three thousand dollars in money and checks. Frantic, he telephoned back to the hotel, and two bellboys searched the lobby to no avail. But one of the boys remembered having seen Mabel, the hotel cat, playing with something earlier that afternoon. They checked the cat's home under the back stairs, and sure enough, there was the missing pocketbook with the checks and money scattered about. Knowles was so grateful he rewarded Mabel with the expensive collar.

But Davis was nowhere to be found, and the deputy was forced to leave without serving the papers. The hiding place of the shortstop was becoming the subject of considerable debate in baseball circles. It was thought that perhaps McGraw had outsmarted the American Leaguers by hiding Davis in Indiana until he could be slipped into Chicago on Sunday, when legal papers could not be served on him. Or McGraw might have sent his shortstop on to St. Louis, the next stop on the Giants' trip, to avoid the process servers in Illinois.

Or perhaps the real explanation for the absence of Davis could be found in McGraw's declaration to newsmen that the shortstop was not in the proper condition to play ball. McGraw even confided to some of his friends that he regretted starting the trouble over Davis in the first place. "Charlie Babb is playing better than Davis," admitted the Giants manager.

Another prominent ballplayer also was conspicuous by his absence that day. In Washington, the train carrying the Senators finally arrived in town in the early hours of the morning, and the weary ballplayers got off to discover their bats and other equipment had not made it home with them. Nor had Ed Delahanty, whose wife, Norine, was at the station to meet him as he had instructed. She was not concerned at first, but then some of the players told her of Ed's behavior on the trip and she began to worry that something was wrong.

That morning, fourteen hundred newsboys, orphans, and other disadvantaged youngsters were admitted to the Washington baseball grounds for the first part of the Fourth of July doubleheader. They drank large glasses of lemonade poured from huge vats set up behind the stands and ate free peanuts and popcorn. When a policeman went onto the field to escort Cleveland's Larry Lajoie from the game for attempting to throw the ball at umpire Bob Caruthers during an argument, the orphans taunted "King Napoleon" and showered him with peanut shells.

It was a terribly muggy and oppressive day, and in the early innings Umpire Caruthers himself passed out from the heat and had to be taken to the clubhouse. Harry Mace, a former Washington pitcher, came down out of the stands to call the remainder of the game, which was won by the Senators, 10–3.

A thunderstorm hit the city that afternoon, washing out the second game of the doubleheader.

The whereabouts of Ed Delahanty remained a mystery.

Norine dispatched telegrams to Philadelphia and Cleveland seeking information on her husband, but in both cities their friends knew nothing. Washington manager Tom Loftus also sent out telegrams to various locations, all to no avail. In Buffalo, J. E. Croke, an uncle of the famous ballplayer, received a wire which read: "Let me know at once if Ed is in Buffalo. Mrs. James Delahanty." But the uncle had no knowledge of where Del might be.

At first, the newspapers made light of the ballplayer's disappearance.

John Luitich of Washington wrote in the *Sporting News*, "After a count of noses was taken that one that is attached to the King of Swatville was conspicuous by its absence."

The *Detroit News* guessed that Delahanty had gone to New York, and noted sarcastically, "Probably Del is still so full of booze that he forgets the war is over."

But the longer Delahanty remained unaccounted for, the greater the concern for his safety. "Where Is Del?" asked a headline in a Washington newspaper. "Baseball Player's Disappearance Still a Mystery," stated another.

It was speculated that perhaps Del had jumped to New York or to the outlaw team his brother played for in Denver, but there was no sign of him in either city. The chief of police in Washington, D.C., asked a law officer in Mount Clemens, Michigan, to investigate the possibility Delahanty was at the steam baths there. A two-day search of the town turned up nothing.

All the while, Norine remained at the Oxford House in Washington, waiting for word of her husband. Many of the Washington players went to visit her there. They all agreed Ed should never have been left alone when they last saw him.

• • •

For three days, a black handbag and a suitcase remained unclaimed at the Pullman Car Company in Buffalo. It was not until Monday morning that John K. Bennett, district superintendent of the company, began to wonder if perhaps the baggage belonged to the mysterious stranger who had disappeared from the International Bridge.

He opened the suitcase, curious to discover what he might find inside. There were several minor articles, as well as a suit of clothes. He looked at the label on the inside of the coat and saw the name of a tailor in Washington, D.C.

In the handbag, Bennett found a pair of lace-up, high-top baseball shoes, made by the Waldo Claflin company in Philadelphia. He dug around some more and pulled out a season-pass booklet for the Washington Senators. He inspected it more closely and noticed it was numbered 26.

Bennett looked at the pass book some more, certain that it held the key to the identity of the stranger on the bridge.

• • •

There was no escape from the wrath of Ban Johnson. At noon Tuesday, Cleveland manager Bill Armour received a telegram from the American League president informing him that second baseman Larry Lajoie was suspended indefinitely for his conduct toward umpire Bob Caruthers three days earlier. Lajoie was outraged at such treatment. He insisted that Caruthers had a widespread reputation as a poor umpire and once had gone so far as to eject Philadelphia's Topsy Hartsel from a game because the player dunned him for some money he had lent him several years earlier. King Napoleon angrily threatened to write Johnson a letter about his "incompetent staff of umpires" that would "burn his eyes when he read it." Perhaps he would do so from Atlantic City, where he was headed to wait out his suspension.

But such a letter would not be necessary on Caruthers's account. He failed to show up at the Washington ballpark on Monday and again on Tuesday. In his place, catcher Lew Drill of the Senators called balls and strikes and pitcher Bill

Bernhard of the Naps umpired the bases during a 5–2 victory by the Senators on Tuesday. Caruthers was found still laid up in his room following his collapse from the heat. As soon as he was well again, he was fired by Ban Johnson.

That same Tuesday, another telegram was delivered to Washington manager Tom Loftus, alerting him that while in Detroit, Ed Delahanty had bought a railway ticket from that city to New York.

A few hours later, Loftus received a dispatch addressed to the president of the Washington ball club. He opened it and saw that it was from a John K. Bennett, manager of the Pullman Car Company for the Buffalo district. The letter recounted the removal of the passenger from a Michigan train and the man's apparent death on the International Bridge.

"A dress suitcase and black leather bag were found on our train afterward," continued the letter, "and are supposed to belong to this gentleman, and I find in the suit case a complimentary pass, No. 26, of your club."

Loftus knew immediately what this must mean, but he wanted to be certain before he revealed the information. He went out in search of team secretary Walter Hewitt, and the two men finally returned to the Oxford at midnight. They went to Hewitt's room, where the secretary took out his memorandum book. His hands were shaking as he turned to the section regarding complimentary pass tickets and found what he was looking for. Next to the entry for pass No. 26 was written the name Edward J. Delahanty.

• • •

The water poured over Niagara Falls at the rate of 204,000 cubic feet per second, creating a mighty roar as it crashed into the river below in great clouds of mist. This was the voice of Oniagrarah, "the Great Spirit of the Falls." Or so believed the Seneca Indians, the original inhabitants of the region.

In earlier days, the Senecas regularly gave parts of their

crops and food from hunting as offerings to Oniagrarah, and each spring they would select the fairest maiden of the tribe to be offered as a human sacrifice to the Great Spirit. According to the legend, one year it was Lelawala, the beautiful daughter of Chief Eagle Eye, who was chosen for this ritual. While the chief watched with sadness, she was placed in the traditional white canoe laden with flowers and fruits, and the tiny craft was set adrift toward the falls. Just as Lelawala was swept into the rushing current, she glanced back at her father one last time. Overcome with grief, Chief Eagle Eye jumped into his own canoe and set out after her. Moments later, both were swept over the falls.

From that day, it has been said that in the spray that rises from the Great Falls the form of the fair Indian maid can be seen. She is known as "the Maid of the Mist."

This also was the name given to a steam-powered craft which in 1846 became the first to successfully negotiate the gulf below the falls. There followed another *Maid of the Mist*, and by the turn of the century this second vessel was taking thousands of tourists into the churning water for a close-up look at the spectacular waterfall.

The landing for the boat was on the Canadian side of the river, just down from the falls. It was there that William LeBlond, who lived in the nearby town of Drummondville, happened to be working on the morning of Thursday, July 9, when he spotted a body floating in an eddy near the landing. With some help, LeBlond was able to tow the body to the shore, where he fastened it with a cord and hurried off to summon the authorities.

Mr. Morse, the undertaker, was the first to arrive, and he took the corpse to his establishment in Drummondville.

By now, it was known that the man who fell from the International Bridge probably was the great baseball player Ed Delahanty, so the discovery of the body created considerable excitement in the community. A reporter from the *Cataract*

Journal in Niagara Falls, New York, hurried to the undertaker's office to see if it was in fact Delahanty who had been pulled out of the river.

The man was greeted by a gruesome sight. The body was badly decomposed, and the face was almost black while the trunk and legs also were severely discolored.The stomach had been torn open and the entrails bulged out. The left leg was almost severed near the thigh.

The only clothing still on the dead man was a slate-colored necktie with a white dot around the neck, a pair of black open work socks with a trademark red dot, and a pair of lace-up shoes. The socks were held up by a pair of garters.

It was believed the rest of the clothing had been torn off by the force of the water, and that the leg had been mangled by the propeller of the *Maid of the Mist*. The advanced state of decomposition, said the undertaker, probably was due to the man's state of intoxication when he fell into the water.

There was one other noticeable feature about the body which caught the reporter's attention. The fingers were bent and twisted with abnormally large joints, and the little finger on the left hand was especially crooked.

The reporter looked at Undertaker Morse and commented, "Ballplayer fingers."

• • •

M. A. Green, a stockholder in the Washington ball club and a friend of Delahanty, arrived at Morse & Son Undertakers that afternoon. Green had been in Buffalo when Del first disappeared, and he had remained there to assist in the search for the missing ballplayer. A *Washington Post* correspondent alerted him that a body had been discovered below the falls, and the two men quickly set out for Drummondville on an old farm wagon. The ride had been long and hot, and there was sweat on Green's face as he viewed the body.

Green recognized the necktie and the socks as those belonging to Del. He saw the gold-crowned tooth which he often had noticed when in the company of the ballplayer, and he could see the disfigured fingers which Ed had showed him many times. The facial features were unrecognizable, but Green had no doubt as to the identity of the man.

There were tears in his eyes as he turned away from the body and declared it was that of Ed Delahanty.

• • •

That same Thursday afternoon, the Giants were in St. Louis, where there still was no sign of the controversial George Davis. In his absence, Charlie Babb continued to play shortstop, and John McGraw even made a rare appearance as a pinch batter for Christy Mathewson. He singled and scored during a fierce ninth-inning rally which netted the Giants three runs and a dramatic 4–2 victory over the Cardinals.

At a hotel dining room in New York, Kid Elberfeld got into a heated dispute with a waiter, whose name was Albert Becker. Elberfeld called Becker "a thief," so the waiter refused to serve him. The Kid retaliated by picking up a bottle and using it to club the man over the head. This resulted in the arrest of Elberfeld, who was taken to the police station and fined three dollars and costs. He was released in time to play in that day's game.

In Washington, the ballplayers were about to leave for the ballpark when word came of the discovery of Delahanty's body. Jimmy Ryan and Smiling Al Orth were especially distraught when they heard the news, as was catcher Deacon McGuire of the Tigers.

Del's teammates suspected that in his confused state Ed inadvertently had boarded the wrong train. Possibly, his train had stopped in Buffalo and he got off to get some food or drink. In his rush to get back on, he could have boarded a westbound train and been put off on the other side of the bridge once the conductor noted his mistake. When he tried to cross the bridge on foot, the guard might have suspected he was a smuggler, resulting in a scuffle that led to Del's fall into the river. At least, that was the theory advanced by many of the players.

The flags on the ball club's office building and grandstand were lowered to half-mast in memory of Delahanty, and the Washington players tied strips of black crepe to their left arms. As a final tribute, the Senators knocked out an astounding twenty-four hits, including three home runs, two triples, and a double, to beat the Tigers by the score of 17–4. It was the kind of game Big Ed would have enjoyed.

• • •

There were other visitors to view the body at Morse & Son Undertakers that day. One was a young man who had dark hair and many of the same features as Ed Delahanty, although at five feet nine inches and 160 pounds, he was smaller in stature than the famous ballplayer. His name was Frank "Pudgie" Delahanty, and he was the fifth of the famous Delahanty brothers in professional baseball. Only twenty years old, he played the outfield for Syracuse of the New York State League. Two days earlier, he had left his ball club to join in the search for his brother. He was the first member of the family to find him.

Pudgie recognized Ed immediately, but wishing to leave no possibility of doubt he inspected the body closely for several minutes. In doing so, he found several private marks which verified the identification.

He also made some other observations which left him suspicious about the events surrounding his brother's death. The necktie still was in place around Ed's neck, tied in the four-in-hand fashion, but the diamond tie pin which Del was known to have been wearing was missing. The authorities said it, along with Ed's other valuables, probably had been torn off by the force of the water when the body went over the falls.

But Ed also wore two rings which were not on him when he had been found. Neither Frank Delahanty nor anyone else in the family ever would believe it was possible for those rings to have been swept off in the river.

E. J. McGuire of Cleveland, a brother-in-law, and J. E. Croke of Buffalo, an uncle, were with Frank. They also had their doubts about exactly what had happened the night Ed Delahanty was put off the train.

The three men were joined by M. A. Green, and they went to the International Bridge to retrace Ed's steps. What they saw made them even more dubious. In Sam Kingston's original report to the police, he said the man he confronted on the bridge was unarmed. After speaking to the bridge foreman, Kingston changed his story and claimed the man appeared to have some sort of weapon in his hand. Finally, this weapon came to be described in the newspapers as "a big lump of coal in his hand." Yet, neither Green, McGuire, nor Frank Delahanty could find any trace of coal in the vicinity of the bridge.

Frank Delahanty also was troubled by another discrepancy in the guard's statements. At first, Kingston claimed the man ran toward the American side of the bridge and fell off the open draw. After the police discovered the draw on the sixth span was guarded by automatic gates, the guard's story was modified to have the man fall or jump from the fourth span, where he would have gone off the side of the bridge.

The younger Delahanty was even more skeptical of the bridge guard after confronting him on the pretense of regaining his brother's hat, which no longer was in Kingston's possession. To the surprise of Frank Delahanty and his two companions, they found a man who in Green's estimation was "fully seventy years of age."

Afterward, Green put into words what they all were thinking. "It seems almost incredible that one so old should have gotten the best end of a scuffle on the bridge."

• • •

The activities of the train conductor, John Cole, also came under scrutiny. He recounted to the police the actions of Ed Delahanty on the train ride across Ontario which resulted in his ejection at Bridgeburg. Cole repeated his contention that the man, whom he later learned to be the famous ballplayer, did not appear drunk, rather he "seemed despondent and anxious to make mischief."

The conductor also claimed that in addition to pulling women out of their sleeping berths, the man was threatening passengers with a straight razor. Delahanty's family insisted Ed did not own such a razor and instead used a safety razor.

As to the diamonds and other jewelry which the Delahanty family claimed were missing, Cole stated there had been no such valuables in sight during the train ride. He believed that if Ed Delahanty had been robbed of the diamonds, the theft must have taken place in Detroit.

Meanwhile, Conductor Cole continued to make his daily runs aboard the Michigan Central train on its trips from New York to Detroit and back.

It was while on a westward run to Detroit that he was approached by two men during a short stop in Buffalo. They introduced themselves as E. J. McGuire and Frank Delahanty, and asked if they might talk to him about Ed Delahanty. When Cole nodded his agreement, the younger man, who identified himself as the ballplayer's brother, spoke up.

"It occurs to me," said Frank, his voice rising in anger, "that inasmuch as you took care of my brother from Detroit, you could have brought him across that bridge. If you had done that, Ed would probably be alive today."

Although taken aback by the accusation, Cole stood his ground.

"Perhaps if I had known that Ed Delahanty was going to jump from that bridge, I would have made more of an effort to have brought him across the bridge. But I didn't suspect he was up to anything like that.

"God knows I tried to take care of that man. I watched him all the way from Detroit, and with that train filled with passengers I did all I could to keep him quiet. But when he pulled the razor on the Pullman car conductor and dragged people from their berths, I had to put him off."

The conductor looked at the younger Delahanty, and it was easy to see the resemblance to the man who had caused such a commotion on that now memorable train ride one week earlier.

"Suppose it was your mother or your sister that was in one of those berths," said Cole, "and some man came along and pulled them out. What would you have me do in a case like that?"

Neither Frank Delahanty nor McGuire had an answer for him.

• • •

Undertaker Morse worked all that Thursday night and into Friday morning to have the body of Ed Delahanty ready to be shipped to his home in Cleveland. At six o'clock in the morning of Friday, July 10, the "King of Batters" was placed aboard a Michigan Central train which would take him from Niagara Falls to Buffalo, where he would be transferred to the Lake Shore line for the final leg of his journey.

In Buffalo, Frank Delahanty watched as the casket was removed from the Michigan Central car. He did not try to hide his anger at the railroad over its role in his brother's death.

"I have some suspicion about how Ed went off that bridge," he told newsmen. "The poor fellow is dead now, and he can never tell his side of the story, but the others can tell just what they please.

"You can say this much for me—that the railroad is responsible for Ed's death. They had no business putting him off where they did.

"Even if he killed a man they should have brought him to Buffalo and turned him over to the police. If he was drunk and disorderly aboard that train, they should have taken care of him. He drank and paid for the whisky they sold him, and it was their whisky he got drunk on. Then why didn't they carry him here?"

Across the river in Canada, Police Chief Griffin promised "a rigid investigation" into the death of the ballplayer. In this endeavor, he had no shortage of theories to explain what happened that night on the International Bridge.

There were many people who believed Delahanty committed suicide, as bridge guard Sam Kingston continued to insist whenever he gave his version of events. "He must have climbed over the girders, then onto the pier and jumped off," Kingston said repeatedly.

Or perhaps Ed Delahanty, confused and drunk, simply fell from the bridge in the dark while trying to evade the guard.

Another, more ominous, rumor was contained in a story published in the *Cataract Journal*, a Niagara Falls, New York, newspaper: "Railroad officials say that he jumped from the bridge but there is another surmise that he was held up by the bridge tender, then an altercation and struggle ensued between the two men and that Delahanty either fell off or was shoved off the bridge."

Back in Drummondville, Undertaker Morse returned to his establishment and resumed his chores. James LeBlond, the man who first discovered Delahanty's body below Niagara Falls, continued to perform his duties at the *Maid of the Mist* landing as he had done before the excitement of the past week. That was where the riverman was on Saturday morning when to his surprise he spotted another corpse floating in the eddy.

Just as he had done the week before, LeBlond pulled the body to shore and summoned the authorities. This time, the dead man turned out to be John C. Cherry, a sixty-two-year-old farmer who lived between Black Rock and Tonawanda on the American side of the river. He had last been seen the previous Tuesday, when he set out from his home to walk to Buffalo. He had about fifteen hundred dollars with him when he left, but that money was nowhere to be found.

The best the authorities could figure, the man had been beaten and robbed, and his body thrown into the river. This would have happened near the International Bridge, not far from the spot where Ed Delahanty had met his death just five days earlier.

• • •

In St. Louis, the New York ballplayers sported eighteen-dollar Panama hats bought for them by John Brush. It was a reward for their good play, and the Giants president even went so far as to promise his men new suits if they returned from their western trip still in second place. The ballplayers could not wait to get home to New York.

It was another hot afternoon at the ballpark Friday, and the members of the two teams expended much of their energy yelling and cursing at each other and exchanging angry threats.

The Cardinals thought they had the game won in the ninth inning, but another last-ditch rally by John McGraw's team resulted in a run which tied the score at 3–3 and forced an extra inning. In the bottom of the tenth, St. Louis put two runners on base when yet another argument broke out. There was more shouting and gesturing when suddenly St. Louis pitcher Mike O'Neill, a rugged Irishman who had been born in the old country, ran onto the field and punched New York shortstop Charlie Babb in the jaw. The force of the blow knocked Babb backward, and he staggered all the way to the bench as if he were about to collapse. Instead, he grabbed a bat and sprinted back onto the diamond to chase after O'Neill. This brought members from both teams as well as fans and several policemen swarming onto the field. In the confusion, the big St. Louis first baseman "Sunny Jim" Hackett was able to wrestle Babb to the ground and get the bat from him before any harm was done.

When play was resumed, Hackett hit his fifth single of the game to score the winning run, and it was with great difficulty that the police were able to escort the Giants through the angry mob to the safety of a waiting bus. The mood still was tense when the bus pulled away and began its journey downtown to the Southern Hotel.

After a few blocks, the driver of the bus, a man named Octa Scully, believed the danger was over and slowed the pace of the horses pulling the vehicle. Scully, who had transported ball clubs to and from the playing grounds for five years without incident, was more concerned with the effect of the heat on his animals than he was with any danger from unruly baseball fans.

About halfway to the hotel, he came to a fountain, and there he stopped to let his horses drink. When he did, the players shouted at him and told him to keep moving. Scully ignored their protests, which only made the ballplayers angrier. He thought nothing of it until he felt himself being grabbed by the throat and thrown roughly to the floor of the bus. A fist smashed into his face, then he felt himself being kicked repeatedly. One of the players, later identified as Frank Bowerman, grabbed the reins and began driving back to the hotel. Scully, who was held down and cursed by several players, including John McGraw, could do nothing about it.

Shortly afterward, the New York ballplayers, dirty and sweaty, paraded off the bus and swaggered into the hotel to prepare for their departure from town. Scully, bruised and scratched, scrambled to safety and flagged down a nearby policeman to report the attack.

McGraw and some of his companions still were in the hotel lobby when the cop confronted them. Muggsy sneered at the driver's accusations and swore that the man was drunk.

Without any evidence, the policeman could take no action. And by the time Scully was able to go to the police station and press charges, the Giants already were out of town, on a train headed east.

• • •

Kid Elberfeld's legal problems were not over. On Friday, a sheriff served him with an injunction from the Supreme Court of New York, preventing him from playing for the New York Americans. He also was ordered to show cause why he should not be bound to the contract which he had signed with the New York Nationals. The Kid stormed around the hotel cursing, but he should have seen the trap being laid for him.

A few days earlier, he had received a telegram from John Brush ordering him to report to Giants manager John McGraw in St. Louis. Elberfeld ignored the letter. Brush used it as evidence when he went to court to argue that he was being deprived of the services of a player under contract to him.

It was Brush's retaliation for the injunction against George Davis. It was also part of his plan to force a legal fight with the American League.

What was lost in all the uproar over Elberfeld's status was the effect Brush's actions had on yet a third player involved in the dispute between the two leagues.

It was believed Brush also sent a telegram to Ed Delahanty in Detroit ordering him to report to the Giants. Several members of the Washington team, including Kip Selbach and Jimmy Ryan, speculated that was why Delahanty jumped the team in Detroit and embarked on his fatal train ride. The letter to Elberfeld indicated a similar message also would have been mailed or wired to Delahanty. This led the Washington players to place the blame for Del's death on John Brush and John McGraw. As Delahanty's teammates pointed out, Ed was not headed to Washington when he died. His ticket was for New York.

• • •

There were many who shared this view. It was reported in *Sporting Life*, "the American League players as a mass sincerely mourn Delahanty's unfortunate death, and attribute it to the management of the New York National League Club."

Fred Postal, owner of the Senators, was more blunt in his assessment. "John T. Brush, president of the New York National League baseball team, is responsible for the death of Edward Delahanty," stated Postal.

In turn, John McGraw placed the blame on Ban Johnson for his treatment of Delahanty at the peace conference and afterward.

The New York correspondent for the *Sporting News* maintained there was plenty of guilt to go around.

"While not wholly to blame for Delahanty's death," he wrote, "I think the Cincinnati Peace Committee was indirectly responsible for it. Its alleged ideas of the restoration of peace are certainly crude to say the least. . . .

"There were several men on that committee who had it in good and hard for the New York Club, and they dealt out their impartial justice with as lavish a hand as they were capable of administering."

Another of Del's friends, Frank Patterson of Baltimore, said it was the gambling mania which led to Delahanty's tragic end.

"I always believed Delahanty would never have been tempted to sign with McGraw last spring," wrote Patterson, "if he had not been 'broke' at the Bennings meeting and crazy to keep up the game that eventually led to his ruin and death. It ought to be a warning to ball players, but it won't."

• • •

Ed Delahanty was laid to rest on Saturday morning, July 11. Monsignor Thorpe led the services at the Church of the

Immaculate Conception. He spoke of Ed's "past life, his admirable disposition, and his unstained character."

The other Delahanty brothers listened solemnly. Jim had his arm in a sling as the result of a shoulder injury suffered while playing for Memphis of the Southern League. He already had been headed north to Cleveland to recuperate when he got word of his brother's death. Joe had come from Little Rock, where he was batting almost .400 in the Southern League. Frank had come from Syracuse of the New York State League, and Tom from Denver of the Western League. Norine sat quietly with her young daughter, Florence.

Magnificent floral arrangements completely covered the casket, which remained closed. There was a bat made of red and white roses, sent by the firemen at the engine house where Ed first gained renown as a ballplayer. There was a basket design of roses and carnations from Sheriff Barry, another of Ed's many friends. A wreath of lilies mixed with white carnations and roses had been provided by the Cleveland baseball team. Ed's former teammates on the Phillies sent a floral tribute, as did the New York team of the American League and Tom Delahanty's Denver ball club.

In the audience were many of Del's baseball acquaintances, including one from almost every one of the sixteen major-league teams.

A member of the choir began to sing "Lead, Kindly Light," and the eight pallbearers slowly carried the casket from the church for burial in Calvary Cemetery. One was a short, stocky man, and even with the great weight he helped bear there was a noticeable cockiness in the way he walked. Of all the famous guests at the funeral, he was the most prominent. John McGraw had come to help bury his friend.

VII
AFTERMATH

At the close of last season there was a benefit
game at which gold scarf pins and silk para-
sols were distributed; this year verbal punches
were parceled out. How the mighty have
fallen!

John Luitich

There was no pause in the baseball season in the days following the funeral. In Philadelphia, Rube Waddell left the
pitcher's mound in the middle of the ball game and jumped
into the stands, where he smashed the nose of a heckler before
turning him over to the police. The crowd cheered as the cops
dragged the man, a well-known ticket speculator, across the
field, his nose bleeding and his clothes torn, and tossed him
into a waiting patrol wagon.

The New York Giants arrived in Pittsburgh, where so many
toughs showed up to curse and threaten Frank Bowerman for
his role in the assault on Fred Clarke that the big catcher left
the field and refused to return. John McGraw found him hiding in the clubhouse, too frightened to play.

From Washington, letters were sent to all American and
National League clubs requesting money for a relief fund for
Ed Delahanty's widow. She was said to be in destitute circumstances. The cash and jewelry Ed had with him had disappeared. None of the twenty-four-hour insurance policies he
had purchased on the road trip were in effect at the time of
his death. Ed was a member of Erie Lodge No. 42, Fraternal
Order of Eagles, in Philadelphia, but he had not kept up his
dues so his widow would receive no benefits from that organization. The Washington ball club refused to stage a benefit
game to raise funds for Mrs. Delahanty, claiming it already
had spent fifty-three hundred dollars in lost wages and legal
fees on Big Ed. It would be up to the ballplayers to come to
the aid of their fallen comrade.

"When anyone raised a flag of distress, Delahanty was the
first to contribute," said Del's friend, Jimmy Ryan, "and we
propose to do all in our power to help his widow and
orphan."

The horses that Delahanty loved so much continued to run
at the various racetracks around the country. At the Brighton
Beach track in New York, the bookies gathered in the betting

ring between races and exchanged their wagering slips with the bettors. George Davis, the elusive shortstop, was standing in this crowd on the afternoon of Wednesday, July 15, when he felt someone tap him on the shoulder. Davis turned to see who it was, and a man stuck a document on his arm and walked off. The paper fell to the ground, so Davis reached down and picked it up. He began to read it and realized too late its significance.

It was an injunction from the U.S. Circuit Court preventing him from playing with any club except the Chicago Americans. The previous injunction, which Davis had managed to avoid by staying out of Chicago, was valid only in Illinois. This one came from a federal court and applied to every team in baseball.

Davis stared dejectedly at the document. There would be no more ballplaying for him this season. He bowed out with just four games and four hits to his credits. It wasn't much for all the trouble of recent months.

• • •

The same day the injunction was served on George Davis, there was a hearing before the Supreme Court of New York on the suit by the New York Nationals against Norman "Kid" Elberfeld. Delancy Nicoll, attorney for the New York National League team, argued that the transfer of the player to the New York Americans was a violation of the Cincinnati peace agreement. Charles Greenhall, the counsel for Elberfeld, countered with the claim there was no provision in the peace compact which prevented such a transaction. Justice Greenbaum interrupted to ask if either side had a copy of this document. Incredibly, no one had thought to bring one.

The justice responded by calling an adjournment in the proceedings and lifting the prohibition against Elberfeld playing until another hearing could be held.

Faced with legal setbacks in the Davis and Elberfeld cases,

the National League owners met in New York on Monday, July 20, to plan their next move.

Just over two weeks earlier, on the day Ed Delahanty's body had gone over Niagara Falls, these same owners had reached a secret agreement to reopen the baseball war for a fight to the finish. Only Garry Herrmann of Cincinnati, James Hart of Chicago, and Frank de Haas Robison of St. Louis had been absent that day.

The mood was different this time. After events of recent days, the owners were in a conciliatory mood. The American League had dealt them a pair of legal setbacks in the George Davis and Norman Elberfeld cases. Worse, the prospect of another war between the two leagues had breathed new life into the Players' Association, which announced plans to meet later in the month. Already, there was talk among the players of asking for more money for the next season.

One by one, the National League owners expressed their weariness with the fighting between the two leagues. Those who had feared John Brush and had been afraid to stand up to the Giants owner no longer supported his claims on the disputed players. They came to see the wisdom of Garry Herrmann and James Hart, who insisted that at the peace conference there had been no written or implied understanding that players must remain with the clubs to which they were assigned.

Finally, the owners proclaimed that Elberfeld's transfer to the New York Americans was not a breach of the peace agreement. They also instructed Brush not to play George Davis. There would be no baseball war.

Having accomplished their business, the magnates went to the Brooklyn ballpark to watch that day's ball game. It was a jovial gathering, and even the usually dour Brush was in good spirits. It wasn't that the Giants owner suddenly had become a gracious loser. To the contrary, reported those close to him, Brush had been convinced by his manager that George Davis was not in the proper condition to help the ball club. It was reported in the *Sporting News* that Brush was "being let out of a bad contract by the cooperation of the league, which is working in his favor without its knowledge."

Even when he lost, it seemed that John Brush came out ahead.

• • •

The settlement of the baseball hostilities came too late for Fred Postal. He had a falling out with his manager, Tom Loftus, who was angry Postal would not spend any more money to purchase new ballplayers. Loftus attempted to get his way on the matter by aligning himself with the other minority stockholders, who also had become disenchanted with Postal's absentee ownership. Word of the revolt reached Postal at his office in Detroit, and in disgust he determined to withdraw completely.

He arrived in Washington in early August and took his usual suite at the Oxford Hotel. There he was met by Ban Johnson and Charles Jacobsen, a minority stockholder in the club. Jacobsen informed Postal he headed a group of four investors who were willing to take over the franchise. His group was willing to buy out Postal's 52 percent interest but it did not want to assume the club's twelve thousand dollars in debts. When it looked as if the negotiations had reached an impasse, Johnson announced he would pay Postal fifteen thousand dollars for his stock and assume all the debts. On the night of August 3, the transaction was completed and the Washington ball club came under direct control of the league itself.

Shortly afterward, Postal learned the full cost he must pay for his sellout. At the "suggestion" of Ban Johnson, the American League teams stopped patronizing Postal's hotels in Detroit. Instead, they chose to stay across town at the Russell House, despite its inferior accommodations.

. . .

On the playing field, John McGraw's Giants lost eleven of thirteen games in July and fell to third place in the National League, behind both the Pirates and the Cubs. In the American League, the ageless Cy Young won eight games in succession and Jimmy Collins's Puritans took over first place from Connie Mack's Athletics by beating the defending champions two out of three games on their home grounds.

It was at this time that the eccentric Rube Waddell walked out on both his wife and his ball club and took up residence in a Front Street saloon in Philadelphia. The Rube was unhappy because he already had overdrawn his salary and the ball club would give him no more money.

After a week, Waddell made his way to nearby Camden, New Jersey, where he got a job tending bar. The Rube also could be found at the local ballpark, where on Saturday, August 8, he pitched for the hometown Camden team. He walked off the field in triumph to be greeted by a couple of men who asked if he was indeed George Edward "Rube" Waddell. When the Rube answered yes, the men informed him they had come to take him back to Philadelphia on charges of bail-jumping.

Waddell spent that Saturday night locked in a Philadelphia jail, faced with prosecution for nonsupport of his wife and for assault and battery against the ticket speculator he had attacked at the ballpark.

By the next day, the Rube had lost much of his bluster. He found someone to post bail for him, and he begged the ball club for a second chance. As soon as he got word Mack was willing to let him back on the team, Waddell caught the first train to Boston, where the Athletics were in desperate need of help in a series against the Puritans.

The joy over Waddell's return was tempered by other events in Philadelphia. While the Rube was being hauled back to town by the bail bondsmen that Saturday, about ten thousand fans were inside Philadelphia's National League Park watching the second game of a doubleheader between the Phillies and Boston's Beaneaters. At fifteen minutes past five o'clock, two drunks staggered down Fifteenth Street just outside the stadium and a gang of neighborhood kids tailed behind taunting and jeering them. Without warning, one of the drunken men wheeled about and hit a little girl, knocking her to the ground.

Joe Stanley had just stepped to the plate for Boston, but the spectators in the gallery overhanging the sidewalk were more interested in the altercation on the street below. There were angry shouts of protest when they saw the drunk strike the girl, and the commotion caused other fans to leave their seats and rush to the top of the stands to see what was happening. In a matter of seconds, there were at least five hundred men and boys crowded against the railing.

Too late, they heard the sharp crack and the awful sound of wood splintering, and they could feel the stands start to give way beneath them. They screamed out in horror as the overhang broke off completely and they plunged helplessly to the street below.

There was a huge crashing sound as the 150-foot section landed in the street, and the unfortunate victims tumbled on top of each other in a writhing mass of humanity. Many were pinned beneath parts of the stands, and there were broken arms and legs and fractured skulls everywhere. The blood ran down the street in streams.

Inside the ballpark, the cries for help from outside were drowned out by the shouts of panic as the remaining spectators, fearing the entire structure was about to collapse, scrambled frantically toward the playing field. In their mad rush for safety, the fans shoved and cursed, knocked down those in their way, and fought with one another. On the playing field, the ballplayers armed themselves with bats to keep from being overrun by this wild stampede.

Word of the disaster was relayed to every police station in the city, and all available patrol wagons and ambulances were summoned to transport the injured to hospitals. The first victims were hauled off on a furniture truck that happened to pass by.

It came to be known as "Black Saturday," the darkest day in Philadelphia baseball history. Twelve people died, and 232 were injured. An inspection of the stands revealed that the supporting beams were rotten, and this was responsible for the disaster. A coroner's jury placed the blame on the ball club's former owners, Colonel John Rogers and Albert Reach. They had neglected to have the structure examined in the eight years from its construction to the ball club's sale to new owners. The Philadelphia ballpark, once the pride of Colonel Rogers, had turned into a deathtrap.

The Colonel was devastated by the news. His friends said that after hearing of the tragedy, he was unable to eat or sleep for several days.

• • •

There were other brushes with disaster that season. On the night of August 28, the Cleveland and St. Louis teams of the American League were en route to St. Louis on the Wabash Railroad when the train derailed at a crossing and plowed into a ditch. The sleeper car turned over, and the players on the top side were tossed onto those who were in the berths on the opposite side.

Charles Somers, the team owner, was in the rear car talking to manager Jimmy McAleer at the time of the accident. Their car did not overturn, and though they were badly shaken they were able to escape unharmed. Somers stepped outside to survey the damage. It was dark, and he began walking toward the overturned sleeper, which was shrouded by steam. At first, Somers could neither see nor hear any signs of life, and he feared the worst. Then he heard a noise, and he saw a figure emerge from the wreckage, followed by others. The ballplayers had been asleep at the time of the accident, and it had taken them a few minutes to realize what had happened. No one panicked, and the players calmly began checking on each other and taking a head count. Miraculously, no one was seriously hurt. Among the Cleveland players, the only injury of significance was a cut face and sprained knee suffered by Larry Lajoie.

King Napoleon recovered from this mishap to finish the season with a .355 batting average, good enough to regain the American League crown won by Ed Delahanty the year before. By coincidence, at the time of Del's death, he and his former roommate Lajoie had sported identical .333 averages. Delahanty was dead now, but Lajoie was just approaching his greatest glory. He would win another batting title in 1904, and become manager of the Cleveland team the following season. By the time he finally retired in 1916, he would be acclaimed as the greatest second baseman ever to play the game.

But there was more to Lajoie's greatness than the three batting titles and the 3,244 base hits he amassed. In October 1903, the Big Frenchman emerged from the Neil House in Columbus, Ohio, where the Naps and Cincinnati Reds were playing in a postseason series. Already Lajoie had paid the tuition as well as room, board, and a clothing allowance to send the young orphan Petie Powers to St. Joseph's Academy in Nottingham, Pennsylvania. But on this day, the ballplayer's attention was drawn to a beggar stationed on the curb outside the hotel.

Lajoie went back inside the hotel, where many of his teammates were gathered in the lobby, and a few minutes later he returned to the curb where the beggar sat. The man was blind, and he did not recognize the famous ballplayer who stood before him and tossed a penny in his cup.

"How much was that?" asked Lajoie.

The beggar felt the coin and smiled gratefully. "A penny."

Then came another coin, followed by another and then another. Soon, the cup was filled with nickels, dimes, quarters, and even fifty-cent pieces. The beggar was so overcome with joy he could not speak, but the smile on his face expressed his gratitude. He had just received every bit of loose change from the Cleveland ballplayers, all of it collected by Napoleon Lajoie.

• • •

That same Tuesday, October 6, a crowd of cheering spectators swarmed out of the stands at Exposition Park in Pittsburgh, hoisted Pirates pitcher Deacon Phillippe onto the shoulders of some husky men, and paraded him around the playing field in triumph. Moments earlier, the Deacon, a six-foot-tall right-hander for Fred Clarke's Pirates, had retired Jack O'Brien of the Boston Puritan on a pop-up to second base to complete his third victory of what was billed as the "world's series."

The postseason playoff was the result of a simple agreement worked out between owners Barney Dreyfuss of Pittsburgh and Henry J. Killilea of Boston. Despite the lingering bitterness between the leagues resulting from the George Davis and Kid Elberfeld disputes, the fans and writers were eager for a championship match between the two pennant winners. By late August, when it was apparent Pittsburgh again would prevail in the National League and Boston would beat out Philadelphia in the American, Dreyfuss boldly agreed to such a showdown. He and Killilea established a best-of-nine format with the receipts to be split evenly, and they sealed the deal with a handshake.

Phillippe beat the great Cy Young, 7–3, in the historic first game in Boston. Two days later, the Deacon beat the Puritans again, and following a Sunday off and a rainout, he posted his third victory to give the Pirates a three-games-to-one advantage and set off the wild celebration in Pittsburgh. Phillippe's triumphant ride on the shoulders of the crowd ended at the clubhouse, where he sat in his uniform for half an hour shaking the hand of every fan and well-wisher who wanted to congratulate the hero of the "world's series."

At this same moment, another star Pittsburgh pitcher found himself in seclusion in his home in Andover, Massachusetts, far from all the excitement and pageantry of the postseason championship. His name was Ed Doheny, and he had won sixteen games for the Pirates before deserting the team late in the season. Doheny had been acting strangely for several days prior to his departure, and it was believed he had suffered a mental breakdown. After a few weeks, he rejoined the ball club, but he appeared to be a nervous wreck and soon was sent home and placed under the care of a physician.

From his home, Doheny, like all baseball fans, closely followed the progress of the series. Phillippe's three victories put the Pirates on the verge of victory, and it appeared the National League champions were too powerful for the upstarts from the American League. As a mock show of sympathy, the Pittsburgh fans presented a large rainbow-colored umbrella to the visiting Boston "Royal Rooters" and their leader, "Nuff Ced" McGreevey, a saloon owner whose name came from his habit of ending arguments with an abrupt " 'Nuff said!' "

But on Wednesday, Jimmy Collins's team rallied behind Cy Young, who was derided by the Pittsburghers as old and washed up, for an 11–2 victory. A day later, Bill Dinneen of the Puritans beat the Pirates, 6–3, and suddenly the series was tied at three games each.

The pivotal seventh game was played on a cold and blustery Saturday in Pittsburgh, and Phillippe's many admirers presented him with a diamond stickpin before he took the mound for the Pirates. But by now, the weary Deacon was no match for Young, the old master, and Boston stormed to a 7–3 victory to take the lead in the series.

News of Pittsburgh's defeat reached Doheny at his home the following morning. This apparently caused the pitcher to snap, and when the doctor called on him that morning, Doheny angrily chased him from the house. Later, Doheny attacked his nurse from behind, striking the man on the head with a poker and knocking him unconscious. His wife grabbed their young boy and ran to the neighbors for help, but by then Doheny was holed up in the house threatening anyone who came near. He managed to hold the crowd at bay for more than an hour before two police officers caught him off guard and wrestled him to the ground. Doheny was declared insane by two physicians and committed to the Danvers Insane Hospital.

Two days later, in Boston, Bill Dinneen of the Puritans threw a third strike past Honus Wagner for the final out of a 3–0 victory in the eighth and final game of the series. The exuberant Boston fans happily carried their heroes around the Huntington grounds while "Nuff Ced" McGreevey and his Royal Rooters waved the multicolored umbrella they had received in Pittsburgh. Barney Dreyfuss, who had been forced to pay his own way into the Boston grounds to see the game, sat in stunned silence watching the celebration. Ban Johnson's league had struck yet another blow against the rival National League.

But the Pirates would get the last laugh. The winning Boston players received shares of $1,182 each for their triumph. By contrast, the losing Pirates were paid $1,316, or about $150 more per man, since Dreyfuss tossed his share of the gate receipts into his players' pool.

The Pittsburgh players were preparing to head their separate ways for the off-season when Fred Clarke, still limping from a leg injury which had slowed him in the series, stopped by to thank the owner for his generosity. Dreyfuss smiled and said it was the least he could do for his boys. He thought back to the events of the past three years. There had been the emergence of the American League, the bitterness of the "Great Baseball War," the player defections, the double dealings, and the many angry legal disputes. Through it all, there had been one constant. His Pirates had won the National League championship each of those three seasons.

"The boys deserved it," Dreyfuss told Clarke. "They've won three pennants for me, and they stuck by me during the American League raids. I'm glad to do it."

• • •

The end of the baseball season found Norine Delahanty in Philadelphia. Practically penniless after Ed's death, she and her young daughter had moved into the home of her sister.

That winter, there would be no travel from city to city following the horses, no more flashy diamonds or fancy hotels, and no more of the glamour that went with being the wife of a famous ballplayer. All that remained now were the questions surrounding Ed Delahanty and his tragic ending.

The investigation by Chief Griffin and the Fort Erie police had run into a dead end. They could uncover no clues that might unlock the mystery. There was no proof of foul play in the death of Delahanty and no arrests ever were made. The missing jewelry never was found—not the diamond tie pin absent from the silk tie which remained on Ed's body nor the rings which his family claimed he wore on his fingers. There were some troubling aspects concerning the behavior of bridge guard Sam Kingston but no real evidence of wrong-doing. He had amended his original statement and somehow had ended up with Delahanty's derby, but the story he told remained basically unchanged. Only Kingston knew what really happened on the bridge that night, and he continued to insist that following their struggle Delahanty had run away into the darkness and either fell or jumped from the side. The Canadian authorities finally determined there was no reason to believe Ed Delahanty's death resulted from anything other than accident or suicide.

But Norine remained unconvinced. She went to a lawyer, and she told the story to him. She explained how Ed had been put off the train in the darkness just five minutes outside Buffalo, how he had confronted the bridge guard, and how his body had been found below Niagara Falls days later.

The lawyer told Norine to go home and write down everything she could remember about the events leading up to her husband's disappearance and his death. She found one of Ed's notebooks in which he kept a record of his horse-race bets. In it, he had listed the names of various horses along with their odds, the amount wagered, and how much he had won or lost. Mostly, the winnings outweighed the losses until one came to the final entries and the amounts wagered and the figures in the loss column became much greater. Norine turned to the first empty page and began writing, starting her recollections with the last time she saw her husband, the day the ball club left Washington on its fateful road trip.

It was three days before Christmas when the lawsuit was filed in Ontario, Canada, by Norine on behalf of herself and her daughter, seeking twenty thousand dollars in damages from the Michigan Central Railway Company for the death of her husband. It was alleged the railroad was responsible for Ed Delahanty's death because it had put him out in a strange place just across the river from Buffalo when by his very actions on the train it was obvious he was unable to properly take care of himself.

The case was heard in the town of Welland, Ontario, in May 1904. It was shown that Ed Delahanty earned his living as a baseball player and was paid four thousand dollars for six months of playing ball. He was said to be "very good and generous to his wife," but he was prone to drinking sprees which might last two or three weeks. Sometimes, it was stated, he would go an entire season sober and "then get on a big spree of four or five weeks' duration, during which he would act like an insane person." In Detroit, just prior to his death, he had gotten on one such spree.

Ed's behavior on the train from Detroit was recounted, and it was told how he was put off at Bridgeburg the night of July 2, 1903. Norine Delahanty listened quietly as the opposing lawyers argued their cases. The counsel for the plaintiff reminded the jury that Conductor Cole testified it did not seem to him that a sane man would have done what Delahanty had done. This showed the conductor must be aware the unruly passenger was not able to take care of himself. A man in such a condition who is put off in a strange place in the middle of the night naturally would follow the train, argued the lawyer, and this is what led Delahanty to his death.

Mr. Saunders, attorney for the defense, dismissed such a notion. To the contrary, he said, when told by the conductor to get off the train Delahanty did so willingly, and when directed to the station he went in that direction. To all appearances, claimed Saunders, this man was able to take care of himself.

The jury deliberated only a short while before returning its verdict. It ruled in favor of the plantiff, awarding Norine Delahanty three thousand dollars and her daughter two thousand dollars.

For the young widow, it seemed to be little compensation for the loss of her husband.

• • •

In the spring of 1904, John McGraw and his Giants rode to the opening game in Brooklyn in two gasoline-powered automobiles rented for the occasion by Charlie Ebbets of the Dodgers. The ballplayers felt giddy as they motored down

Fifth Avenue and across the Brooklyn Bridge to the ballpark. It was a far cry from the rickety horse-drawn carriages used in the old days.

The Giants won that day, and they kept on winning. McGraw saw to that. He showed up at the Polo Grounds one morning early in the season and found his surly catcher, Frank Bowerman, unusually happy.

"Why the smile?" asked McGraw.

"As I came in today," Bowerman answered cheerfully, "I saw a team of white horses pulling a brewery wagon past the Polo Grounds."

"So?"

"That's a good sign. Watch me kill the ball today."

Bowerman broke out of a batting slump that day to help the Giants to victory. McGraw said nothing, but the next day another wagon loaded with barrels passed the ballpark as the players were arriving. The Giants ran up another big score. For the next several days, the players kept seeing the team of white horses and the barrel wagon, and they kept hitting the ball. Only later did they realize McGraw had begun paying the driver to take his wagon past the ballpark at the same time each day. It was only one of his many tricks.

Bullhead Dahlen was acquired from Brooklyn to give McGraw the shortstop he had been seeking. He was thirty-four years old and as rough and cocky as Muggsy himself. The fans in New York began to call him "Bad Bill."

Turkey Mike Donlin, the old Oriole, arrived from the Reds after getting so drunk and rowdy Cincinnati president Garry Herrmann suspended him for a month. He was a notorious drunk and a carouser, and he had a scar running from his left cheek down to his jaw from a knifing, but Donlin knew how to hit the ball. He became the slugging outfielder McGraw had hoped Ed Delahanty would be for the Giants.

In September, the Giants arrived in St. Louis needing just one more victory to clinch the championship. They were met there by an aging "Orator Jim" O'Rourke, a minor-league executive who twenty-eight years earlier had made the first base hit ever in the National League. He was fifty-four years old and had not appeared in a big-league game in eleven years. He wanted one more chance. McGraw gave it to him. O'Rourke's uniform hung on him loosely and his head was balding, but Orator Jim went behind the plate and caught everything they threw at him. At bat, he hit a single and came around to score a run. When the game ended, and the Giants had won the championship, the old man still was in there.

News of the Giants' victory preceded a dramatic showdown in New York between Clark Griffith's Highlanders and Jimmy Collins's Puritans with the American League pennant on the line. On the mound for the Highlanders that day was the spitballer Happy Jack Chesbro, winner of an amazing forty-one games during the season. He battled into the final inning with the score tied when Boston advanced a runner to third base. There were two outs and two strikes on the batter. Chesbro smeared saliva on the ball and fired another spitter toward the plate. To his horror, the ball rose uncontrollably from the added moisture and sailed high over the catcher's head and toward the backstop as the man on third base raced home with the game-winning run. In the stands, a Fulton Market fish dealer by the name of Edward Leach was so shocked at seeing the game decided on such a play he let out a gasp and swallowed his lit cigar, ashes and all. He was in extreme discomfort, but when he had recovered from his harrowing experience and could speak again, his first words were, "It was nothing to losing the pennant."

There had been hope of another "world's series" between the champions of the two leagues, but this year there would be no such showdown. For John Brush and John McGraw of the Giants, the old hatreds and jealousies still were too great. Brush contemptuously dismissed Ban Johnson's organization as "a minor league." McGraw bitterly denounced his one-time friend Johnson and his tactics. "I know the American League and its methods," he said. "I ought to, for I paid for my knowledge. They still have my money."

It was not until the following season that the National Commission, created by the Cincinnati peace agreement, agreed upon the arrangements for an officially sanctioned World Championship Series. The first such World Series was played in the fall of 1905. McGraw's Giants, wearing pitch-black uniforms and white caps designed especially for the occasion, defeated Connie Mack's Athletics for the championship. Each one of the five games ended in a shutout, with the great Christy Mathewson throwing three of them.

Baseball was changing. The old sluggers of the past were no more. It was the era of the dead ball, and the bunt became the great offensive weapon.

The elusive George Davis returned to Chicago, and there he led a White Sox team known as "the Hitless Wonders" to the 1906 American League pennant and a stunning upset of the powerful Chicago Cubs in the World Series. He continued playing until 1909, when he ended a brilliant twenty-year career with 2,667 hits and 615 stolen bases. Even after he left baseball, Davis remained a shadowy, mysterious figure. He kicked around a few years, coaching the baseball team at Amherst and working as an automobile sales agent, before dropping out of sight in 1918. It was said he went back to New York to play bridge for a living, taking with him a wife who always wore "a fistful of diamonds." But little is known about what happened in his later years, other than he was committed to a Philadelphia mental hospital in 1934 and died there six years later.

The same year Davis retired from baseball, 1909, Harry Pulliam returned to his room at the New York Athletic Club one evening and stripped down to his shoes, socks, and underwear. The constant bickering and criticism he faced as president of the National League had taken its toll. He pulled out a five-shot revolver, pointed it at his right temple, and pulled the trigger. Even in this last act of desperation, Pulliam failed to do the job successfully. The bullet passed through his brain and blew out both his eyes, but when he was found two hours later he still was breathing and semiconscious. He continued to linger in agony for several more hours before dying the next day.

It came time to choose a full-time successor for Pulliam, and through a strange twist of fate the old revolutionary John Montgomery Ward emerged as the leading candidate for the position. He appeared to have a sufficient number of votes to be elected, but the events of 1903 and the George Davis case again took their toll. Ban Johnson cited Ward's role in the controversy and proclaimed he was not the "clean" man the National League deserved. It was Johnson's threat not to sit with Ward nor serve with him on the National Commission that effectively ended the former ballplayer's candidacy. In retaliation, Ward sued the American League president for libel and eventually was awarded two thousand dollars in damages. The money helped him buy his way back into the game as owner of the Boston National League club in 1912, but it did not ease the betrayal he felt.

• • •

The 1912 season found Jim Delahanty in Detroit as a member of the Tigers. He was the last of the famous Delahanty brothers, who had been a part of the game for the past twenty-five seasons. Ed had begun his career in 1888. Tom had played three seasons in the 1890s. Jim had reached the big leagues to stay in 1904, the spring after Ed's death. Frank had arrived in 1905. Joe finally made it two years later, at the age of thirty-two. A sixth Delahanty, Willie, might have made it, too, had he not met with misfortune. He was playing in the New England League and was sitting on a porch one Fourth of July.

Someone threw a firecracker, and the explosion caught Willie in the eye.

None of the brothers ever approached Ed in greatness, but Jim came the closest. He was a tough, scrappy ballplayer who kicked around with half a dozen teams before arriving in Detroit in 1909. The turning point in his career came when he was moved from the outfield to second base. Jim helped the Tigers to the American League pennant in 1909 and batted more than .300 in their World Series loss to the Pirates.

The star of the Detroit team was outfielder Ty Cobb, who had surpassed Honus Wagner and even Napoleon Lajoie as the greatest hitter in the game. Cobb was a man possessed, and he played the game with savage fury. He cut infielders with his spikes, ran the bases with wild abandon, and fought anyone who dared cross him. Opposing ballplayers feared him and many of his own teammates despised him. No one, not even the fans, was safe from Cobb's angry assaults.

One day in May 1912, the vicious taunts of a heckler in New York drove Cobb into a frenzy. Without warning, he leaped into the stands behind the dugout and began savagely beating the man. The other Detroit players stepped from the dugout armed with bats to keep the other fans back. Afterward, it was learned the man Cobb had attacked was a former printer who had lost three fingers in an industrial accident. The man's physical infirmity did not matter to Cobb. "I don't care if he has no feet," sneered the Detroit ballplayer.

By chance, Ban Johnson happened to be at the ballpark that day to witness the incident. His response was to suspend Cobb for ten days without pay. The Detroit players, believing Cobb had been provoked into the attack, walked out in protest. As word of the players' action spread around baseball, it was said Jim Delahanty had led the players in the walkout.

In their place, Tigers manager Hughie Jennings fielded a team of amateurs and recruits out of the stands to play the Athletics in Philadelphia. Aloysius Travers, a theology student at St. Joseph's College in Philadelphia, stood on the mound in a Detroit uniform and prepared to pitch to Connie Mack's world champions. He looked over at the Philadelphia bench and saw such sluggers as Frank "Home Run" Baker and Eddie Collins. He shut his eyes and whispered to himself not the familiar command "Let's play ball!" but rather the words "Let's pray ball!" The Mackmen showed no mercy. They bunted the ball past the helpless pitcher, stole bases with ease, and won the game by a score of 24–2. Ban Johnson was furious. He fined the strikers one hundred dollars each and threatened to ban them from baseball if they did not report to their next game. It was Cobb himself who finally urged his teammates to return to work while he served out his suspension.

Cobb became a martyr. Jim Delahanty was branded a troublemaker and an insurgent. He insisted he was no more responsible for the uprising than the other players, but he took the brunt of the blame. Not long afterward, he lost his starting position and was benched by Jennings. At the end of the season, he was released by the Tigers. Jim Delahanty was thirty-three years old and just two seasons earlier had batted a career-best .339, but he could find no American or National League team interested in his services. It was the end of an incredible streak. After a quarter of a century of continuous service, there would not be a Delahanty on a major-league roster in 1913.

The Delahanty brothers would make a comeback in 1914 with the founding of the Federal League, which became the third major league. Frank and Jim Delahanty joined the new circuit and played two seasons before its collapse. The end of the new league also marked the last of the Delahantys in baseball.

• • •

Ban Johnson continued to make his annual hunting expeditions to Camp Jerome in the woods of Wisconsin. One year,

Garry Herrmann and some Cincinnati politicians were invited as Johnson's special guests. As a prank, some local Chippewa Indians were hired to stage a "raid" for the benefit of the visitors from Cincinnati. There were wild screams and shouts, and fires lit the night sky as the frightened guests scrambled for cover inside the cabin. To add to the effect, the veteran campers cried out in panic. "Don't let them get me, Commy!" someone shouted to Charlie Comiskey. "We'll burn like rats!" came another scream. It was only when one of the pranksters let out a laugh that Herrmann and his friends caught on to the gag.

Another year, Johnson went on a fishing trip and caught so many bass he had some shipped to Comiskey at the Chicago ballpark. When the fish arrived, Commy beamed proudly and called out to some friends, "Look what Beebee sent me."

By chance, later that same day a messenger arrived to inform Comiskey that Johnson had suspended Chicago outfielder Ducky Holmes for an altercation with umpire Silk O'Laughlin the day before. Comiskey, who already had another outfielder on suspension, was furious at the timing of the action, which left him short of players prior to a Sunday game before a large crowd. In a rage, he lashed out angrily at Johnson.

"What does that fat so-and-so expect me to do? Play this string of bass in left field?"

With that, Comiskey tossed the fish out of his office window, reportedly striking a passerby on the street below.

That marked the final break between Comiskey and Johnson. The two men never again were friends.

• • •

Napoleon Lajoie finally was able to play for Connie Mack in 1915, when the Big Frenchman was sold to the Philadelphia Athletics and allowed to return to the city where he had begun his brilliant career twenty years earlier. Lajoie batted below

.300 that season and again the next, and so he retired at age forty-two in 1916, ending the reign of "King Napoleon."

The following spring, the preacher Billy Sunday brought his revival crusade to New York and was greeted at Pennsylvania Station by eight thousand people singing the hymn "Brighten the Corner Where You Are," which was his favorite tune. For ten days, the former ballplayer preached his message in a hastily constructed building on upper Broadway. He darted about the stage, shadow-boxed with "the Devil," pounded his fists on the pulpit, fell to the floor, stamped his feet, and leaped on top of the pulpit. Sunday was fifty-four years old, balding, and slight of build, but he remained as flamboyant as he had been as a young man on the baseball field. He took off running and threw himself feet first toward an imaginary home plate in the famous "Chicago slide." He was a sinner trying to slide into heaven only to be called out by the Lord.

Sunday's style of preaching was such that he normally made his listeners smile and not cry. But on this occasion, he recounted in dramatic fashion his curbside conversion thirty years earlier, and many in the audience had tears in their eyes as he told his story. Sunday talked of his companions on that fateful day when he first heard the gospel band on Van Buren Street in Chicago. With him had been the famous White Stockings catcher Frank "Silver" Flint and shortstop Big Ned Williamson. Sunday recalled years later being summoned to the deathbed of Flint, where the once-great catcher, stricken by consumption, looked up and whispered to him in a feeble voice that barely was audible.

"He said, 'There's nothing in the life of years ago I care for now. I can hear the bleachers cheer when I make a hit that wins the game. But there is nothing that can help me out now, and if the umpire calls me out now, won't you say a few words over me, Bill?' He struggled as he had years ago on the diamond, when he tried to reach home, but the great Umpire of the universe yelled, 'You're out!' and waved him to the clubhouse, and the great gladiator of the diamond was no more.

"He sat on the street corner with me, drunk, thirty years ago in Chicago, when I said, 'Good-bye, boys, I'm through.' "

Sunday paused briefly to look out across the audience, and it reminded him of the huge crowds which he once played before as a member of Cap Anson's White Stockings. He thought of his famous teammates Flint, Williamson, and the incomparable King Kelly, all of them ruined by alcohol.

"Did they win the game of life," asked Sunday, "or did Bill?"

Minutes after the conclusion of his sermon, the men and women streamed forward by the hundreds asking for salvation. It was called "hitting the sawdust trail," a reference to Sunday's years of tent revivals on ground covered by sawdust in rural America. By the end of the ten days, the ranks of converts in New York had swollen to a phenomenal 98,264. It was the pinnacle of Billy Sunday's success.

John McGraw also was at his peak in 1917. Little had changed about him. He was widely acclaimed as baseball's greatest manager—a cocky, belligerent man who demanded hustle and heads-up play from his ballplayers. Muggsy was a throwback to the old days of baseball, and his preference for the old way of doing things was accentuated by his loyalty to the men who used to play the game. McGraw liked to surround himself with former players, hiring them to do odd jobs around the ballpark. Big Dan Brouthers served as a watchman at the Polo Grounds. Mickey Welch worked as a gatekeeper. Bad Bill Dahlen got a job as a maintenance man. Arlie Latham became a part-time coach. Silver King swept the infield.

One year, Mcgraw got word that Amos Rusie, once the most feared pitcher in the game, was scratching out a meager living in Seattle. Muggsy brought him back to New York and made him a special officer at the Polo Grounds. The first time Rusie stepped onto the field, the fans stood and cheered him and tears came to his eyes. "It's like climbing out of your grave and going to a dance," he said in a voice choked with emotion.

Not long afterward, McGraw told a young reporter about Rusie's exploits and suggested he do a story on the old man. The writer found the aging pitcher living in a rundown shack not far from the ballpark. Rusie, as big and gruff as ever, refused to even let the man inside.

"You writers told the fans I was a bum, so I owe you nothing!" he screamed. "Get out!"

The writer turned and fled.

The Giants won the National League championship in 1917, the sixth of ten pennants they would win in McGraw's thirty-one years as manager of the team. That fall, they lost the World Series to the Chicago White Sox. After the final out, White Sox manager Clarence "Pants" Rowland ran all the way across the field to offer his hand to McGraw.

"Mr. McGraw," said Rowland, "I'm glad we won, but I'm sorry you had to be the one to lose."

Muggsy just looked at him and scowled. "Get away from me, you goddamned busher!"

Two years later, in 1919, Comiskey's White Sox were back in the World Series. It was supposed to be the most powerful team in baseball history, but instead it became the most infamous. The heavily favored White Sox were beaten by the lightly regarded Cincinnati Reds, owned by the popular Garry Herrmann. Afterward, it was revealed that eight of the Chicago players, unhappy with Comisky's cheap tactics and low pay, had conspired to throw the Series. They came to be known as the Black Sox, and Comiskey never recovered from their disgrace. The man who had done so much to advance the cause of ballplayers through his loyalty to the brotherhood and his role in the formation of the American League would be remembered instead for how he betrayed his players and they in turn betrayed him.

• • •

In Cleveland, Frank Delahanty passed the state bar examination and opened a small legal practice. Not long afterward, in 1918, he capitalized on his famous name to be elected to the state legislature of Ohio from a state congressional district in Cuyahoga County.

"When I quit baseball, I was an old-timer," he jokingly told friends. "I was past thirty years of age. In my new profession, I am considered a young man at thirty-four."

Often, Frank thought of his brother, Ed, and the mysterious circumstances surrounding his death. The family's suspicions about what really happened on the International Bridge that night had become even greater when guard Sam Kingston changed his story yet again to claim there had been no physical confrontation and that Ed Delahanty simply had ignored his shouted warnings and walked off the bridge.

Frank also wondered what might have happened had Ed reached his destination that night.

"We couldn't prove anything," Frank would tell reporters, "but I understand what started the whole thing was that he was going to leave the train and go to New York to play for the Giants. He was going to jump back to the National League. If he had made it, the baseball war between the two leagues would have started all over again."

It was several years after his brother's death, near the time when his own baseball career was drawing to a close, that Frank Delahanty began to do some thinking about his plans for the future. Throughout most of his days in baseball, Frank had heard much talk about contracts, but he had paid little attention to these legal documents. But in his last couple of years as a ballplayer, he began carefully reading through his own and other players' contracts. It was this interest that led Frank to begin the study of law during the off-season.

His famous name helped him attract clients, and it was not

long before Frank Delahanty was making more money than he
ever had in baseball. He owed it all to his fascination with
baseball contracts. It was a topic his brother Ed also had come
to know quite well.

• • •

Big Ed Delahanty was elected to the Baseball Hall of Fame
in 1945. His career batting average of .346 is the fourth best in
baseball history, and he still is the only player to win batting
championships in both the National and American leagues.

BIBLIOGRAPHY

Books

Adams, Edward Dean. *Niagara Power* (New York, 1927).

Alexander, Charles. *John McGraw* (New York, 1988).

Allen, Lee. *100 Years of Baseball* (New York, 1950).

Axelson, G. W. *Commy* (Chicago, 1919).

Bartlett, Arthur. *Baseball and Mr. Spalding* (New York, 1951).

Bealle, Morris A. *The Washington Senators: An 87-Year History of the World's Oldest Baseball Club and Most Incurable Fandom* (Washington, 1947).

Braider, Donald. *The Niagara* (New York, 1972).

Brunell, F. H., publisher. *1890 Players' National Base Ball Guide* (Chicago, 1890).

Callahan, Bob, editor. *The Big Book of American Irish Culture* (New York, 1987).

Church, Seymour R. *Base Ball: The History, Statistics and Romance of the American National Game* (San Francisco, 1902).

Condon, George E. *Cleveland: The Best Kept Secret* (New York, 1967).

Convention and Visitors Service of the Niagara Falls Chamber of Commerce. *Immortal Niagara* (Niagara Falls, New York, 1941).

Denison, Merrill. *Niagara's Pioneers* (1953).

Dow, Charles Mason. *Anthology and Bibliography of Niagara Falls* (New York, 1921).

Durso, Joseph. *The Days of Mr. McGraw* (Englewood Cliffs, New Jersey, 1969).

Ellis, William T. *Billy Sunday: The Man and His Message* (Philadelphia, 1914).

Graham, Frank. *McGraw of the Giants* (New York, 1944).

––––––. *The New York Giants* (New York, 1952).

Grayson, Harry. *They Played the Game: The Story of Baseball Greats* (New York, 1944).

Hynd, Noel. *The Giants of the Polo Grounds* (New York, 1988).

James, Bill. *The Baseball Book 1990* (New York, 1990).

Kennedy, MacLean. *The Great Teams of Baseball* (St. Louis, 1928).

Langford, Jim, compiled by. *Runs, Hits & Errors: A Treasury of Cub History and Humor* (South Bend, Indiana, 1987).

Lewis, Franklin. *The Cleveland Indians* (New York, 1949).

Lieb, Fred. *The Boston Red Sox* (New York, 1947).

Lieb, Frederick G., and Stan Baumgartner. *The Philadelphia Phillies* (New York, 1953).

Lowenfish, Lee, and Tony Lupien. *The Imperfect Diamond* (New York, 1980).

Lowry, Philip J. *Green Cathedrals* (Cooperstown, New York, 1986).

Mack, Connie. *My 66 Years in the Big Leagues* (New York, 1950).

Mathewson, Christy. *Pitching in a Pinch* (New York, 1912).

McGraw, Mrs. John J. *The Real McGraw* (New York, 1953).

Miller, Carol Poh, and Robert Wheeler. *Cleveland: A Concise History, 1796–1990* (Bloomington and Indianapolis, 1990).

Morison, Samuel Eliot, and Henry Steele Commager. *The Growth of the American Republic*, volume two (New York, 1942).

Murdock, Eugene C. *Ban Johnson: Czar of Baseball* (Westport, Connecticut, 1982).

Phillips, John. *The 1895 Cleveland Spiders: Temple Cup Champions* (Cabin John, Maryland, 1990).

———. *The '99 Spiders: The Story of the Worst Baseball Team Ever to Play in the Major Leagues* (Cabin John, Maryland, 1988).

———. *The 1903 Naps* (Cabin John, Maryland, 1989).

———. *When Lajoie Came to Town: The Story of the Cleveland Blues of 1902* (Cabin John, Maryland, 1988).

_____. *Who Was Who in Cleveland Baseball in 1901–10* (Cabin John, Maryland, 1989).

Porter, David, editor. *Biographical Dictionary of American Sports: Baseball* (New York, 1987).

Povich, Shirley. *The Washington Senators* (New York, 1954).

Roff, Elwood A. *Base Ball and Base Ball Players* (Chicago, 1912).

Rose, William Ganson. *Cleveland: The Making of a City* (Cleveland, 1950).

Seymour, Harold. *Baseball*, two volumes (New York, 1960).

Shannon, Bill, and George Kalinsky. *The Ballparks* (New York, 1975).

Smith, Robert T. *Baseball: A Historical Narrative of the Game, the Men Who Have Played It, and Its Place in American Life* (New York, 1947).

Spalding's Official Base Ball Guide, 1888–1904 editions (New York).

Tiemann, Robert L., and Mark Rucker, editors. *Nineteenth Century Stars* (Kansas City, Mo., 1989).

Van Tassel, David D., senior editor, and John J. Grabowski, managing editor. *The Encyclopedia of Cleveland History* (Bloomington and Indianapolis, 1987).

Voigt, David Quentin. *American Baseball*, two volumes (Norman, Oklahoma, 1969).

White, Sol. *Sol White's Official Base Ball Guide* (Philadelphia, 1907, reprinted Columbia, South Carolina, 1984).

Williams, Edward T. *Niagara Falls* (1925).

Williams, Marjorie F. *A Brief History of Niagara Falls* (Niagara Falls, New York, 1972).

Wolff, Rick, editor. *The Baseball Encyclopedia*, eighth edition, revised (New York, 1990).

Articles

Ayotte, John U. "Napoleon Lajoie: New England's Greatest Ball Player" (*Yankee*, April 1969).

Claudy, C. H. "Signals and Signal-Stealing" (*St. Nicholas*, June 1913).

Crane, Sam. "Sam Crane Writes Series of Stories on Fifty Greatest Ball Players in History" (*New York Journal*, series of articles, 1911–12).

Fitzpatrick, Frank. "A Baseball Mystery Is 85 Years Old" (*Philadelphia Inquirer*, July 3, 1988).

Fullerton, Hugh S. "Batting" (*The American Magazine*, 1910).

Geyer, Orel. "Billy Sunday's First Prayer" (*Baseball Magazine*, May 1915).

Hoffman, Arthur Sullivant. "The Tzar of the Sleeping Car" (*The Chautauquan*, June 1904).

Hudgins, Mary D. "Days of the 'Diamond Jo' " (*Arkansas Gazette Magazine*, July 1934).

Johnson, Rick. "Amos Rusie: 'The World's Greatest Pitcher' " (*The Indianapolis Star Magazine*, October 1973).

Johnson, William E. "Railroad Temperance Regulations" (*The Chautauquan*, June 1904).

Lieb, Frederic G. "Napoleon Lajoie: The King of Modern Batters" (*Baseball Magazine*, August 1911).

Lockley, Fred, as related to by "Ma" Sunday. "How Billy Sunday Became a Famous Ball Player" (*Baseball Magazine*, June 1920).

Murdock, Eugene C. "Life of Tom L. Johnson" (Ph.D. dissertation, Columbia University, October 1951).

Murphy, J. M. "Napoleon Lajoie: Modern Baseball's First Superstar" (*The National Pastime*, Spring 1988).

Nevard, Norm. "The Strange Fate of Ed Delahanty" (*Baseball Digest*, July 1953).

Royal, Chip. "Delahantys Top Brother Act" (*Baseball Digest*, March 1943).

Sangree, Allen. "Fans and Their Frenzies: The Wholesome Madness of Baseball" (*Everybody's Magazine*, September 1909).

Shanley, J. J. "The Way Station Agent: Suggesting An Epic" (*The Chautauquan*, June 1904).

Soden, E. D. "The Greatest Baseball Family in the History of the Game" (*Baseball Magazine*, September 1912).

Summers, Robert J. "His Ticket Said New York City, But Fate Said Niagara Falls" (*Buffalo Courier-Express*, September 8, 1974).

Waters, Theodore. "The All-Star Base-Ball Team" (*Everybody's Magazine*, 1903).

Zueblin, Charles. "The Civic Renascence [sic]: Washington, Old and New" (*The Chautauquan*, April 1904).

Newspapers

Buffalo News, July 1903.

Cataract Journal (Niagara Falls, New York), July–August 1903.

Cleveland Plain Dealer, 1902–03.

Cleveland Press, 1903.

Detroit Evening News, 1903.

Detroit Times, 1903.

The (Philadelphia) Inquirer, 1903.

New York Herald, 1903.

New York Times, 1903.

New York Tribune, 1903.

Niagara Falls Gazette, July–August 1903.

Philadelphia Press, 1903.

Sporting Life, 1888–1904.

The Sporting News, 1888–1904.

Washington Post, 1902–03.

Welland (Ontario) Tribune, May 1904.

BIBLIOGRAPHY

Special articles

Menke, Frank. Series of articles on the formation of the American League. National Baseball Hall of Fame Library.